PENGUIN BOOKS

Kate Forsyth wrote her first novel aged seven and has now sold more than a million books worldwide. Her novels include *Beauty in Thorns*, which tells the extraordinary love story behind the Pre-Raphaelite artist Edward Burne-Jones's famous painting of 'Sleeping Beauty'; *The Beast's Garden*, a retelling of 'Beauty and the Beast' set in the underground resistance to Hitler in Nazi Germany; *Bitter Greens*, a retelling of 'Rapunzel', which won the 2015 American Library Association award for Best Historical Fiction, and *The Wild Girl*, which tells the story of the forbidden romance behind the Grimm brothers' famous fairy-tales and was named the Most Memorable Love Story of 2013. Kate won the 2017 William Atheling Jr Award for Criticism, and was recently awarded the prestigious Nancy Keesing Fellowship by the State Library of New South Wales. Kate has a doctorate in fairy-tale studies and is an accredited master storyteller.

T0363023

KATE FORSYTH

THE BLUE ROSE

PENGUIN BOOKS

PENGUIN BOOKS

UK | USA | Canada | Ireland | Australia
India | New Zealand | South Africa | China

Penguin Books is part of the Penguin Random House group of companies
whose addresses can be found at global.penguinrandomhouse.com

| Penguin
Random House
Australia

First published by Vintage in 2019
This edition published by Penguin Books in 2021

Cover illustration by Cat_arch_angel/Shutterstock
Cover design by Louisa Maggio © Penguin Random House Australia Pty Ltd
Typeset in Goudy Old Style by Midland Typesetters, Australia

Printed and bound in Australia by Griffin Press, part of Ovato, an accredited
ISO AS/NZS 14001 Environmental Management Systems printer

 A catalogue record for this
book is available from the
National Library of Australia

ISBN 978 0 14378 617 7

penguin.com.au

For my darling sister Binny – the French Revolution
story I always said I would write!

Part I

Blue Blood
July–December 1788

Sang bleu: Of high aristocratic descent. The words are
French, and mean blue blood, but the notion is Spanish.
The old families of Spain who trace their pedigree
beyond the time of the Moorish conquest say that their
venous blood is blue, but that of common people is black.
The Reverend Ebenezer Cobham Brewer
Dictionary of Phrase and Fable (1870)

1

C'est Impossible
13 July 1788

'*Mais non! C'est impossible!*' Madame de Ravoisier threw up her pudgy hands. 'All these riots. It is far too dangerous.'

'But, madame, I do not wish to go anywhere near the riots.' Viviane gazed at her great-aunt pleadingly. 'I only wish to take part in the festival for Saint Anne, here in Paimpont. We shall all carry lighted candles in a procession to the abbey . . .'

'No, no! Your father would never permit it.'

'But he is not here, madame. He is in Versailles where they feast and dance every night. We have so few festivities here, and you know it is Saint Anne's holy day . . . I wished to light a candle for my mother . . .' To her dismay, Viviane's voice quivered. Her puppy Luna whined, and laid her front paw on Viviane's lap. Gratefully Viviane caressed her soft red ears.

'Your mother died the day you were born, Viviane. Do me the courtesy of not pretending to an affection for a woman you never knew.'

'It is possible to miss what you do not have,' Viviane answered.

'Well, if you must fall prey to such foolish sentimentality, you may do so here, in our own chapel.'

'But then I would be all alone, like always. The parade will be so pretty, and there'll be music and dancing afterwards . . .'

'You shall not dance with peasants! You forget who you are. Must I write to your father and inform him that you have not lost your taste for low company?'

'No, madame.' Viviane looked down at her clenched hands.

'Very well. We shall speak no more of it. You must see that it is quite impossible for the daughter of the Marquis de Valaine to be seen cavorting with the *canaille*.'

Viviane did not answer.

C'est impossible.

It was all she ever heard. It seemed to Viviane that her life was bounded by impossibilities. She could not pick up her skirts and run, or gallop a horse, or dance with whomever she pleased, or even dare to dream of love.

Her eyes smarted with angry tears.

'It is more important than ever that we of the nobility maintain certain standards.' Madame de Ravoisier unfurled her chicken-skin fan angrily. 'All this disrespectful clamouring for rights and freedoms. I wonder that the king has not clapped them all in irons! Why, I heard just yesterday that the Comte de Molleville was forced to flee Rennes. They say the musketeers refused to fire on the crowds and he barely escaped with his life.'

'Well, what did he expect?' Viviane cried. 'The comte is the king's intendant here. He came with a dozen *lettres de cachet*, left blank on purpose, ready to throw into prison anyone who opposed the king's will.'

'It is ridiculous. No-one should oppose the king's will.'

Viviane began to protest, and her great-aunt held up one hand imperiously. 'I do not wish to hear it, Viviane. You spend too much time with your head in a book instead of practising your curtsey and sewing your trousseau. It is not fitting for a girl of your noble birth to spout such preposterous notions.'

'But, madame . . .'

'Not another word, I said.'

Viviane picked up her sewing, her brain seething with all the words she wanted to say. It was all so unfair. A searing-hot summer meant the fields and orchards were parched. If there was not rain soon, the harvest would fail yet again. The peasants were hungry, and there was much muttering against the king and queen ensconced in the gilded palace of Versailles.

Viviane could understand why. She had been overwhelmed by the opulence of the court during her brief stay there in the spring. It seemed so wrong that the king and his nobles should powder their wigs with the whitest of flour, while the tax-burdened poor struggled to earn enough to buy a loaf of bread.

But Viviane could not speak her thoughts. It was another thing forbidden to her.

Gradually her great-aunt's head nodded forward, till her chins rested on her bosom. She began to snore. One silken slipper hung from her pudgy foot. Luna sniffed at it, then seized the slipper in her mouth and raced away. Viviane kicked off her own shoes so that she could chase after the puppy. Luna eluded her, shaking the slipper from side to side as violently as if it had been a rat.

'Come here, *mon chouchou*,' Viviane whispered, one hand reaching for the amber collar bound about Luna's neck.

The puppy swerved, and banged against a fragile side-table. A priceless vase rocked. Viviane caught and steadied it, as Luna leapt over the back of the couch, sending a cushion flying.

Madame de Ravoisier harrumphed and shifted her weight. Her wig slipped forward over one eye. Viviane stood tense and motionless, one hand held out entreatingly to the puppy. Luna stood, head tilted, brow wrinkled in enquiry, the slipper dangling from her jaws.

The snores rose once more.

'Good girl,' Viviane whispered. She swung her own shoes by their blue satin ribbons. 'Here you go, play with these.'

Luna watched the shoes swing back and forth, then dropped Madame de Ravoisier's slipper and pounced, trying to reach Viviane's.

Viviane picked her up and dashed out of the drawing-room.

'You are nothing but trouble,' she told Luna sternly, then kissed her smooth white head.

The puppy was too large to be carried far, so Viviane dropped her to the ground. As she hurried down the corridor, carrying her shoes, Luna bounded beside her, not at all troubled by having only three legs.

Viviane had found the puppy two months earlier, caught in one of the mole-catcher's traps. The foreleg had been too badly mangled to save, and the kennel-keeper had reluctantly decided she must be drowned, Monsieur le Marquis not wanting to feed a useless dog. Viviane had castigated the keeper for his cruelty, then helped him to amputate the injured paw. The pup had survived, and had been named Luna for the whiteness of her coat and the huge patch on her side, as round and red as a harvest moon. Ever since, Luna had been Viviane's constant companion, following her about all day and snuggled at the end of her bed each night. Viviane would have been very lonely without her.

She slipped through a double set of doors into the ballroom, shadowed by shutters and swathed in dust cloths. Viviane began to slide along the parquet floor in her white stockings. Luna pranced beside her.

'Why, monsieur, I thank you,' Viviane said, curtseying to an imaginary gentleman. 'I would love to dance.' She executed a few neat dance steps, her skirts billowing. She twirled and stepped and curtsied, and Luna played about her, springing and bowing as if she too moved to imaginary music.

At last Viviane came to a standstill, her arms still raised, one toe pointed. 'I do think it is too bad of Monsieur le Marquis to forbid my dancing lessons,' she said to Luna. 'The days are so long with nothing to do but sew and be scolded by Madame.'

Luna wagged her tail, then trotted to the door, turning to look back at Viviane.

'You are quite right, *mon chouchou*! Why sit and sew on such a glorious day? Let us go out, by all means. I am sure Madame will not miss us.'

Viviane began to glide down the polished floor in long, swooping steps, pretending she was ice-skating like the queen and her ladies. She executed a graceful spin, before slipping out the doors. A long corridor lined with gloomy paintings led to a round tower room. Books filled the shelves from floor to ceiling.

Viviane crossed to the corner of the room and pressed one of the carved roses on the panelling. A faint click, then she pushed the panel back, opening a low hidden door. She and Luna slipped inside, and shut the door behind them.

Beyond was a narrow spiral staircase that wound down into shadows. Luna ran ahead, her body jerking as she managed the steep steps with only one foreleg. Viviane followed, the stone cool under her stockinged feet. Three turns, and she reached the ground floor, unlatching another secret door that led into the stillroom. Viviane could hear the chatter of voices and the banging of pots and pans from the scullery. She tiptoed towards the kitchen, keeping her hand on Luna's collar.

Viviane peered around the doorway. Briaca Cazotte, the château's cook, was plucking a guinea fowl. She was a thin woman with deep-set eyes and an anxious look. All her hair was hidden under a severe linen cap. At the other end of the table, her son Pierrick sat playing solitaire. He wore a pale-blue waistcoat embroidered with flowers and a white-powdered wig. Pierrick was the château's head-footman, and so served the ladies of Belisima-sur-le-lac at supper, and ran errands and took messages as required. He was also meant to accompany the ladies of the château on any visits they undertook, but since Madame de Ravoisier and Viviane never went anywhere, he spent most of his days lounging round, paring his nails and playing piquet with the under-footman.

Briaca had once been Viviane's wet-nurse, and so Pierrick – only four days older than Viviane – was her milk-brother. As babies they had nursed together, and taken their first steps pushing a wheeled chair around the uneven flagstones. Once they turned seven, however, Viviane was banished from the kitchen. They had spent the dozen years since with Pierrick standing ramrod-straight against the wall while she sewed a fine seam, or walking three paces behind her while she strolled with her governess, or serving her soup while she pretended not to know him. Their stiff formality was only abandoned when they were alone, and their old friendship could show itself in natural, unaffected banter and laughter. But Viviane and Pierrick were rarely alone, and so they had – over time – developed a silent language of grimaces and gestures that served them well for quick and covert communication.

Now Viviane called his name softly. Luna whined, straining against her hand, wanting to bound forward joyfully, as Pierrick looked up and smiled in greeting.

'Mamzelle!' his mother cried and cast a quick look around. 'You must not be here. You know it is not permitted . . .'

'Hush, Briaca, I am just passing through.'

'If Madame was to find out you came down to the kitchen . . . mamzelle, it is not fair, you must not risk my position.'

'I'm sorry. I just wanted to borrow some sabots. My shoes are not made for walking in the forest.'

Pierrick grinned at her. 'I'll mind them for you till you get back, *cherie*.' He kicked off his own silver-buckled shoes so he could jam his feet inside hers, which were made of silk brocade with red spindly heels and extravagant blue ribbons.

'Pierrick! Do not be so familiar with Mamzelle. Take off her shoes at once!'

In answer, Pierrick jumped up and began to mince across the kitchen, one hand on his hip, the other swishing an imaginary train. 'Ça alors, I do believe Mamzelle's shoes look far better on me! Perhaps I will not give them back.'

'You are welcome to them,' Viviane said, slipping her feet into some sabots. 'I swear cobblers make shoes to hobble us poor women. I'd much prefer a sturdy pair of boots so I could go walking or riding as I please. But no! It is not permitted.' She mimicked her great-aunt's shrill aristocratic tones.

Pierrick lifted one foot admiringly. 'I do like the ribbons. I think I chose well.'

'You always do,' she replied, laughing. 'You must read all the latest fashion gazettes before you bring them for Madame.'

'But of course!'

'Pierrick, that is enough. What would Madame think if she saw you wearing Mamzelle's shoes? Or Monsieur Corentin? He would write to Monsieur le Marquis and we would be thrown out and end up begging in the streets. Mamzelle, please, you must go before you are seen.' Briaca looked nervously towards the scullery.

Viviane and Pierrick exchanged rueful glances. Born in the same week, fed at the same breast, raised in the same château, and yet they were supposed to never acknowledge each other's existence. It seemed most unjust.

'I am sorry, Briaca. I'll leave now. Don't tell anyone where I'm going.' Viviane clomped out the back door, Luna at her heels, as Pierrick picked up her shoes and hid them in the pantry.

Beyond was the kitchen garden. Straw-woven bee boles sat within embrasures along the high walls. Rows of cabbages, artichokes and scarlet runner beans wilted in the blazing heat. Sunflowers drooped their black-ened faces, like a pilgrimage of penitent sinners.

Through another archway was the orchard. Luna raced around happily, chasing butterflies. The old mill was overshadowed by an immense oak tree, its branches bowed with age. One heavy limb rested upon the outer wall, which had broken under the weight. The *pigeonnière* nestled near the gate, the air full of the doves' soft cooing.

Viviane went through the gatehouse and across the bridge. Below her the mill-race foamed through the arches of the bridge and turned the creaky old mill-wheel. Beyond, the golden flax fields rippled under a catspaw of wind, seedpods rattling. Scarlet poppies danced. The sun burned through the silk of her dress, and she was glad to reach the shade of the forest.

If only it would rain, she thought. *I could not bear it if the harvest failed again. We cannot feed them all.*

She remembered the beggars who had camped beyond the château gate last summer, too weak to even raise their cupped hands. Briaca had cooked great cauldrons of cabbage soup to feed them, but there had been too many. Eventually the steward had driven them away, threatening to set the dogs on them. Viviane had begged him to be merciful, but he said Monsieur le Marquis, her father, had given his orders.

Monsieur le Marquis must always be obeyed without question.

Viviane's father did not care for the people of the estate, or indeed for her. For most of her nineteen years he had scarcely acknowledged she existed. She wished he had never remembered and taken her to Versailles. Then she would not have disgraced herself. Her father would not have ordered her great-aunt to come and live at Belisima, watching everything Viviane did and reporting back to him. He would not have forbidden her from going down to the kitchen in the evenings, listening to Briaca's old tales, of magic and saints and miracles, of perilous quests and cruel enchantments, while she helped the cook make dumplings for the pot-au-feu.

One of Viviane's favourite tales was that of her famous ancestor, the Lady of the Lake. The enchanter Merlin had first met her, and fallen in love with her, at a magical spring of water deep in the Paimpont forest. Briaca said that water flung from the Fountain of the Fairy upon the Stone of Merlin had the power to summon a storm.

Remembering that old story, Viviane's step quickened.

It's only a story, I know, she thought as she took the path towards the old spring. *But there is often truth in old tales . . .*

Viviane loved Belisima with all her heart. She had inherited the estate from her mother the day she was born and had lived here all her life. Its soil was her soul. As she hurried through the green shadows of the beech trees, Luna prancing at her heels, she imagined rain soaking into the scorched land, a rich and bountiful harvest, the gratitude of the hungry serfs, the approval of her father as his pockets filled once more. It was an entrancing vision.

She came at last to the Fountain of the Fairy. It was a long gash of dark water, enclosed within steep stone walls and overshadowed by trees. A huge boulder lay nearby, laced with golden lichen. The Stone of Merlin.

Kneeling, Viviane reached down with her sabot and scooped up some water and threw it upon the boulder. Twice more she flung the water, silently praying all the while for rain.

Then she hurried for home.

She would be in trouble, she knew. Gone so long. Wandering alone in the forest. Madame would be angry. She broke into a run, till a stitch stabbed her ribs, then walked, then ran again, Luna loping ahead.

The shadows grew long. The abbey's bells rang the Angelus. The wind was rising, shaking the canopy of leaves overhead. It blew the puppy's ears inside-out.

Suddenly an old man slouched out of the forest. He was dressed in a moleskin waistcoat over a tattered shirt and soiled leather breeches. His long grey hair and beard were matted with leaves and twigs, and grime was deeply engrained in the furrows of his face. Over one shoulder he carried a pole hung with the limp bodies of dead moles, their pale paws dangling.

His name was Maugan. He had haunted Viviane's nightmares since she was a little girl. It was in one of his mole-traps that Luna had lost her foot, and it was clear the puppy remembered for she growled at him.

'Out of my way!' Viviane cried.

'Damned aristo!' Maugan spat at Viviane's feet. 'You think you rule the world, but a storm is coming, a storm like the world has never seen before, and then heads shall roll.'

The mole-catcher had a reputation for strange mad prophecies, and indeed his eyes were fixed and crazed. Viviane remembered that her father had once had Maugan flogged for daring to predict the Marquis's young wife would die without bearing him the much-desired son. Well, he had been right. Viviane had been born, a mere girl, and her mother had died in the bearing of her and the Marquis left with no-one to pass down his name.

Viviane pushed past the filthy old man and ran headlong down the path towards home. Clouds loomed behind the château like a giant's anvil. The lake scudded with white waves. Lightning fractured the sky.

Viviane hurried forward through the flail and hiss of hail.

2

The Lord's Vengeance
14–29 July 1788

'Ring the warning bell!' Viviane cried to one of the grooms, as she ran through the gate. The dogs in the kennels barked, and the horses neighed and reared in fear. 'A storm's about to hit. Hurry!' He ran to do her bidding.

Viviane gave Luna – frightened and whimpering – to the kennel-keeper, then ran through to the orchard and began to call down her doves. They wheeled above her head, their wings white against the menacing sky, then flew through the tiny windows under the *pigeonnière*'s pointed roof. When all were safe within, she pulled down the shutters and locked the heavy door.

In the kitchen garden, an old man in an indigo smock and leather gaiters was flinging sacks over the precious glasshouse. Hailstones huge as fists pelted around him. 'Yannic!' Viviane cried. 'Be careful!'

She threw a sack over her head, and ran to help him. The old man guarded his domain zealously, despite the arthritis that threatened to cripple his fingers and knees. She wished once again they could afford a strong young man to help him.

Thunder boomed, then lightning struck like adders' fangs. Sleet pelted down. Viviane could scarcely see the château's towers through the torrent. 'Get inside!' she called to Yannic. 'It's not safe out here.'

'Mamzelle!' Pierrick shouted from the kitchen door. 'We need you.'

She picked up her wet skirts and ran.

A man had stumbled in from the fields, blood pouring from a gash in his scalp. Viviane tended him with steady hands. The kitchen was soon full of frightened mothers and sobbing children. Viviane served them bowls of hot bouillon.

'Do not be afraid,' she said. 'The Château de Belisima has stood here for six hundred years – it's not going to break under a few hailstones.'

'Mamzelle,' a cold voice said.

Viviane looked up and saw Agathe, her aunt's maid, standing in the doorway. Her nose was tilted high as if she could not bear the smell of cabbage soup and wet peasants' hair.

'Yes?' Viviane answered.

'Madame wishes you to attend on her. You know how much she dislikes storms.'

Viviane made a swift gesture at the crowded kitchen. 'Please tell Madame that I regret I am unable to come at present.'

Agathe's lips thinned. 'Madame will not be pleased.'

'I am sorry for that,' Viviane replied, 'but these are my people and I must have a care for them.'

Agathe inclined her head and went away.

Briaca looked up, frightened. 'Mamzelle, please, she is right. Your father . . .'

'Is not here,' Viviane said. 'And even if he were, I still would not sit by and do nothing!'

'Please, mamzelle.'

Viviane bent and hugged her. 'Don't be so worried, Briaca. You cannot really expect me not to help, can you?'

Just then the door slammed open, and four men carried in a white-faced boy on a stretcher made of a sack stretched over sticks. His arm was bent at an unnatural angle.

'Quick, take him into the stillroom,' Viviane cried. 'Briaca, I will need splints. Can you find me some long straight sticks? Pierrick, get me some brandy!'

As everyone hurried to do her bidding, she cast Briaca a swift determined look. 'Unless you'd prefer me to go and sew a fine seam with my great-aunt in the drawing-room?'

By dawn, the storm had passed away.

All was quiet. People lay sleeping on the floor, rolled in coats or covered with shawls. Viviane trudged down the corridor, unutterably weary. The boy was sleeping now, but it had been an exhausting few hours. She had never splinted a broken arm before, and could only hope she had done it right.

Viviane had begun taking care of the local people's ailments some years before, after discovering her mother's notebooks in the stillroom. She started in small ways. Binding up a burned finger. Gathering lavender, sweet marjoram and rosemary to make healing bouquets. Mixing rose oil and calendula into beeswax to make a balm. Gradually, following the steps outlined in her mother's recipes, she had learned to do more. She found the people of the château preferred to come to her than to call the doctor, who was a rotund man with a bulbous red nose, dirty fingernails and a huge wig that he was always scratching.

Soon, people were bringing her injured birds or asking for relief for a fussy baby. Viviane would ask for help from those on the estate who knew about such things. The falconer showed her how to set a broken wing, and the beekeeper's wife suggested cool chamomile tea and rubbing honey on sore gums. Viviane helped Yannic in the garden, and listened to his long lectures on the properties of herbs and flowers. Burdock to purify the blood, comfrey to help bones knit, meadowsweet for heartburn, sweet cicely to lift the spirits and bring new energy. Briaca taught her how to make nettle soup and raspberry leaf tea and elderberry wine and bone broth, and made Luna a collar of amber to keep the fleas away. The Abbé came from Paimpont every Sunday to hear her and Madame de Ravoisier's confessions, and to give Viviane religious instruction. A gentle and enlightened man, he had always encouraged Viviane to study and learn, and had brought her many books from the monastery library, as well as his own Latin dictionary so she could decipher the botanical nomenclature of plants. Viviane carefully wrote down all she learned in her remedy notebook. Slowly her knowledge grew. The hours she spent in the garden and stillroom were the happiest of her day, for Viviane loved the feeling that she was of some use to the world.

Seeing the warm flicker of a candle from the kitchen, she turned that way, wondering who could still be awake.

It was Briaca. She was slowly and laboriously writing on a piece of paper.

'Briaca, you should be in bed,' Viviane said.

The cook jumped so violently she knocked her ink-pot over. She dropped her quill and leapt to her feet, seizing a cloth to mop up the spilt ink.

'Oh, I didn't mean to startle you,' Viviane said, hurrying to help her.

'I thought you were in bed, mamzelle,' Briaca gasped, screwing up her piece of ink-stained paper and throwing it on the fire.

'I'm sorry,' Viviane said. 'You will need to write it again.'

'It's no matter,' Briaca said, screwing the lid on the inkpot and putting away her goose-feather quill. She had a quaint little box, set with mother-of-pearl, to keep her writing implements in. It had been given to her many years ago by Viviane's mother, who had taught Briaca how to read and write and count. Briaca had in turn taught Pierrick and Viviane, at least until the first of her governesses arrived to take over her education.

Your mother had a heart of gold, Briaca always said. *If she had not taught me my letters and numbers as a child, I could not have become cook here at the château. Things would have gone badly for me, you know, with a baby to feed and no way to earn my living. She could have turned me out to starve on the streets. Many women would have done so.*

Not for the first time, Viviane wondered who Pierrick's father had been and how old Briaca was when he was born. She could not have been much more than fourteen or fifteen. Briaca would never talk about it, even though Pierrick had pestered her for many years. 'It does not matter,' she answered, and, once or twice, 'It is better you don't know.' Pierrick liked to imagine that his father had been a travelling musician who had come to stay at the château and seduced the young Briaca. One day, Pierrick said, his father would come and claim him and they would travel the roads, singing for a crust. The possibility delighted him.

'I must go out and see how the harvest has fared,' Viviane said. 'Try and get some rest, Briaca, you've been up all night.'

'No point in going to bed,' Briaca answered, gesturing at the loaves of bread set to rise on the sill. 'They will all want to be fed again soon.'

Viviane squared her shoulders and went out to view the damage. The sky overhead was clear and bright, but the sodden ground was littered with fallen branches, leaves, dead birds, broken slates, cracked bricks.

She walked out to stand on the bridge, raising one hand to shield her tired eyes. Monsieur Corentin was astride his horse in the barnyard, talking to a group of mud-smeared and exhausted men. He raised his hat at the sight of her, and dismounted so he could come and join her. A hawk-faced man with pock-marked skin, she had never seen him look so bleak. Together they gazed out at the landscape.

On the other side of the lake, the battered fields stretched away, silvered with frost. The flax stalks lay broken, drenched. The forest looked like a giant had smashed his way through it with a club. Trees lay with their roots in the air and their branches buried in mud. The slate roof of the barn was smashed.

Viviane felt it was all her fault. If she had not tried to summon rain, if she had not meddled with forces beyond her ken, perhaps the storm would never have come. She had acted like a child, heedless, caught up in a game, not realising the potential for harm.

Viviane wished to make amends, but it was not going to be easy.

'The harvest?' Viviane asked.

He shrugged and shook his head. 'It is ruined, of course. We saved what we could.'

'What can we do?' she asked.

'I shall write to Monsieur le Marquis. I do not expect I shall receive a reply.'

16

Viviane bit her lip and looked away. Indeed, her father was only interested in the estate for the money he could wring from it.

'I shall write also.'

He regarded her with a faint thawing of his expression. 'I thank you, mamzelle. I pray that your entreaties bear fruit.'

She nodded and tried to smile.

They both knew it was no use.

Two weeks later, a letter arrived from Versailles.

Viviane's heart shrank within her at the sight of the elegant handwriting. Carefully she sliced away the seal, and read the words within.

After a few cold courtesies, her father told her that he had married once again and that his bride sent her new daughter her felicitations. The Marquis went on to say:

> I am grieved to hear of the devastation of the storm of July 13th. We have heard that the damage stretched more than four hundred miles, from Normandy to Toulouse. No doubt it is the Lord's vengeance against the recent traitorous rebellions of a few misguided yokels. I do not believe it is my duty to ease the burdens caused by The Lord Our Father's rightful chastisement. Nonetheless my dear wife the marquise has conceived a great longing for a garden in the English style, which the Queen has made fashionable. So I have engaged the services of an English gardener to build what her heart desires. I believe much land has been cleared by the storm's unfortunate felling of trees. Give this land over to the new garden, and instruct Corentin to pay a few sous to the peasants who have lost their livelihood so that they may labour at the English gardener's instruction.
>
> Yours etc,
>
> Louis-Auguste-César de Ravoisier, the Marquis de Valaine
>
> PS: If you ever disobey your great-aunt again, I shall have you thrashed.

17

Viviane lay down the letter and stared at it in disbelief. How had he known? Who had told him? She cast a glance at her great-aunt, who was eating sweetmeats and reading scandal sheets. She had hoped Madame de Ravoisier would not complain of her to her father, but obviously it had been a vain hope. It was puzzling, however. Viviane had not seen any letters written in her great-aunt's handwriting laid out on the silver salver in the hall for Pierrick to post.

'What does your father say?' her great-aunt demanded. 'May we return to Versailles?'

'My father has married again.'

'Indeed? To whom?'

Viviane read out the name inscribed in her father's letter. 'Mademoiselle Élisabeth-Marie-Clothilde de Jussieu de Charmille.'

'Clothilde de Charmille! Why, she is little more than a child. Younger than you. But then my nephew always did like a pullet. Her blood is of the best, and I believe she has a pretty fortune to her name. I wonder what strings Cesar pulled to arrange such an advantageous marriage? No doubt her father was in debt to him. Cesar was always a devil with the cards.'

'Poor Clothilde,' Viviane whispered.

Her great-aunt clicked her tongue. 'Not at all. She is no doubt thrilled to be made a marquise. Not all girls have such nonsensical romantic notions as you.'

Viviane did not answer. *Perhaps my new stepmother will be a friend to me,* she told herself. *She must be so afraid. Perhaps I could help her . . . comfort her . . .*

Her heart quailed within her. If Viviane was to meet her new stepmother, she must see her father again.

The thought filled her with terror.

3

The Marquis's Daughter
2–4 August 1788

Angry crowds surged about the post-chaise, striking spades and scythes against the lacquered door emblazoned with the shield of the Marquis de Valaine.

David leant from the carriage window. 'What is the problem?' he asked in his clumsy French.

A ragged girl held up her cupped hands. 'A few coins, please, m'sieur?'

'Bread! Give us bread!' a thin woman cried.

'I'm sorry. I have no bread, and very few coins.' He made a rueful gesture, but the crowd was not appeased. An angry mutter arose.

'Damn aristos!' A man flung a stone at the carriage, causing the horses to shy.

Another man seized hold of the door handle, rattling it violently, then hit the carriage with his pitchfork.

'Quick, let's go!' David called.

Crouched low in their saddles, the postilions spurred the horses on. The coach raced away over the cobblestones.

David had heard that there had been riots in Rennes. The local *parlements* had opposed the king when he tried to impose new taxes. So Louis had tried to dissolve the *parlements*. Violence had broken out in Paris, and all through the countryside.

David had not expected to run into any trouble himself. It was the marquis's luxurious coach, he realised. His new employer had offered him the carriage so he could travel in comfort, and David had been pleased to accept.

It had been a mistake.

David had been travelling for five days, and he was eager to see the Château de Belisima-sur-le-lac, and to start planning its new garden. It was David's first-ever commission as a landscape designer, and he wanted to impress the marquis. If he created something truly beautiful and unique, more commissions would surely follow.

The road wound its way through a patchwork of small fields and tiny villages. The men wore billowing linen trousers with wooden shoes on their feet, while the women hoeing the fields had their hair pinned up under huge caps. David saw oxen pulling a plough, and an old woman spinning wool onto a distaff, and felt as if he had somehow travelled back in time.

By sunset he had reached Paimpont, a village built around an abbey on the edge of a lake. Some distance beyond was a set of rusted iron gates, half askew. Battered stone shields showed a hand holding a sword above waves. David put his head out the carriage window. 'Turn here,' he called.

The drive led through ancient woodland, trees as old and gnarled as Father Time.

It was like travelling through a long tunnel. David could see nothing of the sky, or the lake, or the hills.

This is not the way to approach a marquis's home, David thought. *The drive should be broad and firm, and show a new vista at every rise.*

Darkness fell. At last the potholed road led to a cluster of stone houses and barns on the shore of a lake, dimly lit by the moon. A narrow stone bridge supported by three arches spanned the water, leading to a tall medieval fortress built on an island. Sharp-pointed towers, battlements and a gatehouse armed with a heavy iron portcullis made the château seem like something out of an old tale.

The only sound was the song of frogs.

David alighted from the coach and stretched his stiff muscles.

'Wait here,' he told the two postilions, who dismounted wearily and went to the horses' heads.

David crossed the bridge and came to the closed gate. He rang the bell vigorously.

A long tedious pause. He rang the bell again.

At last the gate creaked open. An old man appeared, white-bearded and rumpled, dressed only in a long nightgown and nightcap, his bony feet thrust into sabots. He lifted high his candle, grunted a few unintelligible words, then shut the gate in David's face. Impatiently David rang the bell again, and heard the old man cry, '*Une minute!*'

Some time later, the gate was opened by a tall man with pockmarked skin and a neat brown wig, carrying a lantern in one hand.

'Who is it?' he demanded.

'I . . . I am David Stronach.' His throat was dry. 'I am the gardener from the Jardin du Roi . . .'

'Ah, yes. The English gardener. What are you doing here so late?'

'It took so long . . . I did not expect . . .' David was so tired, he found himself fumbling for the right French phrase.

The man nodded. 'The road is very bad. You would have done better to stay in Paimpont overnight and hazard it in the morning.'

David stammered an apology, but the man said, 'It is no matter. You are here now. I am Monsieur Corentin, the steward of Belisima-sur-le-lac.'

David bowed in greeting.

'You must be tired,' Monsieur Corentin said. 'Let my men look after the horses, and come and wash and refresh yourself.' He rang the bell with great vigour, and men came clomping into the courtyard, jackets thrown on over their nightshirts. Yawning, they went to tend to the horses.

David was so tired he felt an unpleasant swaying sensation.

'Pierrick?' Monsieur Corentin beckoned to a young man in a flowered waistcoat, and gave him some instructions in a low voice. Pierrick nodded and slipped away. He soon returned with a steaming ceramic mug. David took it with thanks and sipped. He had been expecting tea, so was rocked back on his heels by the potent brew within. It was some kind of mulled cider, fragrant with honey and cinnamon, which burned a fiery track down his gullet. David coughed and spluttered, laughing.

'Hot apple cider with apple brandy and fermented honey,' Pierrick said in strongly accented English. 'Is good, yes?'

'Yes, thank you,' David agreed, putting the mug down. It brought new strength and vigour to his limbs, but made his head swim.

'Have some more?' the young man offered. When David declined, he grinned and swigged back the last mouthful himself. 'A shame to waste it,' he explained with a saucy wink.

David frowned, not liking his impudence. He followed Monsieur Corentin across the bridge and into the inner courtyard of the château. It was a large dusty square, with an old cart in a corner and barrels in another. A wide set of stone steps, littered with leaves, swept up to an immense arched door.

A formal parterre garden here, David thought. *Hedges of box and cones of yew, with silver-leafed plants planted within to reflect the grey slate of the roof.*

The Marquis de Valaine wanted David to create a garden of love to celebrate his wedding, so David had already ordered a great many seedlings which he knew had a romantic association. White lilac, for love at first sight. English box for constancy, birch trees for new beginnings, and orange trees for fertility. Lavender for devotion, rosemary for remembrance, forget-me-nots for never-ending desire, and sweet-faced pansies for love's thoughts. He would order more from Paris once he had designed the garden.

In the kitchen, the postilions drank cider and ate soup while a thin woman crept about with a jug, topping up their ceramic mugs. Her dark hair was hidden by a cap, her dark gown by an apron. The old man in the nightgown and sabots was sitting in a rocking-chair by the fire, smoking a long clay pipe. He scowled ferociously at the sight of David.

'Yannic, our head gardener,' Monsieur Corentin said. 'He will show you about the gardens tomorrow.'

David bowed his head in greeting, but the old man only stared at him with suspicious eyes. *He's not pleased to have an outsider coming in to oversee his precious gardens*, David thought. *A foreigner, to boot!*

He tried to smile reassuringly, but the old man was not mollified, puffing so angrily on his pipe that clouds of smoke filled the air.

'Madame Cazotte, can you prepare Monsieur Stronach some supper?' the steward asked, and the thin woman ducked her head in agreement.

Pierrick showed David through to a small sitting room, where he laid the table with a starched white cloth and silver cutlery, then brought a jug of warm water, a bowl, and a bar of soap wrapped in a linen hand-towel. David was glad to wash the dust from his face and hands, and was even gladder when Pierrick came back with a bottle of wine and a fine crystal glass. His mother slipped in after him, carrying a plate covered with a silver cover. Silently she lifted it to show cold pigeon pie, served with a wild mushroom fricassee and a salad of greens dressed in oil and vinegar. Dense brown bread was accompanied by primrose-yellow butter studded with crystals of salt.

As David sat down to eat in solitary splendour, he could hear the sounds of jocular conversation from the kitchen beyond. He was, he knew, in a strange no-man's-land as far as social etiquette went. Too lowborn to be invited to sup with his employers, too well-bred to break bread with the peasants.

Laughter came from the kitchen, then the sound of song.

David ate in silence.

Mist wrapped the château, muffling all sound.

As David guided the raw-boned gelding he had borrowed towards the forest, he was surprised to see two high-heeled shoes set neatly side-by-side on the gatepost. The shoes were made of cerulean-blue brocade, with red heels and silken ribbons. He glanced back at them as he rode past, puzzled. They seemed so incongruous in this sylvan setting.

As the sun rose, it struck through the mist in long rays that his grand-father had always called God's fingers. He came to the edge of a meadow.

A young woman and a three-legged puppy played together with a stick. She was dressed in a loose white dress and had a crown of wildflowers set crookedly on her long dark curls. Wild roses and ox-eye daisies and the airy umbrels of bishop's lace. Her slender feet were bare. The dog was white with red ears and feet. David dimly remembered a tale his grandfather had once told him, about the red-eared fairy hounds of Annwn, who rode with the Wild Hunt on certain nights of the year. To hear their baying was a warning of death to come.

At that moment, the puppy looked towards him, lifting the stump of her foreleg. David saw she had a great round spot on her side, like a target. The young woman glanced up. Her face was narrow-boned, her nose high-bridged, her eyes black as sloes. Seeing David on his horse, she bent and caught up a wide-brimmed straw hat, filled with wildflowers as if it was a basket. With the dog at her heels, she ran for the forest, her bare feet and ankles showing under the hem of her gown.

'Wait!' David called. 'I'm sorry, I did not mean to startle you.'

But she had gone into the mists.

Slowly David rode back along the path. The girl had looked like a fairy queen from one of his grandmother's stories, he thought. As if she rode upon a white hart and lived within the hollow hills. David grinned ruefully. It was just the medieval atmosphere of the château, he told himself. She would be a peasant girl from one of the cottages, playing truant instead of doing her spinning.

As he rode back to the château, he saw the high-heeled shoes were gone from the wall.

'I thought a formal parterre in the inner courtyard,' David said.

Yannic shuffled along, leaning on a stick and scowling. 'Mamzelle won't want all the old cobblestones dug up. Her ancestors laid them, and she'll want them left just the way they are.'

'But it would look so beautiful, looking down from the château,' David argued.

'Pffff!' The old man blew out his breath in disgust.

David saw, on the far shore, a grove of willow trees trailing their long tendrils in the water. 'We could put a Chinese temple there. Lacquer-red, with a pagoda roof and golden dragons.'

Yannic made the derisive noise again. 'Mamzelle won't hold with that. Heathenish.'

'But Chinese temples are *à la mode*,' David protested. 'Monsieur le Marquis said he wanted all that was fashionable.'

'Mamzelle don't hold with fashions,' Yannic said.

David took a deep breath. 'Is it possible for me to speak to this Mamzelle?'

'She'll be in the stillroom. That way.' Yannic pointed a gnarled finger.

David went through the archway to the kitchen courtyard. To his surprise, it was crowded with people. A woman cuddled a fretful baby. A man waited, a bloodstained handkerchief tied about his hand. Two boys sat in the dust, playing with sheep knuckles. One had a black eye, the other a split lip.

When David asked the way, the boys pointed to a low-roofed stone building jutting out into the garden from the base of the tower. 'Have you hurt yourself?' one of the boys asked sympathetically. 'Don't worry. Mamzelle will fix you.'

David tapped on the blue-painted door. A low sweet voice called, 'Come in.'

Within was a long, cool room with a flagstoned floor and windows that looked out to the courtyard on one side and the kitchen garden on the other. Most of the room was taken up with an old wooden table, with shelves against the stone walls and a sink with a water-pump.

An old man sat on a chair, one arm outstretched on the table. Before him stooped a slight figure, a big apron tied over her white muslin dress. Her sleeves were rolled up to the elbow, and she had a kerchief tied over her dark curls.

She glanced up, and smiled. 'You need my help, monsieur?'

It was the young woman from the meadow. Blood rushed through his body.

'Pardon me, mademoiselle . . . I was looking for the daughter of Monsieur le Marquis,' he said in careful French.

'I am she,' she answered, in his own language. 'You must be the English gardener.'

'I'm not English, I'm Welsh,' he answered, then cursed himself for sounding like a fool.

'Indeed? Is Wales not part of England?' She spoke English well, with a charming French accent. Her eyes were the blackest he had ever seen.

'Not according to the Welsh.'

She smiled. '*Ah, oui*. Like our Bretons here. They think themselves Breton first, French second. But you must not let my father know. English gardeners are *le dernier cri* . . . how do you say? The latest fashion? He will be most displeased if he knew he had a Welsh gardener instead of an English gardener.'

David found himself smiling. 'I will be sure not to tell him.'

'If you will excuse me, please?' she said. 'Monsieur Bernard here has burned himself most badly. I have made a . . . what is the word? A balm?'

'A salve?' David suggested.

'*Bon*. A salve. I have made for him a salve that will help.'

As she anointed the old man's angry burn with the sweet-smelling ointment, David looked about the room. On the table was a large stone mortar and pestle, a set of scales, and various pots and jars, filled with wild roses, ox-eye daisies, chamomile, feverfew, selfheal and bishop's lace. David remembered how he had seen her dancing in the dawn, wildflowers in her hair. She had been collecting medicinal herbs, he realised.

The deep stone windowsills had been turned into a kind of cabinet of curiosities. David saw oak galls, feathers of all sizes and colours, seeds, pine cones, butterfly wings, tiny skulls, old birds' nests, fossils. It reminded him of his own windowsill when he had been a boy, spending most of his days out on the hills.

The marquis's daughter was gently bandaging the old man's arm. Monsieur Bernard gave her a toothless grin and patted her cheek. She helped him up and passed him his walking stick.

He said something to her in thick Breton patois, and she answered him in the same language as he shuffled out the door.

'Tell those little rascals to come in next,' she called after him in French, then turned to David, switching without a moment's hesitation into her charmingly-inflected English. 'I am so sorry, I hope you will pardon me, but I must not stop. Many people need my help today. I presume you wish to speak to me about the garden, yes? I will not be free until this afternoon, and then only if my great-aunt takes a . . .' She paused and waved a hand in the air. 'I cannot think how to say it. *Une petite sieste.*'

'A nap?'

'*Oui*, but something about a cat . . . a nap of the cat.'

'A catnap.'

She laughed. 'It is an expression of the most ridiculous, yes? But exactly right for my great-aunt who is like a very fat, very lazy cat.' The next moment, her face filled with dismay. '*Je suis désolée, monsieur!* I should not have spoken so. Always I am told I must turn my tongue seven times in my mouth before I speak, and always I forget!'

David had seen Madame de Ravoisier being carried to chapel in her velvet-hung sedan-chair. She had barely managed to squeeze inside. 'Truth will out,' he replied solemnly.

Her eyes flew to his in startled laughter. 'That is Shakespeare, is it not? I do not believe my father would accept such a sentiment as an excuse for my disrespect. He is of the opinion that a maid should be seen but not heard.'

She began to tidy away the salve and soft cloths.

David did not want their conversation to stop. 'How did you learn to speak English so well?'

Her face sobered. 'When I was a little girl, I had a governess who was most strict, most unkind. She cared only that I sat up straight and sewed a neat seam. She did not like me to read books, or visit the farm animals, or play with Pierrick, who is my milk-brother, you know. So I was always running away and hiding from her, and she was always tying me to my chair to keep me still.'

David gazed at her, appalled. He could not imagine tying a little girl to a chair.

'Then, when I was of the age fourteen, Pierrick and I made an explosion most spectacular, concocting fireworks for the dauphin's birth.' She smiled at the memory. 'My father, Monsieur le Marquis, he was displeased. He told Madame Malfort she must go. So then I had a new governess. Her name was Miss Hayward. She looked exceedingly stern and forbidding, for she had such a nose! Like an eagle's beak. And she wore only black, for she was mourning her one true love who had died most romantically saving his commander in battle. She was kind, though, and had a great many English books that she used to read to me at night. And her French was not good, even worse than yours. And so I learned English to please her.' She sighed. 'When my father sent her away, I was desolate.'

'Why did he send her away?' David asked.

'Monsieur le Marquis said she was too soft and had filled my head with foolish notions unbefitting one of *la noblesse*.'

He would have liked to have known what so-called foolish notions her English governess had taught her. The idea that all people were born equal in the eyes of God, and should share the same rights and privileges and protections? He hoped so.

'After Miss Hayward went back to England, I had a new governess, from Austria,' the marquis's daughter went on. 'Frau Schwarz was not soft, not at all, she liked cold baths and stout boots and a good hard tramp in the forest, but my father did not like her teaching me biology or how to gallop and so he . . . how did your Shakespeare say? He sent her packing. After Frau Schwarz, there were no more governesses. I was sent to Versailles instead.'

All the humour had vanished from her face. Her hands clenched.

David wanted to know more, but just then the door opened and the two boys tumbled in. A breathless woman accompanied them. 'I'm sorry, mamzelle, I could not find them! They were in the orchard, pelting each other with apples.'

'Wicked boys!' the marquis's daughter said. 'For punishment, you shall gather up every bruised apple and give it to Briaca to make gâteau. And you must help her roll out the pastry and sprinkle the sugar.'

The boys looked at each other in delight.

She made a swift gesture of dismissal to David. 'You must go now,' she said in English once more. 'If my aunt has the catnap, I will meet you in the garden when the abbey bells have rung.'

'Wait!' he cried. 'I do not know your name.'

'I am Héloïse-Rozenn-Viviane de la Faitaud de Ravoisier,' she answered with immense verve.

'No wonder everyone calls you mamzelle,' he said.

She laughed. 'The Abbé calls me Viviane. It is easier, *non?*'

'I'm David Owen Stronach,' he said. 'Not nearly so impressive.'

'It is a pleasure to meet you, Monsieur Stronach,' she said quaintly, holding out her hand to him. He bowed over it and went away in a daze.

The hours until he could see her again dragged past at a snail's gallop. David ate the lonely repast the cook prepared for him, his thoughts full of the marquis's daughter. She was not what he had expected at all. There had been no cold hauteur, no disdainful pride. She had been as natural and frank as a boy. Perhaps it was because she had spent her childhood in the Breton country, so far from the rigid etiquette of the royal court. Perhaps it was just her nature. He remembered how she had laughed and played with her dog in the dawn. She had been filled with what his grandmother called *joie de vivre*.

At last the abbey bells sounded out across the valley. David went at once to the kitchen garden, but there was no sign of her slim figure. He paced back and forth as the shadows grew longer. A dandelion growing in a crack in the flagstones began to close up its yellow petals. He bent and dug it up and threw it on to the garden.

'You think it nothing but a poor weed?' a merry voice called from behind him. 'I've heard you gentlemen gardeners want nothing to do with the common old flowers anymore, only wanting strange exotics from foreign lands.'

David's heart gave a strange thud at the sound of her voice. He turned to face her. 'It's just a dandelion. Called common for a reason.'

Viviane laughed. 'Is that what you call it? Such a funny name! It's not just a weed, though. We eat its leaves in our salads and make wine from its flowers. And I make a medicinal cordial from it to help old men pass water.' Her look of mischief grew. 'For here in France we call it "pissenlit", did you know?'

David could not help grinning. 'We call it "wet-a-bed" too, sometimes. But mainly dandelion. When it's in seed, we call it a "fairy clock".'

'I like that!' she cried in delight. 'Do you make wishes when you blow?'

'Yes. At least, I did when I was a boy.'

'What did you wish for?'

'To make my name, I suppose.'

'Is that why you are here? To make your name creating a garden for Monsieur le Marquis?'

He nodded.

'Do not pin your dreams to my father,' she said in a low voice.

Her voice, her whole manner, had changed. Her hands were clasped together, her jaw clenched tight with tension.

'Why not?' David asked, troubled.

Viviane hesitated, then shrugged her narrow shoulders. '*Pardon*. I should not have spoken so.'

'Have you had dreams of your own quashed?' he asked, greatly daring.

'It is not my place to have dreams. I am a mere daughter, subject to my father's will. It would be foolish to hope for a different kind of life. Such a thing . . . *alors, c'est impossible*.'

Her face was so sombre, David wished that he could comfort her somehow. He said gruffly, 'My grandmother always said, "For a valiant heart, nothing is impossible."'

She glanced up at him, her lips parted in surprise. 'I wish that were true.'

'Aye, well, next time you see a fairy clock, you'll know what to wish for,' David said, trying to lighten the moment. 'For the impossible.'

She smiled once more. 'Then I shall! Every single time. Shall we look for a fairy clock?'

Picking up her muslin skirt with one hand, she began to walk through the garden, her eyes on the ground. 'Look! Here is one.' She picked the dandelion puff, closed her eyes and blew. Delicate seeds sailed out on to the breeze. 'I wish . . .' she whispered.

'You need to say, "Dandelion seeds away, make my wish come true some day."'

She repeated the little rhyme, smiling.

'Here's another!' David picked it and presented it to her with a little bow. She blew once more, till she stood haloed in shimmering winged seeds.

'You will have dandelions cropping up everywhere now,' David said.

'That is good! More dandelions, more fairy clocks, more wishes.'

'Well, I hope all your wishes come true,' he said.

'And yours too. You shall create a garden most beautiful, and so make your name and your fortune.'

'Will you help me?' he asked. 'Tell me what your father likes, what will please him?'

She was silent for a moment, then said slowly, 'My father is very proud. He likes all that is most rare and costly, so that other men might be jealous of him.'

'Then we shall make a garden that everyone will envy,' David said. 'People will travel from far and wide to see it.'

Her face lit up. 'Maybe even from other lands.'

'From everywhere!'

'I would like that,' she said.

For some reason David put out his hand, as he would to a friend, as some kind of pledge or promise.

Laughing, she took it and shook it vigorously.

'To believing in the impossible!'

4

Romance of the Rose
5 August 1788

Viviane stood on the battlements, looking out across the barren fields.

It was going to be a hard winter.

Perhaps David Stronach's dream of a garden was the answer. They could employ the men in clearing the dead trees and tumbled stones, and rebuild something new and beautiful from the ruin.

He had expressed a desire to see the château grounds from above, so Viviane had asked Pierrick to bring him to the top of the watch-tower, on the south-eastern corner of the château. It was the only turret open to the elements. From here, one had a bird's-eye view over the surrounding fields and forest.

She heard his quick, impatient step and turned. He came towards her eagerly, a telescope in one hand, his cocked hat tucked under his arm. Tall and broad-shouldered, he wore buff breeches and a sober waistcoat under a dark blue coat cut in the English style. His eyes were a clear grey-blue, as changeable as water, and his unpowdered hair glinted with fiery bronze lights in the sunshine. He wore it tied back with a leather thong, like a peasant, but his tall boots were polished to a high shine and he wore a gold signet ring on the little finger of his left hand.

'*Bonjour*, mamzelle,' he said.

'Good morning, sir,' she answered.

He grinned. 'Your English is very much better than my French, I admit, but how am I to improve if I cannot practise it?'

'You can speak French to everyone here at Belisima but I can only practise my English on you,' she answered. 'So, you see, my need is greater than yours.'

'And I must admit it's a relief to speak in my mother tongue.' He laid down his hat and stood with his hands braced, gazing out across the meadows. 'What a beautiful view. I can see for miles.'

As he opened his telescope and scanned the landscape, Viviane made a little gesture to Pierrick who was standing by the door to the stairwell.

You can leave us, her gesture said.

But your great-aunt? Pierrick answered with an eloquent shrug of his shoulders.

Never mind my great-aunt, go! She made a pushing motion with both hands.

La la la, you like this clodhopper! Pierrick responded, both eyebrows shooting up. He appraised the gardener with an appreciative eye. *I can see why!*

Go, go, she responded, smiling and blushing and shaking her head.

David glanced at her and she bent to pat Luna so he could not see her face. When she looked up, Pierrick was gone.

After a while, David dropped his telescope and said, in a neutral tone of voice, 'The land is not in good heart.'

Viviane knew it was true. 'The flax exhausts the soil. And it gives us the greatest return, so my father insists we continue to plant it instead of allowing the fields to lie fallow. Then he takes all the profits and does not allow us to invest it back into the land.'

He glanced at her.

She could not meet his gaze. 'Life at court is expensive.'

He frowned. 'Have you tried planting winter turnips? They return nourishment to the soil, and can be harvested as fodder for your animals to help them through the lean months.'

'No,' she answered, excitement quickening through her.

'You will not be able to plant flax for a season after the turnips, but other crops will do well.'

She shook her head, her spirits deflating. 'My father will not permit it.'

'There is no profit to be made from empty fields. If we worked to fertilise the soil and planted winter crops, we can stave off hunger over the winter, and replant in the spring. Surely your father could not disapprove of that?'

'No,' she said slowly. 'But . . . how are we to fertilise the soil?'

'I've heard there is no place in Bretagne more than one hundred miles from the sea,' David answered. 'Why do we not go and harvest some seaweed?'

She gazed at him in wonderment. 'Seaweed? Of course! Why did I not think of that?'

'Farmers in Wales have used seaweed as fertiliser for a long time. Whenever there was a great storm, everyone would take their horse and cart down to the seashore and fork it up. I always loved to help.'

'I've never been to the sea.'

'Then you must go.'

Viviane did not answer. She knew she would never be permitted.

David went on eagerly, 'Perhaps we could go to Saint-Malo. That is where my grandmother was born.'

'Your grandmother is French?'

He nodded. 'Yes, though she left France when she was only eight. Her family were linen weavers, but they fled to England to escape the king's persecution of Protestants.'

'Your grandmother was a Huguenot?'

'Yes. They lost everything. She still remembers the journey from Saint-Malo to Plymouth, even though she was just a child. She thought the sea would swallow her up. She and her family found their way to Wales, and settled near Caerphilly. There were so many French there, the village was called Fleur-de-Lis.'

Viviane laughed in delight. 'A village with a French name in Wales?'

'Yes indeed. I suspect they couldn't wrap their tongues around the Welsh. There are villages nearby with names like Pontnewynydd and Llanbradach and Troedyrhiw.'

Her black eyes widened comically. 'Say those names again?'

He obeyed with gusto.

'I will never be able to say such words,' she declared, then spent the next few minutes trying. 'No wonder they named their village Fleur-de-Lis,' she said at last, limp with laughter.

'My grandmother still has trouble speaking Welsh, even after sixty-odd years. We all grew up speaking French as much as English.'

'We?'

'Me and my sisters,' David answered. 'Ceridwen is eighteen and Angharad is twenty . . .'

'One is a year younger than me and one a year older! Well, almost. I turn twenty in a few months.'

'I think you would like Angharad. She loves animals too.' He nudged a sleeping Luna with one boot. 'After my grandfather lost his living, she decided to raise rabbits for the pot but then grew to love them so much she refused to let them be killed. They are the fattest, happiest rabbits you've ever seen.'

'I would like her!' Viviane exclaimed. 'I am like that about my doves. And what about your younger sister? What is she like?'

'Oh, she is the merriest-hearted girl you've ever met. Always laughing and singing and dancing about.'

'And your parents?'

His face darkened. 'Our parents died when I was just a boy.'

'I am so sorry. It is hard to grow up without your parents. My mother, she died the day I was born. I never knew her. And my father . . . well, he lives at court and so I rarely see him.'

There was a long silence, then Viviane said softly, 'What happened to you all after your parents died?'

'My grandparents took us in.'

'Which is why you speak French so well.'

He nodded. 'That is how I got the job at the Jardin du Roi. They wanted an English gardener but had trouble finding one whose French was good enough.'

'They got a Welshman instead of an Englishman,' she said, smiling.

'Well, yes. But I don't think they know the difference. All they cared about was that I had my degree in botany . . .'

'You went to the university?' She gazed at him with eager interest. 'Oh how I wish that I could do such a thing! But women, they are not permitted.'

'No. Nor are grandsons of poor parsons, usually. I was lucky. The local squire was a man named Morgan and he had a son much my age named Richard. My grandfather tutored Richard for college, and Mr Morgan was happy for me to sit in the lessons too. They thought it would keep me out of trouble.' He grinned at the memory. 'Anyway, when Richard went off to Magdalen College in Oxford, I went with him. He studied law and I studied botany, under Humphry Sibthorp, who is famous for having taught but the one course for thirty-odd years.'

'This Monsieur Morgan, he paid your fees? That was most kind of him.'

'Oh yes. It made all the difference. My grandfather is not very worldly, you see. He . . . well, he travelled about, preaching to all the poor people in the mountains who had no church of their own. He'd preach in a field if there was no barn, and on a street corner if there was no field, and he'd teach all the poor children how to read and write, all for no pay, because he thought it the right thing to do.'

'He sounds like a wonderful man.'

'Oh he is! You've never met anyone so good! But not at all practical, I'm afraid. He displeased the church, who thought he was neglecting his own flock. They did not like him writing hymns in Welsh, or preaching on the streets, and so they cast him out of the church a few years ago.'

'*Comme c'est barbare!*' she exclaimed.

'Yes, indeed. He was heartbroken. Indeed he has been blue-devilled ever since.'

She frowned. 'Blue-devilled? This term I do not know.'

'It means he's had a fit of the blue devils. You know, down in the dumps.'

Her puzzlement only grew.

He laughed. 'He's in the doldrums, poor fellow, his heart in his boots.'

'His heart in his boots?' She gazed at him quizzically. 'Are you making a joke with me?'

'It means he's low-spirited. *Malheureux*.'

'Oh I see. I am so sorry that he is beset with these blue devils. It is very sad for him.'

'It is. He does not know what to do with himself. And the worst thing is that my grandparents were already as poor as church mice, and have the three of us to provide for.'

'And so you must make your fortune so that you may support them all.'

A flush rose in his lean cheeks. 'Yes, indeed. That is why . . . well, that is why this job is so important. I must create something very beautiful and romantic, something your father will want to boast about.'

'What did you have in mind?'

'An enclosed rose garden . . . sweet-scented . . . with a fountain or a statue . . .'

'A garden of love to celebrate my father's wedding.'

'Yes, indeed.' He looked at her closely. 'Do you mind . . . about your father marrying again?'

'Not at all,' Viviane said. 'Particularly if it means he is no longer so deep in debt.'

'I just need to find the right spot,' David mused, lifting the telescope to his eye again.

Viviane looked down at the roofs of the château below. Suddenly her eyes lit up in excitement. 'What about the outer bailey? See?'

She pointed down at a long broad strip of rough turf that ran the entire length of the château, separated from the lake by a low wall.

'Why, that could be perfect,' he said. 'Would I be allowed to use it?'

'It's not used for much else anymore. Come, I will show you.' She led him down through the dim stairs and corridors, Luna trotting along at her heels as usual. David looked about him with great interest, noticing the chandeliers in their muslin shrouds, the murky paintings in tarnished frames.

'This is the banqueting hall,' Viviane said, showing him into a long gloomy room with shuttered windows all along one side and huge damp-spotted mirrors along the other. An immense table stretched the entire length of the hall, covered with a heavy dust-cloth.

'This room is only used when my father is in residence,' she told him, going across to the windows and beginning to fold back the shutters so light streamed in. David went to help her. 'It looks straight out onto the outer bailey.'

Below the windows was a long stretch of grass and weeds.

'We could build the rose garden at the heart of a maze,' David said, his grey eyes glowing in excitement. 'You would be able to see the shape of it clearly from up here. People could watch those who try to make their way through. We could construct it to illustrate a story, like the king did with Aesop's Fables at Versailles.'

'Oh yes! *Ce serait merveilleux!*' Viviane cried, then her face sobered. 'Was not the maze at Versailles ripped out, to make an English garden? My father would want to be à la mode.'

He looked at her in surprise. 'Well, yes. That was in the days of Capability Brown, though. He removed all planned elements from a garden, wanting everything to look as natural as possible. The newest trend in English landscaping is to have three sequences of gardens. The first is inspired by formal geometry, with parterres and topiary and avenues of trees. The second is the transitional garden, with lawns and secret paths winding through groves of shrubs and trees, and vistas cut through to eye-catching landmarks, like temples or statues or fountains. The third level is the wild and the natural, with field and forest and mountain.'

As he spoke, David gestured with his hand to the view, sketching in the air how he imagined redesigning the landscape. 'That is how the garden at the Petit Trianon is laid out, and also how the Marquis de Laborde is planning his garden at the Château de Méréville. He has employed Hubert

Robert, designer of the king's gardens, to lay out the grounds, but your father was determined to have an Englishman, as you know.'

Viviane knew that her father had a long unfriendly rivalry with the Marquis de Laborde, whom he considered an upstart and a commoner. Laborde had been born into a lowly bourgeoisie family, but had made his fortune importing sugar, rare plants and slaves. He bought himself a title and a fine estate, only to lose his château to the Duc de Penthièvre after a game of musical chairs. Laborde had simply bought himself another château and was, by all accounts, pouring money into making it the finest property in the country.

'Well, then, if the Marquis de Laborde is building such a garden, my father will want one even bigger and better,' Viviane said. She began to fold the shutters back into place, plunging the banqueting hall back into shadow.

'So I believe,' David said. 'I plan to give it to him. Will you show me down? I'd like to start work planning it right away!'

David paced out the length of the outer bailey.

Once he reached the end, he pulled out a battered notebook from his capacious pocket and began to make sketches with a pencil stub.

Pigeons swooped through the air, darting in and out of the little windows at the top of the *pigeonnière*. Viviane called to them, cooing like a dove, and they fluttered down and rested on her head and shoulders and arms, hoping for corn.

When Viviane had been a little girl, her father had ordered her locked in the *pigeonnière* as punishment. The tower had been filthy and dark, filled with the sound of rustling and scratching. He had expected her to be terrified. Instead Viviane had been found curled asleep in the straw, a dove snuggled in her arms. The birds had been her special pets ever since.

David cast her an amused look. 'If I closed my eyes, I'd think you were a dove too. However did you learn to do that?'

She smiled. 'Oh, I just listen and then try and repeat it. Pierrick and I used to compete to see how many different noises we could make.'

'And who won?'

'I did, *naturellement*.'

'You are close to Pierrick?'

Viviane smiled and shrugged her shoulders. 'Oh la, *naturellement*! He is my milk-brother. Though we are not meant to speak now, *bien sûr*.'

David looked as if he meant to ask more questions, so Viviane hopped to her feet, shaking out her skirts. 'So what story shall you illustrate, with your maze, *monsieur*?'

'I was thinking of the story of Fair Rosamund, confined within her tower in the centre of the maze.'

Viviane did not like stories of girls confined in towers. '*Non, non!* Does she not die? Besides, it is an English tale. My father dislikes the English. It should be a French tale, a Breton tale. I know! You shall build a garden inspired by *Le Roman de la Rose*.'

'What's that?'

'Come! I will show you.' With Luna prancing alongside her, tail wagging, Viviane led the way back towards the château. She glanced back at David over her shoulder, laughing. '*Vite! Vite!*'

She took him to the library. He looked about with interest at the walls lined with books, and the huge faded tapestry above the fire. Fresh flowers in an antique Chinese vase filled the air with faint fragrance. The large windows looked over the orchard to the mill, and the quaint squat tower of the *pigeonnière*.

'*Le Roman de la Rose* is an old medieval poem.' Viviane unlocked a drawer in a cabinet and drew out a heavy leather-bound book in a brown morocco case. 'Some say it is set here in Bretagne. My family has an illustrated copy. It is very old, very rare. One of the treasures of my mother's family.'

She laid the book on a lectern, and carefully began to turn the pages. They were hand-lettered, with intricate drawings of birds and flowers and animals in the margins. David exclaimed in pleasure, and bent to examine the text more closely. Viviane was intensely aware of his closeness, his warmth, the smell of his skin. She stepped back and let him turn the pages himself.

'The poem was written by a man named Guillaume de Lorris in the early thirteenth century but he died before he finished the tale,' she told him. 'Someone else completed it, half a century later, but here at Belisima we do not have that later text, only the original unfinished poem.'

'What is the poem about?' David paused to admire a painting of a young man in a blue medieval robe and red hose seeking entry to a walled garden.

'It tells of a young man's quest for the rose, which symbolises true love. He finds a walled garden, where minstrels sing for fine ladies. In the centre of the garden is a fountain where grow the most beautiful roses he has ever seen. He is shot by arrows by the God of Love, and falls for the rose, *le coup de foudre*. How do you say? Like a thunderbolt.'

'He falls in love with a rose?'

'It is an allegory, *imbécile*. The rose is a young woman, of course. The Lover must be tested before he can win her.'

David grinned at her. 'I'm an imbecile, am I?'

'*Mille pardons, monsieur*. My tongue, it runs away with me sometimes. Though is that not yet another absurd saying you English have? As if a tongue has feet.'

He laughed and returned his attention to the book. 'I think it could work,' he said after a while. 'The maze could lead to a fountain in the centre, planted about with red and white roses like in this picture. There could be a statue of the God of Love, with his bow and arrows raised . . .' David pulled out his battered notebook and began to make sketches.

'We could plant the garden with fruit trees to attract the birds,' Viviane said, 'and all the sweetest scented flowers.'

'With banks of thyme and chamomile, like they used to plant in medieval times.'

'We need to plant a fig tree too,' Viviane said, reaching over his shoulder to point at a verse.

'I cannot read it – the medieval French is too difficult for me. What does it say?'

Viviane began to read aloud, bending closer to read the strange cramped handwriting. 'The God of Love, who watched me constantly, had

41

followed me with his drawn bow. He stopped near a fig tree and, when he saw that I had singled out the bud that pleased me most, he took an arrow and shot it at me with such great force that the sharp point drove straight through my eye into my heart. Then a chill seized me . . .'

She paused to turn the page, touching with one finger the painting of the winged god with his gold-tipped arrow.

'Pierced thus by the arrow, I fell straightway to the earth. My heart failed. It played me false. For a long time I lay in a swoon, and when I returned to my senses and reason, I was so very weak I thought that I must have shed a great deal of blood. But the point that had pierced me drew no blood whatsoever . . .'

Viviane paused, trying to find the right words. 'I took the arrow in my two hands and began to pull it free. I drew out the feathered shaft, but the barbed point called Beauty was so fixed inside my heart that it could not be withdrawn. It remains within. I still feel it, and yet no blood has ever been shed. I was in great pain and anguish because of my doubled danger: I didn't know what to do, what to say, or where to find a physician for my wound, since I expected no remedy for it, either of herbs or roots. But my heart drew me toward the rosebud, for it longed for no other place.'

Viviane paused and looked up. David's eyes were intent upon her face. Blood rushed up her skin. She moved away, trying to speak lightly. 'So do you like the poem? Do you think you can build a garden inspired by it?'

'Yes, indeed,' he answered, smiling at her. 'It is perfect.'

5

Ghosts of the Past
6 August – 8 October 1788

'**G**ood morning, sir!' a sweet voice called.

David turned, smiling. '*Bonjour*, mamzelle.'

'So you ride for Saint-Malo today?'

'*Oui*, mamzelle.'

With Luna prancing at her heels, Viviane made her way across the courtyard, where a parterre garden had been planted in triangles of box, enclosing cones of dark yew. Enclosed within the hedges were flowering bushes of lavender and Russian sage.

'It looks so pretty,' she said. 'My mother would be so pleased to see her old home being made beautiful once more.'

'This was your mother's home?'

'Yes, indeed. Belisima has been passed down mother to daughter for generations, ever since the time of the Lady of the Lake.'

'Lady of the Lake?' he asked, perplexed. 'You mean the fairy who gave King Arthur his sword?'

'*Oui*. My ancestress.'

When David made a scoffing noise, she looked at him with frowning eyes. 'Do not laugh. It is true. Her father served the Duke of Burgundy and was given this forest in reward. She met Merlin when she was only twelve years old, and he was enchanted by her. He taught her his magic and built her a crystal palace in the lake. On a day like this you can almost see it, can't you?'

David gazed out across the lake, where the reflections of the château's towers stretched long across the sparkling water. 'Yes, one can understand how such tales come to be invented, in a place like this.'

'The tales are not invented,' Viviane cried. 'They are true. It is my family heritage. Merlin met Viviane in the forest, and knew at once that she was his destiny. When Viviane was grown to womanhood, he tried to seduce her but she was afraid . . . and so she used the magic he taught her to confine him within a hollow oak tree.'

'We have similar tales in Wales,' David said. 'I know of at least three lakes where the Lady of the Lake is meant to have offered Excalibur to King Arthur.'

The look she gave him was comically cross. 'Perhaps. But those are just make-believe stories. This one is true.'

'And you are meant to be descended from her?'

'My mother's name was Viviane de la Faitaud. It means "kin to the fairy",' Viviane said. 'And indeed, the château is full of strange stories. Like the marquis who diced with the Devil.'

David repeated her words incredulously, and she laughed.

'It was Lent, but the marquis could not go so long without gambling, so he invited a few friends to join him in secret on the night before Good Friday. A stranger in black joined them and won every hand. He challenged the marquis to a game of all or nothing. The marquis agreed, but then in his haste dropped the dice to the floor. When the marquis bent to pick up the dice, he saw the stranger had cloven hooves. But it was too late. The Devil seized him and carried him away to hell. To this day, when the lord of the château is about to die, you can see the windows of the highest tower glaring with red light.'

'You are making this up!' David exclaimed.

She shook her head. 'No, no, it's true. The château has been here many hundreds of years, monsieur, you must expect a few ghosts of the past to linger.' She gave a little shiver. 'The saddest story is that of the young woman who drowned herself and her baby in the lake. People see her, the babe in her arms, dripping wet, on All Souls' Day.'

David gazed at her, frowning. 'Surely you do not believe in ghosts?'

She looked away. 'I did when I was a child. Sometimes I thought I could hear them creeping closer in the night. I used to hide under my bedclothes, afraid a cold claw would seize me and drag me away. I had to try not to cry out, in case anyone heard me and was angered.'

'Did you not have someone to run to?' David thought of his own grandmother, and how she had comforted him in the night whenever he woke up afraid.

Viviane shook her head. 'Madame Malfort would have been most displeased at such foolishness.'

'Monsieur Stronach!' the steward called from the stableyard. 'It is time to leave.'

The men had harnessed the horses to the carts, and Monsieur Corentin had brought out the rawboned gelding, bridled and saddled.

'I'm sorry,' David said. 'I must go.'

'I wish that I could go with you,' she said wistfully. 'But Madame did not permit.'

'I am hoping to find some wonderful exotic plants in the Saint-Malo nurseries. Their ships sail all around the world, to the Americas, and even to Bengal and China.'

'I tried to run away to Saint-Malo last spring. They call it the city of corsairs, you know. It sounded so romantic and exciting. I thought I could stow away on a boat and travel the world like Jeanne Baret. She was the first women to circumnavigate the globe. She dressed like a man and pretended to be her lover's valet . . .'

David could not help grinning. 'Is that what you planned to do?'

Viviane laughed and shrugged. 'Oh, well, perhaps not. I just meant I would dress like a boy, and no-one would ever guess I was a girl. I've wanted to sail the seven seas and have adventures ever since I was little and first read the encyclopedia.'

'Me too,' David admitted. 'One day I shall go and make my fortune. I'll discover a wondrous new flower and Linnaeus will name it after me.'

'Sometimes I wish I were a boy,' she sighed and stepped away from his stirrup.

I am glad you are not, David thought, but did not say.

A few nights later, Viviane was reading in bed by the light of a candle.

A knock on her window startled her so much she gave a little scream. Luna leapt up, wagging her tail. Viviane saw a glimpse of a grinning face. She threw a shawl on over her nightgown and went to unlatch the window.

'Pierrick! What are you doing?'

He scrambled in over her windowsill and stood, swaying slightly and dripping water all over her floor. 'Such news!' he slurred. 'Just wait till you hear!'

'Where have you been? Why are you wet?' She caught up a linen towel from her wash-table and flung it at him.

'Had to swim the mill-race and climb the wall. Gates were shut for the night. I didn't want old Corentin to know I'd been out.'

'But where have you been?'

'Rennes,' he answered, struggling out of his wet coat. 'Stop fussing, Viviane, and let me tell you my news.'

She perched on the end of the bed. 'Go on then. Tell me. But keep your voice down. We don't want anyone discovering you in my bedroom.' Viviane grinned at the thought of the furore it would cause.

Pierrick began to rub himself dry with the towel. 'The king has called a meeting of the Estates General. For the first time in centuries!'

Viviane stared at him. 'Really?'

Pierrick unknotted his lace cravat and wrung it dry over Viviane's wash-bowl. 'Yes, can you believe it? There was a riot in Grenoble. The people hurled tiles at the soldiers and blocked the streets. Then they all gathered together at a château – nobles and priests and common folk together – and demanded that the king call the Estates General and hear their grievances.'

'And the king said yes?'

'Yes. But that's not all. They demanded that the king double the number of representatives for the Third Estate.'

Viviane tried to absorb this. The Estates General was a general assembly meant to represent the three estates of the realm. The First Estate was the clergy, the Second Estate was the nobility, and the Third was everyone else. The first two estates together numbered about half a million people, while the latter – the peasants, the workers, the artisans and the bourgeoisie – came to more than twenty-three million people.

She wondered why the Third Estate would ask for double the number of representatives. Each estate of the realm was only allowed to cast one vote. The clergy and the nobility obeyed the king, so their two votes always cancelled out the single vote of the common people.

She voiced her confusion, and Pierrick nodded, his black eyes dancing with wicked joy. 'Yes, but you see, they wish the voting to be counted by head, not by estate. So if the Third Estate have double the number of votes than the other two, they have a real chance of making some changes.'

Viviane felt a thrill of excitement. 'But surely the king has not agreed?'

Pierrick weaved his unsteady way towards the door. 'No, naturally not. But he will have to eventually. There is no more money left in the treasury, and no grain left in the barns.'

He made a ludicrous show of checking no-one was watching, then lurched out the door. Viviane climbed back into bed with a sigh, thinking of their own empty coffers. If it was not for the fat purse her father had set with Monsieur Stronach, to pay for labour and plants, they would be in desperate straits.

Monsieur Stronach had been hard at work these last few weeks, setting the men to plough ash and manure and seaweed into the soil. The blacksmith had been set to work making grand new gates, and a new driveway cut along the lake shore. It was astonishing to see how quickly the château grounds had been transformed.

Monsieur Stronach knew exactly what he wanted and how to achieve it, she thought admiringly, and he was not afraid to spend her father's money.

Viviane was just worried about where the money came from. Her father the marquis was always in debt. The money must have come from his new wife's dowry, but what would Clothilde think about her endowment being put to use in a remote little château nearly two hundred and fifty miles from Paris?

Even more frightening was the nagging question of why Viviane's father was investing so much money into the Château de Belisima. He had never done so before. Not even to make sure the fields and orchards kept producing income for him. He must have some kind of plan for the château.

Which meant he had some kind of plan for her.

David trudged back towards the château, his tools over his shoulder.

It was a warm summer's evening, stars glinting to life overhead. He felt pleasantly weary in every limb. He had spent the day helping the men plant *tilia tomentosa* along the avenue. Already the linden saplings looked beautiful, with their silvery heart-shaped leaves tossing in the breeze. They would grow fast, and by autumn would be a blaze of gold reflected in the lake. In spring, the honey scent of their starry flowers would be carried by the wind to the château, sweetening the air of every room.

He wished that he would be here to see it. That was the worst of being a gardener-for-hire. You imagined and planned and planted a garden that would blossom for other people's eyes.

It was late, for David had wanted to work till the last of the twilight had faded. He put away his tools and pulled up a bucket of water from the well, washing himself vigorously. His stomach growled. He looked towards the kitchen, but all was dark.

'Monsieur Stronach?' A soft voice spoke behind him.

He looked around, and saw a slender figure silhouetted in the doorway of the stillroom.

'Mamzelle?'

'*Oui*. Are you hungry?'

'I'm so hungry I could eat a horse.'

'Eat a horse? Why would you want to eat a horse?' Her voice rippled with laughter. 'What odd terms you English have! Come in. I have saved you some supper.'

'Glory be, but you're a marvel. Thank you.' David followed her into the stillroom, but saw no sign of any meal on the table.

Viviane took up the candle and led the way towards the corner, Luna at her heels.

'My great-aunt has gone to visit a neighbour tonight, so I am all alone, and Pierrick told me you missed your dinner. I know it is not *de rigueur*, but I thought . . . that is, if you do not mind . . . that we could sup together.' She looked back over her shoulder at him. 'You do not mind, do you? I know I can trust you not to take advantage.'

'No, not at all . . . I mean, yes, yes, of course you can trust me,' he answered, blushing and stammering like a schoolboy.

'I am about to show you one of the secrets of the château. You must swear on your parents' grave to never reveal it to anyone.' Viviane gazed at him expectantly.

David said at once, 'I swear, honour bright, never to tell.'

She was pleased with his response. 'Honour bright. I like that. Now, see the panelling on the wall? If you press the third rosette like so . . .' She demonstrated. To David's surprise, a low hidden door in the panelling sprang open, revealing a narrow turn of steps within.

'It leads up to the library,' Viviane said. 'We can be comfortable there. Come on, follow me.'

The stairs were nearly as steep as a ladder, and very tightly wound. David had to duck his head and hunch his shoulders, and almost lost his footing as Luna dashed through his legs. At last he crept out another small door into the library.

'I found the secret door quite by accident when I was a child,' Viviane explained to him. 'No-one else knows about it. Except Pierrick, of course.

He used to come and rescue me when Madame Malfort left me tied to a chair for hours. She always rested in the afternoon, you see. We had to be sure to be back by the time the abbey bells rang the Angelus, else she would discover me gone. Once we barely got back in time, and she could not understand how my hair could be so tousled and full of seeds, and my dress so grubby.' She laughed.

David felt a familiar pang of mingled pity, dislike and jealousy. Pity for Viviane, so lonely and constricted. Dislike for her governess, who sounded like a harpy. And jealousy towards Pierrick, who featured in so many of her tales.

Viviane danced forward, waving her hand to show him a small table set with white linen and old silver. 'I did it all myself,' she said. 'To keep our supper secret, *tu vois*. Madame would be most displeased if she knew.'

She lit the candles with a long taper kindled at the fire, and then poured them each a glass of ruby-red wine. 'Sit,' she said. Then she ladled small bowls of brown soup, and shaved what looked like horse manure over the top. She picked up her spoon and tackled it with enthusiasm, but David hesitated.

'Try it,' she coaxed. 'I promise, it is *très bien*.'

'What is it?' he asked.

'Chestnut soup with truffles,' she answered. 'Eat!'

He did as she ordered, and was pleasantly surprised.

'You English do not know how to eat,' Viviane said. 'Boiling your beef till it is grey, and then those horrible pudding things cooked in dripping.'

'I'm Welsh, remember. You should try our *bara brith* before you scoff.'

She held her spoon suspended over her bowl. '*Bara brith*?'

'Fruit soaked in hot tea and sugar, then baked with flour and spices and glazed with honey.'

'You and your tea. Pierrick told me how disappointed you were to discover we do not drink it here.'

'Only coffee and cider. Most uncivilised. Though I must admit this wine is very drinkable.' He smiled and lifted his glass to her.

'I raided the cellar,' she admitted. 'I'm glad you like it.'

'What's next?' he asked as she removed the bowls and put down a plate before him.

She lifted the silver lid. 'It's lamb from the salt meadow, served with white beans.'

'What does that mean, from the salt meadow?'

'The lambs are raised on the salt marshes near the sea, where the grasses are bitter.'

The flavour was exquisite. David ate eagerly.

'I wanted you to taste some of our Breton delicacies. Usually our meals are ordered by Madame, but she does not like our local food and so I must always eat as if I am at court. So much food, and all so rich and laden with cream. This is much better.'

'So where is Madame tonight? She does not often leave the château, does she?'

'Oh, no, never! She is far too lazy. She is all worried and upset about the news from Versailles, however, and so has gone to gather gossip.'

'What news?' David asked, sipping his wine.

'Well, the king is bankrupt now, they say.' Viviane topped up his glass. 'And so he's recalled Monsieur Necker, who was the former director-general of finance. The king had banished him from Paris with a *lettre de cachet* but has now changed his mind and wants him to return . . .'

'What's a *lettre de cachet*?'

Viviane regarded David with sombre black eyes. 'They are letters signed by the king and counter-signed by one of his ministers, which have no right of appeal. If a *lettre de cachet* is issued against you, why, you can be sent to prison without a trial, or locked away in a convent or a mad house, or transported to the colonies, or condemned as a galley-slave, or exiled. And there's nothing you can do about it.'

'*Quelle barbare!*' he exclaimed, using one of her favourite expressions.

'*Exactement.* And the worst of it is the king will sometimes sign *lettres de cachet* sight unseen for his favourites, so they may imprison or banish who they please, with no legal consequences.'

David looked up. 'That really is barbarous.'

'Yes. It is one of the things most disliked about the king. Anyway, Monsieur Necker was banished with such a letter but now he has been reinstated. All Paris is celebrating, for they hope he will save the country from bankruptcy. Madame is most angry, however. Monsieur Necker is a commoner, you see, and a Protestant, and he believes in reform, all of which Madame hates.'

'So Madame would hate me too.'

'*Oui, naturellement.*' Viviane smiled at him. She cleared away the dirty dishes, piling them neatly on a tray, then made coffee in an ornate silver pot over a hissing flame. She brought him a small cup, black and strong, and sat by the fire, picking up her sewing. She was embroidering red roses on pale pink silk.

'What is that you are making?' David asked, coming to sit nearby.

'A new waistcoat for Pierrick. It is our birthdays in a few weeks. We turn twenty.'

Jealousy pricked him once more. David tried to repress it. He knew it was wrong of him. Viviane had known Pierrick all her life. She thought of him as a brother. And, Lord knew, David had no right over her affections. Yet he could not help wishing that he did. The few moments he spent with her each day were like bright notes in a minor key.

'What do you wish for your birthday?' he asked, after a long moment of silence.

'If I could have anything?'

He nodded and Viviane considered, her head tilted to one side. 'I'd like a flying carpet that could take me wherever I wanted in the twinkling of an eye, but still bring me home in time for supper.'

'Where would you go?'

'I would go to all the wild and hidden places,' she decided. 'Places where hardly anyone has been before. I'd go to Madagascar, and the Caribbean, and the South Sea Islands, and the Americas, and New Holland. Imagine the rare beasts I would see, the new flowers and fruits, the strange customs of the natives . . .'

'You'd be following in the footsteps of the botanist-gardeners from the Jardin du Roi,' David said.

She clasped both hands together in a characteristic gesture of eagerness. 'Would I?'

'Yes, indeed. Monsieur Thouin, the head gardener at the Jardin, has sent men all over the globe. They bring back plants from everywhere.'

'I would like to see the Jardin du Roi one day. I have heard it is most beautiful.'

'It may be your best chance of seeing the rarest and most exotic plants,' David said, 'since you do not have a flying carpet.'

'One day perhaps I will go,' Viviane said.

David hated the way melancholy shadowed her face. He said impulsively, 'I will take you there! You would love it so much. It was originally a medicinal garden, and so many of the herbs and plants there have healing purposes. But there is a Cabinet of Curiosities, too, and all sorts of romantic follies. A labyrinth, and a dovecote, and secluded rose bowers.'

'It sounds most romantical.'

David went red. He took a gulp of his coffee to hide his embarrassment, then made a face at its bitterness.

'So where would you go, if you had the magical flying carpet?' she asked.

'To China, so I could get a decent cup of tea,' he said ruefully.

'China,' she whispered. 'Yes, it's the great last unknown, isn't it?'

'You know they call it the Flowery Kingdom? Merchants come back with the most extraordinary plants. Gigantic peonies, azaleas, camellias, lilies, chrysanthemums, repeat-flowering roses, mulberry plants . . . no tea plants as yet. Smuggling out tea is apparently punishable by death.'

'I have read that there is a massive wall there, four hundred leagues in length and twenty-five feet high, that scales mountain heights and valley depths,' Viviane said. 'I would like to see that.'

'It must be extraordinary,' David said.

'One day, perhaps, it will be possible,' she whispered, and set another stitch in her sewing.

*

On the evening of her birthday he waited in the garden for a long time, a bunch of wild flowers in his hands, but Viviane did not set a candle in the window of the tower, as a signal she was alone.

Miserably David went back inside. As he began to prepare for bed, he saw a faint glow from the courtyard through his tiny mullioned window. Curious, he glanced out and saw Viviane walking towards the chapel. She was dressed in black, and had her hair bound back severely. In her hands she carried a small lantern. It cast a golden radiance about her head like a halo. Luna limped at her hem.

David caught up his coat, and shrugged it back on. He slipped through the silent corridors and across the courtyard, looking in the chapel's door.

Viviane was praying by the marble sepulchre of a woman with her hands folded upon a book. Her lantern flickered in the cold draught, filling the vaulted roof of the chapel with light, if not with warmth. David watched till he was numb and stiff with cold. At last he saw Viviane rise, and bend to kiss the cold marble lips, then put a little posy of rosemary on the cold white breast.

It was her mother's grave, David realised. Only then did he remember that Viviane's birthday was also the anniversary of her mother's death.

He went inside the chapel. She looked up in surprise.

'I'm sorry,' he said. 'I did not realise . . . it is a sad day for you as well as a glad day.'

'Thank you,' she answered simply. 'Everyone else tells me not to be ridiculous, that it is stupid to be sad for someone I never knew.'

'It is possible to miss something you've never had,' he said.

She nodded.

'I was only six years old when my parents died, and yet I miss them every day.'

'How did they die?'

'In a carriage accident. We had no warning, no chance to say goodbye.'

'That is very sad.'

'At least I knew them. I have some memories of them.'

'I have only this.' Viviane drew a round miniature painting out of her pocket, small enough to be hidden within a hand. Set within a gilded frame, edged with red velvet, was a portrait of a young woman dressed in blue. Her powdered hair was piled high on her head, under a hat dressed with pink and blue plumes. A tree behind her, a glimpse of blue sky, and just one pink rose, growing beside her.

'Your mother? She's beautiful.' David handed back the tiny portrait.

Viviane turned it over and unfastened the back. Hidden within were two black locks of hair, entwined together. 'My mother's hair and mine, cut from our heads the day I was born and the day she died.' She touched them with a reverent finger.

David drew the gold signet ring from his left hand. 'This is all I have left of my parents. My mother had it made for my father. They were forbidden to marry, you see. She was a squire's daughter, and he was a poor parson. She had it engraved with a fleur-de-lis, can you see? For his French blood and the village he grew up in. And then she had it engraved on the inside with a secret message that only he could see.'

Viviane took the ring and held it to the light. 'This, and my heart, until I die,' she read. 'Oh, that makes me want to cry. So how did they marry? Did they run away together?'

'Eventually her father relented and gave his permission,' David said. 'They were poor but very happy, or so my grandmother says.'

She gave him back the ring. 'It sounds like an old fairy-tale.'

'A fairy-tale that came true,' he said stoutly.

A sudden brief smile illuminated her face. She shook her head and moved past him into the darkness, the white dog pressing close by her side.

'It is good that you live in a world where fairy-tales can come true,' she whispered, so low he barely heard her. 'I, unfortunately, do not.'

6

The Day of the Dead
2–9 November 1788

The Day of the Dead dawned bright and cold.

David rode out into the shadowy forest, flame-coloured leaves flying up from beneath the gelding's hooves.

At home, in Fleur-de-Lis, his grandfather would be preparing a sermon designed to bring comfort to those who grieved their dead. His grandmother would be cooking soul cakes and his sisters would be tying up little treats of gingerbread and treacle toffee, to give the children who would come mumming that night. If David was home, he would have been building a huge bonfire in the garden, ready for the evening festivities. In Welsh, the day was known as Calan Gaeaf, the end of summer, the beginning of winter, the shadowy time when spirits walked the earth.

Here they called it *La Touissant*, or All Souls Day.

David had been at Belisima-sur-le-lac for three months now, and it had all been filled with the kind of purposeful work he had longed for. Yet it had been a lonely time too. The men who worked under his command were distrustful, not liking Englishmen. Monsieur Corentin was polite but distant, while David felt an electric current of rivalry between him and Pierrick. He did not believe that Pierrick thought of Viviane only as a milk-sister. How could he, living so close to her, seeing that glowing vivid beauty every day?

Whenever David thought to himself that Viviane could never love a mere footman, he had to remember that he himself was just a poor jobbing gardener, far too lowly for a marquis's daughter. It did not matter that David believed fervently that all men were born equal in the eyes of God, and that he had as much right to forge his own way as anyone born of noble blood. It only mattered that, in the eyes of the world, she was born of blue blood and he was not.

David gave a sigh that was almost a groan.

He set his horse to galloping, not heeding the lash of twigs across his face. In recent weeks, David had been longing for a steep climb up a cold windy mountain, or a plunge into the icy waters of a black Welsh lake. He was not sleeping well, even after long days of hard labour. He was homesick, he told himself. *Hiraeth* was the word for it in Welsh. A yearning or a longing for that which was gone or which could never be. David bent lower over the gelding's withers, urging him on.

When at last he drew his horse up, both panting and sweating, he found himself in part of the forest he had never explored before. A narrow path ran down between mossy boulders to the lake. And there, framed between the bronze-red leaves of an ancient beech tree, was the finest view of the château he had yet seen. Both bridges were revealed, their arches reflected in the water, and the turret with its battlements, and the tall pointed spires. The white foam of the mill-race through the smaller bridge added a dash of movement and drama to the scene.

At once David imagined building a summerhouse here. A place to have picnics in the warmer months, a retreat for silent contemplation in winter. He pulled out his notebook and began to draw sketches. *I must bring Viviane here*, he told himself.

He rode back to the château more slowly, feeling the wind chill on his skin as the sweat dried. Then he sent a formal note up to the drawing-room, requesting Mademoiselle de Ravoisier to ride out with him that day.

An hour later, Viviane came skipping out to the courtyard, dressed in a trim green riding habit with a tall black hat decorated with a curled ostrich plume. The dress showed her slim boyish figure to advantage, and David found himself once again bereft of words.

They rode together along the winding path through the forest, Luna loping at the horses' heels. The path gave lovely views of the château reflected in the glimmering lake behind them.

'Do you gallop, monsieur?' Viviane asked, when they were some distance away from the château.

'Frequently,' David answered, a little surprised.

'Race me then!' And she leant forward, and gave the mare a little tap with her whip. The mare surged forward into a smooth, ground-eating gallop. Viviane cast back a mischievous look and David spurred his own horse on. Through the autumn forest they sped, fallen leaves swirling up from the horses' hooves. Luna raced behind.

David almost caught up to Viviane, but she leant low over the pommel of her side-saddle, urging her mare on. She reached the clearing first and pulled her mare up with a victorious whoop. 'I won, I won!' she called and waved her whip triumphantly.

'Ladies are not meant to gallop,' she confided, as David drew up beside her. 'But I always want to.'

'I'm sure ladies are not meant to gloat either,' he returned.

She laughed. 'If I had my way, I'd gallop every day.'

'Then why don't you?' he asked in surprise.

She gave a little characteristic twist to her lips. 'I don't have my way very often. *Sacré bleu*, if I was to be seen galloping! Someone would write to my father for certain, and then I'd be in trouble.'

'Well then, you must gallop here in the forest where no-one can see,' David responded lightly.

'I am not supposed to ride at all anymore,' she explained. 'My great-aunt only gave permission today because you said you wished to discuss the garden, and she knows my father wishes it to be the very best it can be. If she had known we were going to ride in the forest, out of sight of the château, she'd never have agreed!'

'I hope you do not get into strife,' he said.

She shrugged. 'It will be worth it, to ride in the forest once more. I have missed it so much.'

The path led them to the small bay with its lovely view of the château.

'I was thinking we could build a summerhouse here.' David pulled his battered notebook out of his coat pocket and showed her his sketches.

Her black eyes glowed with excitement. 'It'll be truly lovely,' she exclaimed. 'I remember coming here with my Austrian governess. She did not mind the scramble at all. We would bring a basket and have a *picque-nique*. She would never let me go any further, though. She said it was not safe. I wonder if it may not be even prettier a little further along? Can you see how the land juts out into the lake there, almost like an island? That may be a better place to build the summerhouse.'

They rode together down into the narrow track, which twisted and turned among tree roots and mossy boulders. It was so rough and overgrown they needed to dismount and lead the horses. Brambles snagged his sleeve. Soon David caught a whiff of something unpleasant. Viviane made a face. Luna began to whine and ran on ahead, nose to the ground. They followed her, David wondering uneasily if they were about to find a dead stag or something even more unpleasant.

The next moment the trail led out to a small peninsula, surrounded on three sides by water. A ramshackle hut was built close to the lake shore, overgrown with ivy and weeds.

'Someone lives here?' David said, dismounting and catching at the gelding's bridle.

'I don't know,' Viviane said. 'I've never come this way before. There was no path. Or, at least, I thought there was no path. Ooof! Doesn't it stink?'

'Look at the view!' David said. 'It is the perfect framing of the château.'

Together they stood staring across the lake. The château looked like a dream of a fairy-tale castle.

'But if this is someone's home . . .'

'It looks abandoned,' David said. 'And if it's not, it should be! The whole thing looks ready to fall down.'

As he spoke, he went across to the rough-hewn door of the hut and pushed it open with one hand. He had to duck his head to enter. Viviane followed him, screwing up her face at the smell.

Inside was a dark room with a hard-packed dirt floor. A rough hearth had been made of rocks against one wall, and was filled with ashes that winked red sparks of fire. A blackened pot hung over the ashes from a tripod, and a few iron utensils hung on the wall, most of them filthy with dust and cobwebs. Three crude stools were drawn up by a rickety table, where a knife lay gleaming next to a dark heel of bread.

'Someone is living here.' As Viviane's eyes accustomed to the gloom, she saw a row of moleskins tacked to a string across the ceiling. Her pulse jumped. 'It's the mole-catcher's home. He's quite mad. He mustn't find us here – I hate to think what he might do. Let's go.'

David, however, had seen a small door set in the back wall. Curiously he pushed it open.

A white shape swung towards him, arms billowing.

Viviane screamed. As David stumbled backwards, she sprang towards him, half-sobbing in her terror. 'What is it? Is it a ghost?'

David put his arm about her and drew her close. 'No, no, look. It's just an old nightgown. Hanging from a hook. It's just the draught that made it sway.'

Viviane uncovered her face and looked. The white thing was indeed a small nightgown, green-stained as if with water, and falling into tatters. Other clothes hung from hooks. A shabby dress of brown homespun. A dirty fichu. A child's linen coif.

The room was simply furnished with a straw pallet covered with an old patchwork counterpane, much chewed by rats who seemed to have nested within. A candle was set upon a stool, the wax melted down in fantastic shapes and thick with dust. At the foot of the bed was a cradle, grey-draped with cobwebs, and a little rocking chair, made as if for a child. Set upon the rocking chair was a handmade ragdoll, eyes and mouth crudely stitched, wearing a dress made of scraps.

'It's a little girl's room,' Viviane said wonderingly.

'But look how dirty. No-one has been in here for many years.' David took a few steps inside, his footsteps smudging the grey fur of dust on the floor.

'I did not know Maugan had a daughter,' Viviane said.

'Perhaps she died, and he shut the door to her room and never opened it again.'

'So sad,' she whispered.

Just then David caught a swift movement in the corner of his eye. He turned. The mole-catcher leapt towards Viviane with the knife in his hand. David called a desperate warning and Viviane jerked away. The knife sliced down her arm, tearing the cloth. She screamed, as David caught her in his arms and swung her out of harm's way. The next moment, he struck a powerful blow to Maugan's jaw. The mole-catcher reeled backwards, dropping the knife. David seized Viviane's hand. 'Run!' he cried.

Together they leapt over the mole-catcher's body and raced for the door. Maugan staggered to his feet and bent to retrieve the knife.

'He's coming!' David flung Viviane up into her saddle and unhitched her bridle, passing her the reins. 'Ride!' he shouted, striking her mare's rump with the flat of his hand. Viviane obeyed, Luna racing behind her. David vaulted into his own saddle, and galloped after her. Looking back, he saw the mole-catcher shaking his fist and shouting curses.

As soon as he was sure they were safe, David drew his gelding to a halt and caught the reins of Viviane's mare. 'Show me your arm.'

'It's nothing. Just a scratch,' she panted, showing him the bare skin of her arm inside the torn fabric of her sleeve. A long red weal oozed blood. He tore off his cravat and bound it firmly. 'Oh, David, you saved my life!'

It was the first time she had called him by his name.

'It was just luck,' he said. 'If I had not seen him from the corner of my eye . . .'

'But you did. You did see him. And you knocked him over. You helped me escape. Thank you.'

Her dark hair was ruffled, her eyes glowing with fervour. David wanted badly to kiss her. He looked away, the gelding prancing and fidgeting from the tension in his fingers.

'Let's get you home,' he said gruffly. 'Then, when you are safe, Monsieur Corentin and I shall take a few men and see what can be done about that madman!'

The air was scarlet with smoke.

Viviane stood at her bedroom window, gazing out at the forest. 'They are burning the mole-catcher's hut.'

'Well, what did you expect? The man attacked you with a knife.' Briaca gently wound a bandage about her arm.

'But it's his home . . . where will he go, what will he do?'

'By all accounts, he is rarely there. He travels about, catching moles for whoever will pay him. Monsieur Corentin said the locals thought that old place had fallen in long ago.'

'I just don't understand. Why did he try to stab me? What have I ever done to him?' Viviane's voice broke.

Briaca was silent for a moment. 'A lot of hate for those of blue blood.'

Viviane thought of the men who had been sent to burn the shack. Many of them had sent her sullen looks, though she had not wanted Monsieur Corentin to take such harsh action. They had not liked to see David riding at the head of the procession either. Some had cursed him under their breaths or spat on the ground.

'If it was not for David, I'd be dead,' Viviane whispered.

Briaca came and put a hand on her arm. 'You should not be so familiar with him, mamzelle. He is a foreigner and a commoner, and not even Catholic. If your father knew . . .'

'Am I not allowed even one friend?' Viviane cried in sudden anger.

'Choose your friends from among your own kind, mamzelle,' Briaca said.

Viviane's shoulders were rigid with tension. 'There is no-one of my own kind here. You know that.'

'Come to bed, mamzelle,' Briaca said.

Viviane resisted the pull of her hand, looking back out the window at the thick pillar of black smoke. 'I never knew the mole-catcher had a daughter.'

Briaca dropped her hand and turned away. 'She died soon after you were born.'

'But how? How did she die?'

'She killed herself.'

'But why?'

'She was hurt . . . she was ashamed . . .' Briaca's face was shadowed.

Viviane frowned at her. 'Was she . . . was she with child?' She remembered the cradle in the girl's room, all spun over with cobwebs.

'She did not want it. Your mother did her best . . . but then she died . . . and for poor Loeiza, all hope died with her.'

'My mother?'

'Yes. Your mother tried to help her but . . .' Briaca sat down on the end of the bed, her head bent down into her hands.

'Briaca? What is it? What's wrong?'

'So long ago. None of it matters now.'

'Won't you tell me?'

Briaca shook her head, and got up abruptly.

'Wait. Please.' Viviane reached out and caught hold of her dress. 'The mole-catcher's daughter. How old was she?'

'Just fourteen years old. Little more than a child.'

To Viviane's amazement, Briaca was weeping.

'I'm sorry,' she whispered, scrubbing her face with her apron. 'It's just . . . I should have helped her. She was my dearest friend. But I was too frightened . . .' Her voice broke.

'Who was the baby's father?' It somehow seemed very important to know.

Briaca got up abruptly. 'It doesn't matter. Loeiza has been dead these twenty years. Let her rest in peace.' She went swiftly towards the door.

'Wait! Briaca, please.'

Briaca turned, one hand on the half-open door.

'How did they die? The mole-catcher's daughter and her baby?'

'She drowned herself in the lake, with stones in her pockets and the baby in her arms. Twenty years ago, on the Day of the Dead.'

'Less than five weeks after I was born. Five weeks after my mother died.'

'Yes.'

'Three babies, born so close. The mole-catcher's daughter's baby, Pierrick and me.'

'Yes.'

'Is that why he hates me? The mole-catcher? Because I lived but his daughter died?'

'That is one reason,' Briaca answered.

'What other reason could there be?' Viviane demanded.

Briaca stood still, her head bent.

'Was my father the baby's father too?' Viviane asked, her mind making a wild intuitive leap. 'And . . . was he Pierrick's father also?'

Briaca put up one hand and smudged away a tear.

'Please tell me.'

Briaca looked at her with haunted eyes. 'I cannot. I swore never to tell.'

'Who made you swear that? My father?' Viviane rushed across the room, seizing Briaca's hand and preventing her from leaving. 'But why?'

Briaca shook her head again. 'He would throw me and Pierrick out into the street to starve if he knew I was speaking to you about it, mamzelle.'

'So it's true? Pierrick is my brother?' Viviane felt a surge of contradictory emotions. Joy and surprise and disbelief and bewilderment, all muddled up together. 'But . . . why then is he nothing but a servant? My father wants a son and heir! Surely that is why he has married again, so late in life? I do not understand.'

Briaca stared at her in incomprehension. 'Mamzelle, don't you know the laws against bastards? A child born out of wedlock has neither kith nor kin, nor any rights at all. Even if Monsieur le Marquis was to acknowledge my son as his – which he would never do – Pierrick would never be able to lay claim to a single *sou*.'

'But that's so unfair,' Viviane whispered. 'He is my father's son.'

'Not in your father's eyes.' Briaca spoke bitterly. 'When I knew that I was with babe, I went to him, I begged him on my knees to help me. And he told me that any child of mine would be born of a soiled womb, and so worthless in the eyes of all. And I knew that to be true. I knew all good people would shun us, and that we would likely die together in a ditch, for a sin that was forced upon me! I was in despair.'

Briaca gripped Viviane's hands with all her strength. 'Then Monsieur le Marquis took pity on me, he said that I could stay, and my child too, as long as I never told anyone the truth. And for twenty years now I have kept my lips sealed, and never said a word. You must promise me to do the same, mamzelle! Please! If Pierrick found out, I do not know what he would do. He hates the marquis, and all of his kind. And you know Monsieur le Marquis would not think twice about casting me off; we would lose everything. Promise me you'll not tell Pierrick the truth!'

Viviane hardly knew what to do or say. Her mind was all confusion.

'Swear on your mother's grave,' Briaca commanded her.

'I swear,' Viviane said falteringly.

Briaca let her hands go, and turned away with a deep sigh of relief. 'It is better Pierrick does not know,' she murmured. 'He is already angry and dissatisfied with his lot. He may begin to wish for the impossible, and that only ever leads to heartbreak.'

Viviane sat down abruptly. Her legs felt weak and trembly. Pierrick was her brother? Her half-brother, she supposed. Yet born out of wedlock, and so born without a name, nothing but a dash in the parish records where his father's name was supposed to go. What would he think if he knew?

Briaca was right, she thought. Pierrick would be angry and resentful. Maybe it was better he did not know.

But the secret burned within her.

Briaca was hunched and anxious. 'Mamzelle, you need to know. Loeiza's father was not a bad man before. A trifle stern, perhaps, for he wanted to keep her safe. But then he found his little girl had been forced against her will, and was with child when only a child herself, and the father giving her nothing but heartache and a ruined name, and the child to be born without a sou to his name when – less than a league away – another child, born of the same father, was to be wrapped in silk and fed with a silver spoon, and bowed and scraped to all her life – well, is it any wonder it drove him mad?'

The words spilled out of her, as if a tie fastening her tongue had been cut.

Viviane stared at her, feeling sick.

'It's enough to drive anyone mad,' Briaca said then, very low, and went out, closing the door behind her.

David stood at his narrow lancet window, a glass of wine in his hand. He felt both bone-weary and overwrought. He kept seeing that moment when the mole-catcher had lunged at Viviane, the knife flashing down in his hand.

Thank God he had snatched her away. Thank God she had not died.

It was a long time before he slept.

The next morning, David was roused by the sound of shouting and running feet. Half-dazed with sleep, he pulled on his breeches and boots and went out to the courtyard. Maids were clustered about the gate, shawls cast over their dresses against the early morning chill. They all looked anxious and upset. One was weeping. 'Poor Mamzelle,' she said. 'How awful.'

David pushed past them and ran through the garden. More people stood, staring towards the orchard. Through the archway, he could see a cluster of people standing near the *pigeonnière*, looking down at something white and bloodied on the ground.

His heart banged hard against his ribs. He broke into a run. *No, no*, he thought. *Please.*

He pushed through the crowd.

A heap of white birds on the ground. Wings bent and stained with red. Heads severed. Claws bent and frozen. Dark eyes staring.

'Someone took to them with an axe,' Pierrick said. For once, there was no ripple of amusement in his voice.

'But why?' Monsieur Corentin said.

'The peasants hate the laws that allow the seigneur to keep a thousand doves that eat their seeds and destroy their crops, but cannot be hunted for food.' Pierrick spoke with great authority, so that David looked at him in surprise. 'It is one of the grievances the Third Estate hope to bring before the king.'

'This is more personal.' David's voice was croaky. 'No, this is the mole-catcher. This is his revenge.'

Pierrick glanced at him, then nodded in swift agreement.

'But how did he get in?' Monsieur Corentin demanded.

'He would have swum the mill-race, then climbed the wall broken by the oak tree.' Pierrick pointed to the far end of the orchard, to where the wall had half-collapsed under the weight of the heavy branch. A half-smile flickered over his face. 'It is not hard.'

Just then, a cry of distress rang through the morning. Viviane ran towards them, a robe flung over her nightgown, her hair tumbling free. 'My doves! What has happened? Oh no! But . . . who? Why?'

She flung herself on her knees and began to turn over the limp bodies of the birds, flinching at the sight of their severed heads. Tears flooded down her face.

'I think it was Maugan,' David said, his voice rough with emotion.

Viviane bent her face into her hands and began to weep. David bent and lifted her to her feet, and blindly she turned into the comfort of his arms, burying her face against his shoulder. He rocked her gently, murmuring words of comfort.

When David lifted his head, it was to find all the men staring at him and Viviane. A hot burn spread up his body. Gently he drew away from her. She clung on tightly.

David saw, over Viviane's head, Briaca standing with the maids.

'Pierrick, will you take Mamzelle to your mother? She is distressed.'

The young man nodded and came forward, putting his arm about Viviane's shoulders and leading her away.

'What do we do with them all?' David asked, staring down at the tragic heap.

Pierrick turned his head, with a flash of his usual grin. 'Eat them, of course!'

Ten days later, a letter arrived from Viviane's father.

She opened it with a sick knot of anxiety in the pit of her stomach.

> Versailles, 6th November 1788
> Mademoiselle,
> It has most regrettably come to my attention that you have entered into a friendship of some intimacy with the English gardener. I hope I do not need to remind you of the honour due to your birth and position. I must inform you that any further conversation with the man in question shall lead to his dismissal, without pay or referral.
> Yours etc,
> Louis-Auguste- César de Ravoisier, the Marquis de Valaine.

7

A Rose as Red as Blood
12–20 November 1788

I n November, the starlings flew from the cold north.

Viviane leant her chin in her hands and gazed out at the twilight sky. This year there seemed to be more than ever before. Swirling and eddying and spiralling against the rose-coloured clouds, black sparks in a rising wind.

Viviane felt she could not bear to be confined indoors anymore. 'Pardon me, madame. I must take Luna out for a moment.'

'Must you always be so restless?' her great-aunt complained. 'Sit still and finish your embroidery.'

'Of course, madame. As long as you do not mind Luna piddling on the rug.'

'Do not be so vulgar!'

'A thousand pardons, madame. I will not be long. Shall I order you up some hot chocolate?'

'And some more sweetmeats,' her aunt sighed, dusting the sugar from her plump fingers.

Viviane went out demurely, Luna trotting behind, then gave her aunt's order to Agathe. She caught up her coat and muff and hat, and ran down the stairs and across the bridge. David was overseeing the paving of the avenue of linden trees. She halted momentarily, then walked swiftly past him, pretending not to see him. He leant on his shovel and gazed at her with bleak eyes.

Viviane walked slowly, feeling the pain of their separation deep within her, like some kind of internal wound. She had not realised how much she had come to rely on him for comfort and companionship. Each day seemed leached of colour and vitality. Even the pastimes that had once brought her joy – her garden, her stillroom, her books – were now nothing but chores to fill in the dead hours of her days.

It was not just David's companionship that she was missing. Viviane hardly dared to speak or even look at Pierrick now that she knew the truth of his parentage. She wished that she could run to him and fling her arms about him and call him 'brother', but feared her father's reaction if the truth was to come out. He would be merciless, she knew.

The fields stretched out, ashy under the twilight sky, fringed with skeletal trees. It was cold. Viviane burrowed her hands into her ermine muff. She felt very alone.

'Mamzelle!'

The sound of David's voice like a bolt of lightning to a metal key. She began to walk faster. He called again. She said, without turning, 'No . . . you must not . . . he will find out.'

'He?'

'Monsieur le Marquis, my father.'

He caught her by the arm and drew her to face him. 'Is that why? Your father? But there is no-one here to see . . .'

'They will have seen you follow me.'

'No. I was discreet. I promise you.'

She allowed herself to look up at him. The strong jaw, a little bristled this late in the day. The thick disobedient hair, the colour of old bronze. His eyes, grey as the sky.

'He will dismiss you without pay.'

'Only if someone sees us.' He caught her gloved hand and drew her fast across the fields, away from the château. Viviane gripped his hand tightly. She felt like running, or dancing, or weeping.

A distant rushing and roaring sound. Viviane pointed up into the sky.

'What is it? A fire?' David gazed at the dark billows swirling above his head.

'No, it's birds. Thousands and thousands of birds.'

A torrent of starlings, pouring through the sky like a vast shape-shifting whirlwind. A swift elusive ballet, birds swooping and swerving and soaring as if they thought and responded with a single mind. For a moment, a spinning vortex was formed, then a shape like a leaping fish, then a parabolic curve, and then a great dragon with wings of shadows. David and Viviane watched, mesmerised, as the birds flashed overhead, so free and jubilant it made her chest ache.

'*Sacré bleu*,' she whispered. 'What would I give to be so free?'

At last the sun sank away, and stars began to prick out. The birds sank away. Silence dropped.

'Why do they fly like that?' Viviane wondered.

'A hawk must have been threatening them,' David said. 'It's an evasive manoeuvre, a feint.'

'I think they do it for the joy of it. I feel it in my bones.'

'Perhaps it is both. A flight for life and freedom, made more urgent by the threat of danger.'

How she loved him. No-one else spoke to her the way David did. He seemed to know her own thoughts before she did herself.

The ground seemed to rock beneath her feet. It is true, she thought. I do love him. I have loved him all this time and not known it. It is like I have found the missing piece of myself.

Her first feeling was one of pure joy. Desolation soon cast its shadow upon her, however. Her father would never permit such a *mésalliance*.

Slowly they began to walk back to the château, Luna frisking away after the scent of rabbits. Viviane's hand was still on David's arm, keeping her steady on the rough ground. She could feel the strength of his muscles, the warmth of his body so near to hers. It was so dark now she could only see the shape of him against the luminous sky. She would have liked to have stepped closer still, into his embrace, but instead she dropped her hand and drew away. Her jaw ached with misery.

'Is your father cruel to you?' David asked suddenly and unexpectedly.

Viviane did not know how to answer.

David stopped and turned her to face him. 'Viviane, tell me. Is he cruel to you? Does he hurt you?'

'He is my father. It is his duty to chastise me,' she said at last.

'Is that why you ran away?' he asked. 'When you tried to go to Saint-Malo and become a corsair?'

She saw the white plume of his breath. Luna came to her, sensing her distress, pressing her body against Viviane's leg.

'I . . . did not wish to marry as my father ordered,' she answered at last.

David's jaw tensed. 'Who did he want you to marry?'

'The Duc de Montmaront. He is much older than my father, but very rich.'

'So you ran away?'

She shrugged. '*Oui.* I stole some of Pierrick's clothes and some food. I made it nearly all the way, sleeping in haystacks and under trees at night. Oh, my feet, they were so sore and blistered! But my father found me and brought me back. He was most displeased.'

'But he relented? He said you did not need to marry the duke anymore?'

'Oh no,' she answered matter-of-factly. 'He beat me till I could not stand, and then he took me to Versailles. I was to be presented at court, and then married. This was last spring, a few months before you came to Belisima.'

'So what happened?'

Viviane looked up at him, trying to see his face in the darkness. 'My father and the king spend every day hunting. They like to see how many poor defenceless animals they can kill. Me, I do not like killing. One day I rode out into the forest on my horse. I made the sound of a hunting horn, like so.' She put both hands to her mouth and gave a startlingly good rendition of a hunting horn being blown.

Luna began to bark in her deep voice.

Viviane laughed and soothed her with loving strokes. 'All the hounds ran after me, as you can imagine, and the hunters too. Oh, I led them a merry chase! Not one stag did they shoot that day, not one sparrow. My father, he was most angry, and the Duc de Montmaront, he said that he would not marry a girl with so little decorum.'

'So you were sent back here in disgrace?'

'*Oui*. My father, he thinks to punish me by keeping me from court, but me, I do not like court and I do not wish to marry anyway. So! He is happy thinking I am being punished and I am happy because I am home. It is only poor Madame who is miserable. She misses court very much. Even though all she ever did there was sleep and eat and play cards, just as she does here.'

'You do not wish to be married? I thought all girls did.'

'Yes, but you are an *imbécile* who knows nothing about women,' she answered, turning away from him and beginning to walk once more across the fields, slashing at the thistles with a stick she seized from the ground.

'Well, yes, so my sisters tell me,' he answered, falling in beside her.

'They are right.'

'But will you not explain to me, then?'

'Why would I wish to marry? I would have to leave Belisima and go away to court, and wear clothes of the most uncomfortable kind, and be bored to tears, while my husband gambled away my dowry and forced himself upon me, regardless of what I wished, all while flaunting his mistresses in front of me and ruining all that I hold dear to buy silk stockings and velvet coats and silver snuffboxes . . .' Tears stung her eyes, and angrily she rubbed them away.

David was appalled. 'But . . . it doesn't have to be like that, does it? What about love? What if you married for love?'

'Those of my kind do not marry for love,' Viviane answered.

They walked along in silence. David had pushed both hands into his coat pocket, and his head was bent.

After a long while Viviane said, a note of pleading in her voice, 'I wish it were not so. Miss Hayward and I used to read novels together, like *La Vie de Marianne* or *Julie*, and I used to dream that one day I too would find a love like that, even if it was to end most tragically. But I know it is

73

impossible. My father would never permit.' She looked up at him, trying to smile. 'So you see, it is better I do not marry at all. I would rather grow old and die than marry someone I do not love.'

'That would be a crying shame,' David said with some difficulty.

Viviane coloured and looked away. 'I must go in,' she said. 'I must not stay out here.' Yet she lingered a moment longer, biting her lip. At last she looked up at him again and whispered, very low. '*Pardon. Je suis désolée.*'

Only then did she turn to run across the fields towards the château. Luna bounded beside her, whining in distress.

At last Viviane reached her room and flung herself down on the bed, hiding her face in the crook of her arm.

Imbécile, she told herself. *He is a gardener. And a Welshman. And a Protestant. Such a thing is impossible.*

But Viviane was tired of being told that all the things she wanted were impossible.

When the roses finally arrived, it was a chilly day in late November.

The sky was leaden, the lake silver. All the men were put to work carrying the roses across the bridge and through to the château's outer bailey. Their thorny branches were bejewelled with rosehips, their roots carefully bound in hessian.

At last the roses were all set in place, ready to be planted in the morning, and the men went inside in search of warm fires and hot cider. David stayed out in the half-twilight alone, smoking his pipe, gazing over what he had created from a patch of turf and weeds.

Suddenly he became aware that Viviane was watching him from the steps of the château, Luna pressed against her leg. She was dressed in a long black velvet coat, lined and trimmed with ermine, with a matching cap trimmed with white heron feathers. Her hands were hidden within a white fur muff. Her face was very pale, her eyes very black. It was the first time he had seen her since the murmuration of starlings, the first time since he had discovered that she could not marry for love.

She must have been watching from the banqueting hall, waiting to find him alone. Her breast was rising and falling hurriedly, as if she had run down three flights of stairs to meet him, out here in the garden where no-one would see. His blood quickened all through his body.

Slowly she came down the snowy steps, Luna limping at her side. Her eyes met his for a moment, then she flushed and looked away.

'The garden looks magical,' she said. 'It's like a miracle, to see what you have wrought out of nothing.'

'Thank you. Come, let me show it to you.'

His hands clenched behind his back to stop himself from reaching for her, David led her towards two stone griffins, their wings laden with snow.

The maze had been planted with more than seven hundred yew trees, six-foot-high and brought by a procession of oxen-drawn drays from Paris. Already David had begun clipping them into shape, so that they walked through dark shadowy corridors hung with tiny red berries. The only sound was the faint crunch of their feet on the snow-powdered gravel.

At last they reached the inner garden, where a long oblong pool had been installed and filled with water piped in from the lake. It was now hazed with ice.

At the northern end of the pool stood a statue of a young woman wearing a garland of marble roses. At the southern end was a sculpture of a young man kneeling, one hand braced on the ground, the other held out in entreaty to the Rose Maiden. The God of Love stood to the east, the tips of his marble arrows gleaming gold, standing beneath a fig tree trained into the shape of a fan. The statues were all caped with snow, and the roses stood in serried ranks of thorny trunks.

'They look dead.'

'They are just sleeping,' David told her. 'In spring, they shall bud again.'

'Spring seems a long time away.' Her voice was subdued, her face downcast. 'And summer even longer.'

Both knew that David's work at the château was almost at an end.

In a soft voice, David began to describe how the garden would look in full and voluptuous bloom when midsummer finally came.

'Imagine to the south, where the Lover kneels, banks of red roses, symbolising passion and yearning. Then to the north, billowing around the Rose Maiden, white roses with golden hearts, meaning purity and innocence and awakening love. Then, to the east and the west, huge pink roses with a thousand petals and the sweetest scent imaginable.'

'It will be lovely in summer. What a shame roses last such a short time!' she said.

'Yes. We will need to plant carefully to make sure there is colour and interest all year round. Red poppies and peonies and columbines to the south, white delphiniums and clematis to the north, and pink lilies with yarrow and apple-blossom beebalm to the east and west. I'd like to keep the flow of colour consistent but not rigid. And, of course, all will be enclosed within low box hedges to tie it all together.'

'I wish we knew what colour the roses were,' Viviane said, fingering a spray of orange hips.

'It is written on their labels,' David said. 'See, the ones with Rosa Alba written on them are white, and the ones with Rosa Gallica written on them are a deep crimson-pink.'

'Not red?' she asked in surprise.

'There are no true red roses,' he answered. 'Not in Europe anyway. I have heard rumours of a ruby-red rose in China, but all attempts to bring one back have failed. Sir Joseph Banks has invested a fortune in trying! But the journey is too long, and there are too many pitfalls for such a delicate flower.'

'But all the medieval romances talk of red roses,' she argued.

'That was only because they did not have a word for "pink",' he said with a wry grin. 'Saying "pink" to describe a colour only began less than a hundred years ago. At first it meant flowers in the Dianthus genus, like carnations or sweet Williams or the common pink, which all have frilled or serrated petals, as if they have been cut with pinking shears. Gradually the word came to mean the colour as well as the flower.'

'The things you know,' she said in wonder.

'My old lecturer Humphry Sibthorp loved stories like that. He knew dozens of fascinating facts about flowers and plants that he insisted on sharing with us at length.'

'And so what colour is this rose?' Viviane asked, bending over a plant that seemed quite different from the other two. She read the label. 'It's called Rosa Centifolia. Is that not from the Latin? Meaning a hundred leaves?'

'Yes, it means a rose with a hundred petals. It's a newly invented rose, and has tightly clustered petals of the loveliest pale pink colour, and a heavenly scent. It will look so beautiful.'

'How can you invent a rose?' she asked.

'It's easy enough. You take the the pistils from the heart of the mother rose, and dust it with pollen taken from the anthers from the father rose, and then you let it swell into a rosehip.'

David suddenly became aware that discussing the sexing of a rose was not at all the type of conversation he should be having with a young, gently nurtured lady.

'Then what do you do?' she prompted him.

He continued, with heightened colour and a constricted voice, 'In spring, you cut open the rosehip and plant the seeds. In time, you will see the new rose you have invented. Hopefully it will have the qualities you want, the rich colour, the sweet scent, the many petalled-shape. Sadly, this does not happen nearly as often as you'd like.'

'If I was to invent a rose, I'd make one that flowered more than once,' Viviane said. 'The rose blooms for such a short period, and the rest of the year it is just a thorny bush.'

'I've heard that roses in China bloom again and again, even when the first frosts have fallen.'

'Really?' She clasped her hands together like an excited child. 'Oh, one day I must go to China. It seems as if all the marvels of the world are hidden behind its high walls and mountains.'

All awkwardness seemed to have passed away. Once again she was at ease with him, as if she was his sister or his friend. But David knew that his feelings for her ran much deeper than that.

Sometimes he indulged himself in a fantasy where he performed great deeds and won her father's gratitude and Viviane's hand in marriage, as if he was a knight out of one of her old stories.

Other times, he spoke to himself sternly. *She is not for you. You cannot afford a wife. Particularly not one brought up in a château. You have your grandparents to support, your sisters to dower. You need to keep her at arm's length. She is a marquis's daughter, with blood as blue as snowmelt. She is used to servants. To fine clothes of silk and velvet and fur, and a vast château to live in.*

A vast cold empty château, the voice inside him whispered. *A lonely loveless château.*

David tried to ignore that voice. He had to be sensible. He had to think of the future. Viviane was not for him. She would go to court and marry for money, and he would seek to make his fortune somewhere else, far away from here.

Yet he could not help imagining Viviane in his life, in his arms, in his bed.

David turned away from her, put his hand upon the handle of a spade, searching for something to say. 'Would you like to plant the first rose?' he said at last.

'Oh, yes, please.' Viviane waited as he dug a hole next to the statue of the Rose Maiden. Then she drew her bare hands out of her ermine muff, and carefully lifted one of the roses into place. As she straightened, one high heel sank into the soft earth and she pitched sideways. Flinging out a hand to save herself, she caught at the rose's branches and cried out in pain as thorns pierced her palm. Beads of blood as red as rubies sprang up on her white skin.

'*Aïe-aïe-aïe!*' Viviane cried. She put her palm to her mouth to suck the blood away.

David drew out his handkerchief and took her hand in his, pressing the white linen against the wound. Immediately her blood soaked through.

Viviane looked up at him ruefully. 'I wonder if that is the colour of the red rose of China? A rose as red as blood that blooms even in frost! I would love such a rose.'

David should have turned away. He should have muttered something inconsequential about the weather.

Instead he took her bare hand and lifted it to his mouth, pressing his lips to her palm. 'One day I will go and find you one,' he promised.

8

Free as a Bird
8–11 December 1788

It was dusk, and the sky was slowly darkening.

Snow lay thick on the château's battlements, and frosted the steep slate roofs of the towers. The lake was a sheet of steel-grey ice, and the mill-race a surge of frozen cascades. The mill-wheel stood immobile, long icicles trailing from the spokes.

David stood on the smaller bridge, staring down at the frozen lake. A solitary figure skated there, pushing along one of the gilt chairs from the banqueting hall. She had been out there for an hour or more, all alone, stumbling and falling often. Luna crouched in the snow on the shore, watching anxiously, having tried to follow Viviane onto the ice until all three legs had slipped in different directions.

David and his sisters and the Morgan children had spent many a happy hour in the winter skating on the fish-pond at Plas Machen, building snowmen and hurling snowballs at each other. It had been great fun. He wondered if Viviane had ever been allowed such innocent play with other children her own age.

Just then, Viviane fell with a thump, skirts billowing up around her. Doggedly she tried to regain her feet, only to fall again.

David went through to the kitchen, and found Pierrick playing cards with some of the men. 'May I have a word?' he asked.

Pierrick looked up at him speculatively. 'When I've won this round,' he answered.

David sat down to wait. Finally – after much smoking of pipes and swilling of hot cider – the game finished and Pierrick came to join him. 'You want something, monsieur?'

'I am wondering if there are any ice-skates I can borrow?'

Pierrick shook his head. 'Mamzelle ordered hers from Paris. It does not often snow here in Bretagne, but they say this is the worst winter in eighty years. Mamzelle has had her heart set on a pair ever since she read that the queen loved to skate on the Grand Canal at Versailles.'

'I wonder if I can get hold of a pair somehow,' David said. 'I often skated at home.'

Pierrick regarded him steadily. 'I can find you some skates, *naturelle-ment*, if you have the coin to pay.'

David sighed. 'I have very little coin left, not having been paid yet.' *And I am saving it to buy something special for Viviane for Christmas*, he thought but did not say.

'Do you have anything to sell?'

'Only some old books,' David replied.

Pierrick made a face, but agreed to take the books to sell next time he went to Rennes to pick up the mail. 'The main difficulty will be finding skates big enough,' he sighed. 'You have feet like an elephant.'

'Better than having feet like a mouse,' David rejoined.

Pierrick returned with the skates a few days later, and – when dusk was falling and the men had come in from the cold – David strapped them on and went gliding out to join Viviane.

Her face lit up as he raced towards her. 'David!' she cried. She let go of the chair and skated towards him, both hands held out. Inevitably one foot skidded sideways and she lurched wildly. David caught her before she fell.

'I never realised it would be so hard,' she panted, straightening her skirt.

'Here, hold my hands,' he said, and began to skate slowly backwards. She stumbled along after him, but after a moment caught the idea and her skates began to move more fluidly.

'Keep your knees bent a little more,' he instructed. 'Push off with the inside edge of the blade . . . that's right.'

David was careful to keep close to the shadow of the château, where they would be less likely to be seen. Mademoiselle de Ravoisier, the daughter of the Marquis de Valaine, skating hand-in-hand with the gardener? *Quelle horreur!*

Yet he had not been able to bear seeing her out on the ice, so indomitable, so alone.

Her gloved hands clung to his. Her cheeks were rosy, her black eyes glowing with excitement. Soon they were moving so swiftly, her muff flew out behind her on its long satin ribbon. The ice hissed beneath their steel blades.

'Oh it's wonderful! I feel like I could skate forever,' she cried, 'all the way to the sea. I'm as free as a bird. Look, David!' And she let go of his hands so she could spread her arms wide like wings, one foot lifted. For a long moment she flew forward, graceful as a swan, then her ankle wobbled. David caught her hands and steadied her. She laughed up at him, and it was all he could do not to pull her into his arms and kiss her.

'It's getting dark,' he said. 'We should go in.'

'I don't want to go in,' she cried. 'Skate with me, David! Skate with me to the ends of the earth.'

So he took her hands and taught her how to spin.

Round and round they whirled, snow swirling down from the dark sky.

At last they came to a halt in the shadow of the bridge, clinging together, laughing, trying to catch their breath.

'That was wonderful!' Viviane gasped, looking up at him. 'Thank you.'

Unable to help himself, David bent his head and kissed her.

Viviane gripped his coat with both hands, lifting her face mutely, pressing her body against his. His hands found the shape of her within the heavy ermine-lined coat. Her mouth was sweet, her skin under his fingers like silk. He lost himself in a delirium of passion.

Then she wrested herself away. 'I can't, I can't,' she said, mouth against his shoulder. 'Oh, David, you must stop.'

He held her, staring down at her as if stupefied.

'I can't,' she said again, even as she lifted herself on tiptoe so she could kiss the clenched line of his jaw. 'My father would kill you if he knew . . .'

David could not think. His body trembled as if he had an ague. 'I did not know . . . it could feel like this.' He kissed her again.

After a long while, she drew away. 'What are we to do?' Her voice was desperate.

David tried to recover himself. He leant his hands on the wall, feeling the burn of the snow on his bare skin. 'I'm sorry,' he managed to say. 'I should never have done such a thing. It was . . . damnable.'

'No, no,' she said quickly. 'It was as much me as you. We could not help it . . . and I am glad!' She caught hold of his hand. 'I just wish . . . oh, but like all my dreams and wishes, it is impossible!'

Her voice broke. David turned and drew her into his arms, kissing away her tears. 'Why? Why is it impossible? Is not every man born free and master of himself? Why cannot we choose who to love?'

'I am not free,' she said. 'And I will never be free. I am my father's chattel, I must do as I am bid. And he will never permit me to marry you.'

David stiffened. 'Am I so ineligible?' he cried, out of the bitterness of his heart. 'I am not rich, it is true. The Lord knows, the Devil could dance in my pocket. But I am young, I am strong, I can work to support you . . .'

'It does not matter. Your blood is not blue. My father . . . we are of the *noblesse ancienne* . . . how do you say, of the old nobility. He is a *grand seigneur* . . . of noble blood from time immemorial. He would consider it an insult of the most unforgiveable. If he even knew that you had kissed me . . . he would run you through with his sword and feed you to the dogs.'

David was silent. His body thrummed with anger and thwarted desire. Words and arguments tumbled in his head. *It is wrong! We are all equal in the eyes of God. No man has the right to lord it over another.*

Yet he knew that all would condemn him for daring to fall in love with a marquis's daughter.

He looked down at Viviane, nestled into his arms as he had wanted her for so long. 'We will run away together,' he said recklessly. 'We'll find a ship and sail the seven seas. You can be my cabin-boy.'

83

She smiled, as he had intended, but it was such a forlorn attempt it smote his heart. He bent and kissed her hair. She was shivering.

'You are cold, Viviane *fach*. You must go in.'

She nodded, but did not move from the shelter of his arms. 'What does that mean?' she whispered. 'What you just called me.'

'It means "little one" in Welsh,' he told her, smoothing her hair away from her face. 'And also, "my dear one". And you must call me Davy *bach*, which is "my dear one" for boys.'

'I like it. I wish you could call me that always. I wish we could stay here, like this, for always. I wish . . . oh, Davy *bach* . . .'

He wiped away her tears. 'They would find us frozen to death in the morning,' he pointed out. 'Entombed in ice.'

'I wouldn't care.'

'Come on, Viviane *fach*. Let me take you in. Remember what my grandmother always said. For a valiant heart, nothing is impossible. We will find a way, I know we will.' David spoke only to comfort her. His own heart was as heavy as lead in his chest.

'There is no way.'

'I will write to your father, plead my case . . .'

'No, no! You must promise me, you will not write . . . he will kill you. Please, David, promise me!'

At last, unhappily, he promised her. She wept in the circle of his arms.

Resting his chin on her head, David gazed out into the darkness. In the corner of his eye, he saw light widen.

Someone was standing in the lit square of a window.

Watching them.

As a child, David had always wanted to know how things worked.

He dug up seeds to see them sprouting and dismantled clocks to examine their inner workings. His heroes were the great rationalists. Thomas Paine, Jean-Jacques Rousseau, Voltaire.

A rational man would never allow himself to tumble head-over-heels into love. A sensible man waited till he was financially secure, then looked about for a suitable young woman of good birth and good sense before asking her father for his permission to court her. After a few weeks of polite conversation, it might be permitted to kiss her hand.

A rational man did not stand in a wintry garden half the night, looking up at a window hoping to see it flower into light.

A rational man did not toss his sheets into a tangle, torturing himself with memories of a kiss in the snow.

A rational man did not take any chance to seize another kiss, knowing that discovery would be the ruin of all his hopes.

Yet David was no longer a rational man. His love for Viviane was lunacy.

A week after Saint-Nicolas's Feast, it was David's twenty-fourth birthday. He thought that nobody knew. Yet when Pierrick brought him in his breakfast, a small packet tied up with ribbons lay on the tray.

'From Mamzelle,' Pierrick said.

David opened the package. Inside was a flat brick of dried, compressed leaves. On top was stamped the image of a Chinese pagoda. David lifted the brick to his nose, then crumbled a few leaves.

It was tea.

David grinned.

'Mamzelle made me ride all the way to Saint-Malo to buy it for you,' Pierrick said. 'In this weather!'

'Please thank her for me,' David said, drawing a small silver teapot towards him. As he had hoped, it was full of scalding hot water. He cut off a hunk of the brick of tea and dropped it inside.

'Why do you not thank her yourself? When you sneak off to see her after supper?'

David felt a sharp stab of consternation. He knew how much Viviane feared her father discovering their love. 'Who else knows?'

Pierrick shrugged. 'Anyone who has eyes to see.'

'My intentions are honourable,' David said stiffly.

'So I should hope.'

'But the circumstances are . . . difficult.'

'Now that's an understatement.' Pierrick's voice was brittle and angry.

The door opened, and Briaca came in with a bowl of pottage.

'The men are going hunting this morning,' Pierrick said in a very different tone of voice, 'for if we cannot find meat we may all starve come Christmas Eve. Will you come with me, monsieur? I know that you can ride.'

He fixed David with a meaningful glare.

David nodded reluctantly.

'Enjoy your tea,' Pierrick said. 'I shall see you in the stableyard when you are finished.'

The hounds milled around the horses' hooves, baying with excitement.

The master of the hunt lifted his horn to his lips and blew a thrilling note. Horses broke into a canter, streaming across the two-arched bridge and into the forest. Ice cracked under their hooves, and the wind was sharp enough to bring tears to David's eyes.

'*Allons!*' Pierrick cried, standing up in his stirrups and gesturing to the west, away from the pale light of the rising sun.

David urged the gelding on. He needed a good hard gallop. It was difficult being confined within the snowbound château. Wanting Viviane and not being able to have her. Seeing no way out of their impasse. He had hardly enough coins in his pockets to buy himself a jug of ale, let alone passage for two back to Wales. He was still owed his wages, the marquis paying his servants at midsummer and midwinter. In a few more days, Christmas would be gone and David would have enough money to pay for tickets for two on the stage-coach to Saint-Malo, and thence on a boat to England.

If only Viviane would flee with him. But she would not. 'My father would find us,' she said in that bleak, hopeless voice that cracked his heart. 'He would kill you, and it would be all my fault. It's no use, David.'

How he loved the way she said his name, in that sweet broken English of hers.

The hounds caught a scent, and began to bay. Their voices were deep and powerful. David felt a quickening of excitement. He kicked his gelding into a gallop, following a narrow winding path through the trees.

It was not long before they saw the stag, antlered head held high. The dogs charged after it, baying like the wild hunt of Annwn. David and the other men galloped after, clods of snow flying from the horses' hooves.

Through the winter-bare trees they raced, leaping over fallen logs, veering around snow-mounded boulders. At last the stag was cornered between a thicket of red-berried holly and an immense bare-branched oak tree. The dogs barked shrilly in their excitement, darting in and biting at the stag's legs and being swept away by the lowered antlers. The master of the hunt dismounted and drew his knife. In moments, the task was done and the stag had fallen to his knees, its lifeblood staining the snow. David looked away. He could not help feeling a kind of grief that so noble a creature should end its life so cruelly.

It was not long before the stag was trussed and ready to be taken back to the château. The master of the hunt mounted up, prepared to see what other sport could be had that day. David turned his horse's head to follow the men back home.

'Monsieur Stronach,' Pierrick called. 'Wait for me.'

David reined his gelding in. The sun was higher in the sky now, but still cast little warmth or colour into the cold day. He blew into his gloved hands.

'Will you ride a little way with me, monsieur?' Pierrick asked. 'There is something I wish to show you.'

David inclined his head, and followed Pierrick as he rode along the frozen stream, the sun casting long shadows before them.

Pierrick led him into a deep shadowy valley, with tall pines rising up to rocky peaks. The rocks were all red. In the centre of the valley was a frozen lake. A bitterly cold wind clawed through the fabric of his coat. David buried his chin in his muffler. In Wales, the old folk called such an icy draught 'the wind of the feet of the dead'.

At the far end of the lake, Pierrick dismounted, tying his horse's reins to a thorny bush. David did the same, both curious and a little wary. Pierrick then led him in a steep scramble to a large outcrop of rocks at the top of the valley. From there, they could see across the dark lake and the forest to the open rolling farmland to the west.

They call these rocks *Le siège de Merlin l'Enchanteur*,' Pierrick said. 'That means . . .'

'Merlin's Seat. Thank you, yes, I know.'

Pierrick sent him a sparkling glance. 'Your French is indeed very good. And see you, the valley below? It is called the Vale of No Return. It is the domain of Morgan le Fay. She imprisons faithless lovers here, never to escape.'

David looked at him, one eyebrow raised.

'It is the truth I am telling,' Pierrick said, laughing. 'Every tree and every rock in this forest has a story, most of them to do with murder and magic and betrayal. The lake is called *Le Miroir aux Fées*. It was once the home of seven fays. One day the youngest fell in love with a mortal man, a knight who came hunting in the forest. Her elder sisters killed him, for daring to love one of their kind. The youngest sister hunted them down, one by one, and cut their throats. She collected their blood in a little bottle and mixed it with her own, and then used it to bring her lover back from the dead. It is said her sisters' blood flowed for seven days and seven nights. It flooded the forest, and dyed the rocks red, as you can see.' He made an elegant gesture with one gloved hand.

'I am in love with Viviane,' David said. 'I do not intend to be false to her.'

'You English! So frank, so lacking in finesse.'

'Is that not why you brought me here? To threaten me?'

'To warn you,' Pierrick said. 'Monsieur le Marquis is not a forgiving man. I do not wish to see your blood – or Mamzelle's – staining the ground red.'

'So it is true what Viviane says, that he will run me through with his sword and feed me to the dogs?' David asked.

Pierrick nodded. 'If he is merciful. It is far more likely that he will have you arrested and sentenced as a galley slave, or thrown into a prison to rot. It is the *puissance paternal*. The law of the father, you would say, I think.'

'I was hoping it was just a turn of phrase Viviane used to make her point.'

Pierrick grinned. '*Non, malheureusement.*'

'So our only hope is to run away together,' David said bleakly. 'Though she swears her father will hunt us down and catch us.'

'He will indeed try. That is why you must go now. Before he hears any whispers.'

'I cannot. I have no money.'

'None?'

'My pockets are to let.' To demonstrate, David turned the pockets of his breeches inside out. 'I will be paid on Chrismas Day, I am told, that being Monsieur le Marquis's usual custom.'

'You will need to break into Monsieur Corentin's strongbox and take what you are owed then.'

David frowned at him. 'I am no thief.'

'Think of it as Viviane's dowry.'

'No. I will not steal. When I am paid what is owed me, I shall go then.'

'You're a fool,' Pierrick said. 'Somehow, though, I am not surprised. Very well then. This is why I brought you here. If you and Viviane decide to flee the château, do not head north towards Saint-Malo. That will be expected. Head west instead, to a small fishing village called Roscoff. Go to the Hotel Le Chat Gris, and ask to speak to a man named Yves. Tell him that you are a friend of me. He will find you passage on a boat.'

'Let me guess. This friend of yours is a good man who does his best to help the poor folk of England enjoy the luxuries of life without the fuss and bother of paying any inconvenient taxes?'

Pierrick bowed with a flourish. 'Perhaps you are not such a fool after all.'

'What does he smuggle?' David asked curiously.

'To England, tobacco, brandy and silk, mostly. To the rest of France, salt. It is a profitable business.'

'So I see,' David said dryly, indicating Pierrick's fine boots and lace cravat.

He smiled. 'Oh, my dear Monsieur Stronach, I am not in league with smugglers! I merely gamble with them. And I have the devil's own luck, as I'm sure you can appreciate. So, if you decide to flee now, let me know and I shall advance you a small sum. With interest, of course.'

'No,' David said shortly. 'I will pay my own way or not at all.'

Pierrick smiled gently. 'On your own head be it. I just wish you to know that if you cause any harm to come to Mamzelle, I shall cut your throat, just as the youngest fairy cut her sisters', and it is your blood that shall stain the ground red.'

9

A Gardener with the Tongue of a Poet
24–25 December 1788

On Christmas Eve, David gave Viviane a ring.

'It's beautiful,' she said with a smile, turning it in her fingers.

It was only a small thing, enamelled with seven roses, that you might buy a child for good behaviour.

It had cost him all his savings.

'Look, each rose lifts up to show a word engraved below.' He took the ring and lifted one of the tiny catches to show her the hidden word.

Impossible, it read.

It seemed like a bad omen, but Viviane only exclaimed in pleasure and lifted the other catches to reveal the secret message.

For a valiant heart, nothing is impossible.

Smiling, she slipped the ring on to her right hand.

David frowned. He took her hand in his, twisting the ring round and round her finger.

'I wish you could wear it on your left hand, to show the world that we are betrothed.'

'I'm sorry,' she faltered. 'But someone would see and tell my father.'

For a moment he did not speak, still twisting the ring around. 'One day I will buy you rubies and pearls,' he said at last, his voice gruff.

'And gold, silver, ivory, apes and peacocks,' she returned at once, laughing. She reached up on tiptoe and kissed his cheek. 'I do not need rubies and pearls. This ring is all I need, and I will treasure it always.'

He enfolded her in his arms, deepening the kiss. At last she stepped away, flushed and breathless. 'I need to give you my gift!' she cried.

Viviane passed him a blue velvet box. Inside was a gold pocket watch with a compass attached. The back had been engraved with the words, *So you may find your way back to me.*

David was troubled. He had done his best to convince her that they must run away together, but Viviane could not believe her father would not track them down and have his vengeance.

'I do not want to leave you,' he said, again finding it hard to steady his voice. 'Will you not come with me, Viviane? I could take you to Wales. You will be safe there, I promise.'

But she shook her head. 'You don't know my father. He would never forgive. He would find me wherever I run, and then he would kill you. We must wait.'

'Wait for what?' he demanded.

'For him to die! For the world to change? I do not know.' She heaved an unsteady sigh, then said, 'In four years I shall be a minor no longer. At least then, we shall have the law on our side. Can you wait for me?'

'If I must,' he said reluctantly, wanting her now, this very minute.

'You can go to China, and find the blood-red rose and make your fortune, and then come back for me,' she said. 'And I will plant turnips and dig seaweed into the soil and wait for you.'

David took the compass and ran his thumb over the inscription. 'I have a better idea,' he said. 'We shall go home to Wales, and my grandfather will marry us, and I'll find work to support you.'

A shadow crossed her face, and she looked back towards the château, its pointed towers silhouetted against a flaming sky.

Eagerly David went on. 'Just one more day, and I shall be paid what I am owed, and then we can leave. We'll go at night. I'll order a carriage to be waiting for us in Paimpont. A few days on the road, and then we'll be safe on the high seas, heading for home.'

'Would I like Wales?' she wondered.

'You will love it,' he promised her and drew her close so he could kiss her again. 'Just one more day.'

At dawn on Christmas Day, Viviane was standing on the bridge, listening to the children sing, when a faint thrumming came to her ears.

She looked up. 'That sounds like . . .' she began.

A dreadful premonition gripped her.

'Hooves,' she finished faintly.

The children broke off in the middle of their song, and clustered at the side of the bridge.

'Look, mamzelle.' One pointed into the distance, where the new driveway curved round the lake. A golden carriage pulled by four black horses could be seen galloping over the hill. 'Someone is coming. Who could it be?'

Viviane stood as if frozen, her lips white.

'Who is it? Is it someone come to stay?' the children clamoured.

At last she managed to speak. 'It is my father.'

'Hurry, hurry, Monsieur le Marquis is almost here!'

David came out of his bedroom, his coat over his arm. 'I beg your pardon? What did you say?'

Pierrick was racing down the corridor, shrugging on his blue coat, his wig askew. 'Monsieur le Marquis is here! You fool, I told you to flee. You should have listened to me.'

David went to the bridge. He stared in fascination at the coach racing along the road. Two men ran like hares before it, carrying long golden poles. The four horses were huge and black, their coats steaming in the cold air. The postilions on their backs were crouched like jockeys, flailing their whips. Behind the golden coach rattled a dozen smaller carriages, roofs piled high with luggage.

'Quick! Quick!' Monsieur Corentin shouted. 'All of you. Line up in the courtyard. Are your aprons clean? Marie, your cap is not straight. Jacques, tuck in your shirt-tails.'

All the servants hurried to obey.

'Monsieur Stronach, you too. Stand at the back here. Take off your hat, you fool.'

David pulled off his hat and clutched it tightly.

The two running footmen crossed the bridge first. They ran right up to the gateway and then collapsed to their knees. Sweat rolled down their faces in great drops, and their gasping breaths were terrible to hear.

Then the coach arrived. It rolled up right to the gateway, the horses blowing, eyes white-rimmed. The postilions slid to the ground, grasping on to the harnesses to keep their feet. Another footman leapt down from the back of the coach and went to open the door.

A tall elderly gentleman in lilac silk and high red heels minced down the carriage steps. He carried a beribboned cane in one hand and a polished agate snuffbox in the other. His wig was very high and very white, and his lined face thick with maquillage. He must be the marquis, David thought, noting his sloe-black eyes and high-bridged nose.

Then a young lady in a huge hat laden with bows and ostrich plumes clambered down. She had to bend to the waist to manoeuvre her head through the carriage doorway. Her pink muslin dress was heavy flounced with lace and caught up at the back to show a multitude of white petti-coats. Although her long ringlets were unpowdered, her hair was so fair that it was at first hard to be sure. Her eyes were pale blue, and her lashes almost white, but her brows had been drawn in thick and dark. She looked at the château with a discontented look on her face.

'Why, monsieur, you have cruelly deceived me. It is positively medieval!'

'I did warn you, my dear. Let us hope the plumbing is not.'

'Do you jest?' she said. 'If not, I shall refuse to stay.'

'My dear marquise, would I make you suffer so? You know I live only to please you.'

'If you wished to please me, you would not have forced me to leave Versailles.'

'Oh, but my dear. The ennui! It simply could not be borne another moment.'

Another elderly gentleman stepped out of the coach. He was magnificently attired in mulberry-red velvet embroidered with gold thread, with a fur cloak flung over his shoulders. His eyes were a cold blue, his lips thin and sneering, his face sagging with lines of dissipation.

'Have we arrived at last?' he asked wearily. 'I had not thought it possible to travel so far in France and not cross a boundary or fall into the sea. No wonder I have never visited before, César.'

'You see why I so rarely make the journey, Vadim. It is wearisome in the extreme. The *chasse à courre* should make up for the inconvenience, though, I am sure. We shall certainly find a few stags, and some wild boar, and perhaps even wolves. It certainly looks like the sort of forest where wolves may lurk, does it not?'

'Wolves?' The marquise gave a little shriek.

'Compose yourself, my dear. If there are wolves, I shall kill them for you and present you with a rug for your bedroom floor.'

She pouted. 'How awful! I do not think it is at all the thing to have wolf skins on one's floor, monsieur. I would much prefer an Aubusson.'

'Of course you would. Your taste is always of the most profligate, my dear.'

She pouted and turned to the gentleman in the mulberry coat. 'What does he mean, Monsieur le Duc? Is he making another jest?'

'César simply means that your taste is exquisite, madame. And expensive.'

'Like my own,' the marquis said. 'That is why we are so well-matched, my dear.'

The marquise's smile seemed forced and stiff to David's eyes. He wondered how many years there were between her and her husband. It must be at least forty.

The marquis had paid no attention to the servants, standing silently in the freezing air. Now he turned towards them, lifting his quizzing glass and surveying them with a faint unpleasant sneer.

'Where, might I ask, is my daughter?' he asked.

At that moment Viviane rushed down the stairs and bent over the running footmen, lying gasping in the snow. 'Oh, you poor things,' she said. 'Can I help you?' She turned to Pierrick. 'They need something to drink! Can you fetch them some mulled wine?'

'You forget yourself!' Her father's voice was like a whiplash.

Viviane flushed and stepped away from the men lying on the ground. Keeping her eyes lowered, she curtsied.

Her father surveyed her through his quizzing glass for a long moment, his face stiff with disapproval and disdain. At last he indicated that she could rise.

'May I present Clothilde de Ravoisier, the Marquise de Valaine and my wife. And my old friend Vadim de Gagnon, the Duc de Savageaux, your husband-to-be.'

David jerked involuntarily. He took a deep breath and tried to compose his face.

Meanwhile, Viviane curtsied and said, in a cool polite voice, '*Enchantée*. Welcome to Belisima-sur-le-lac.'

Viviane sat at the table in the banqueting hall.

Mechanically she ate a few mouthfuls of each of the exquisite dishes put before her, cooked by her father's Parisian chef who had travelled with him from Versailles, along with his valet, his butler, his running footmen, his postilions, his page, a quartet of musicians and the marquise's maids.

Pierrick, resplendent in his blue coat and white wig, stepped forward and filled her empty glass of wine. Viviane drained it dry.

After dinner, everyone on the estate filed in to be paid their wages. The marquis knew every dish that had been broken, every working day lost to sickness, every misdemeanour, and deducted the appropriate amount.

When it was David's turn, the marquis lifted his quizzing glass and examined him slowly from the unruly wave of his hair to the heels of his good leather boots.

'So you are the English gardener?' he drawled.

'Yes, monsieur.'

'You have spent a great deal of money for very little gain that I can see.'

'It is winter, monsieur.'

'The draughtiness of my room and the dampness of my sheets attest to that,' the marquis responded languidly. 'Do not be insolent, else I shall have you flogged.'

'Pardon, monsieur. I simply meant that the garden is dormant. In spring, you shall see a thousand daffodils dancing in the park, and the lilac trees shall cascade with sweet-scented flowers. The roses in summer will bloom most gorgeously. In autumn, the avenue of linden trees will glow as if made of gold. All you need do is wait and let the seasons turn.'

'A gardener with the tongue of a poet,' the marquis said. 'How disconcerting. It is like hearing a toad sing like a nightingale. Very well. I thank you for your service and dismiss you forthwith. I am sure you understand I cannot pay you or give you a recommendation, not having yet seen anything but a few dead sticks.'

David bowed. His face was set, but Viviane could see the spark of dangerous anger in his eyes. 'As you please, monsieur. I shall write to you in the spring when the beauty of your garden shall be clear to even the most uncultured of eyes.'

The marquis held a pinch of snuff to his finely-cut nostrils. 'I doubt that I shall linger here long enough to see it. Such a bore, the country-side. The Duc de Savageaux may still be here, however. Since the Château Belisima-sur-le-lac will be his once he marries my daughter.'

David looked involuntarily at Viviane. She could not meet his gaze.

'In the meantime, your work here is done. Pack your things and be gone.'

David bowed and left the room.

'A gentleman gardener,' the duke commented. 'Indeed the world is changing, César, and not for the better. A game of picquet?'

Viviane endured an evening spent in the company of her step-mama and her great-aunt, who demanded to hear every new scandal of the court.

Clothilde only yawned and declared that Versailles was nothing but a bore, that the king had banned gambling for high sums in an attempt to economise, and that the queen worried over the health of the dauphin, the young crown prince, and so held no balls or picnics.

At last Clothilde retired to bed, saying in a long-suffering tone that she was rattled from head to toe by the dreadful state of the roads and did not think she could possibly sleep a wink. Viviane then listened to her great-aunt's rapturous opinions of the young marquise for another half an hour, before she was at last released and permitted to retire herself.

She went in search of her father, and found him drinking brandy and playing cards with the duke.

'If I may speak with you, monsieur?' she asked, her hands folded, her eyes downcast, Luna pressed close to her leg.

'If you must,' her father answered. 'Please excuse me, Vadim.'

The duke stood, smoothing the wrinkles of his fine velvet coat. 'Of course, César.' He bowed to Viviane. 'Good night, my dear. I look forward to the day when we shall be married.' His eyes lingered on her body in a way that made Viviane feel sick.

'I will not marry him,' she burst out, as soon as the duke had left the room. 'You cannot compel me.'

'Oh, but I can,' her father replied.

'You can beat me as much as you like, or drag me to the altar by force, but I will never consent.'

'There is no need for me to use such crude and violent methods,' the marquis replied. 'You will do as you are bid. You are a minor, and so subject to my will.'

Her legs were trembling but she tried to stiffen them. 'It is not the Dark Ages! There is nothing you can do to make me.'

'I am sure you will see reason once the alternatives are explained to you.'

'Send me to a convent if you must,' she cried. 'I'd rather by far take the veil than marry a man I do not love.'

He smiled. 'I have in my possession a *lettre du cachet*, signed by the king and one of his ministers, for use as I see fit. With its power, I can have you confined in La Salpêtrière in Paris, the prison for harlots and prostitutes. It is not a pleasant place. Filthy, overrun with rats, filled to the brim with the most hardened and diseased women of the street, all forced to work at the most degrading work possible. You would stay there as long as you refuse to do my bidding. Till death, if need be.'

Viviane clasped her hands together. 'I think you must be mad.'

'I do not like my will to be crossed,' he replied, still with that faint smile on his lips. 'Besides, your marriage to the Duc de Savageaux has been arranged to settle what might be called a debt of honour.'

Her face felt stiff. 'A debt? Of honour? You gambled me away?'

He made a tiny gesture. 'Must you be so blunt? Cultivate some finesse, I beg of you. The Duc de Savageaux likes to play high. Last spring, I won a great deal of money from him. This winter he won it back. And now that gambling has been banned at the palace, and the king has abolished so many of our rightful positions and privileges, there is little opportunity for Madame Fortune to smile on me again. The duke has graciously agreed to forgive me my debts in return for your hand in marriage. Your hand, and all your lands, of course. We are all burned to the socket and must recoup our losses any way we can.'

'I will not marry him. Send me to prison if you must. I do not care.'

Her father rose and strolled towards her, swinging his beribboned cane in such a way to make her flinch. He smiled and pinched her chin hard between his fingers. 'I never thought you a fool, Viviane. You may be condemned in public as a whore and sent to the worst prison in the country, or you may become a duchess. The choice is yours.'

Viviane was finding it hard to breathe. Luna whined and looked up at her, her ears and tail sunk low.

The marquis suddenly gave his cane a vicious twist. The ornate silver head twisted free and, with a faint hissing noise, he drew out a slim rapier. He seized Luna's amber collar with one hand and pressed the sharp point to her throat so that blood welled up through her white fur. The puppy yelped and shrank away, but the marquis pressed the blade deeper.

'Your dog offends me. It is an affront to our noble blood that my daughter should choose a crippled dog as a pet. Defy me, and it will die now. Bend your knee to me, and I will let the animal live.'

Viviane sank to her knees, her arm about the whimpering hound. 'Don't kill her. I beg you.'

'So you will marry the duke?' The marquis drew the rapier away, but kept it raised as if for a killing blow.

Viviane said unsteadily, 'What other choice do I have?'

Her father sheathed his sword. 'I knew you would see sense. Next Sunday the banns shall be called. In three weeks, you shall be married.'

Viviane's hands were shaking so much she could not strike a spark from her flint. At last a tiny flicker of flame leapt out, and she was able to light the candles.

She set the candelabra in the library window.

It was very late and very cold. Would David be watching for her? Or did he feel such a disgust for her that he no longer cared?

She saw a dark figure step from the shadows and raise a hand to her. Her knees weakened with relief. She had to sit down, her arms about her dog's neck.

A few minutes later, the hidden door swung open and David stepped through, taking off his three-cornered hat and shaking it free of snow. He was dressed in his long boots and greatcoat, the collar turned up, his leather gloves jammed in its deep pocket.

She flew into his arms.

'You cannot marry him!' He kissed her roughly, angrily.

'I won't! I won't. I'd rather die.'

'But will your father not beat you again? Viviane, you cannot stay here. He will hurt you.'

'No, no, we have to go. I should've gone before. I did not think . . . I did not know how low he would stoop. Oh David, we have to go. Now!'

'Are you sure? I can offer you so little!'

'You are all I want, all I need. Please!'

He caught her to him and kissed her fiercely.

'What a pretty scene,' a drawling voice said from the doorway. 'I am so sorry but I feel as if I must interrupt.'

David and Viviane spun about.

The Marquis de Valaine stood smiling at them. 'Englishman, I fear that you seek to steal something that is mine. I must protest. Unhand my daughter, and prepare to die.'

And with a swift twist and hiss, the sword sprang free from its concealment.

'No!' Viviane backed away, dragging David with her. 'I won't let you.'

'How do you propose to stop me?' The marquis sprang forward, the sword flashing.

Luna leapt, snarling, and the marquis staggered back. Viviane darted forward and twisted the carved rose to open the hidden door. David caught her hand in his, and together they ducked their heads to enter. David, slightly ahead, put up his left hand to brace himself on the wall. The marquis struck out wildly with his sword. David cried in sudden shock and pain. Blood ran down his wrist, staining his cuff.

Then the marquis caught Viviane by her tumbling curls and dragged her back.

'Please,' she sobbed, struggling against her father's vicious hold. 'He will kill you. Go!'

She fought free and pushed David with all her strength through the door, then slammed it shut behind him.

'Open it!' the marquis cried.

Viviane shook her head.

Her father plunged his sword into Luna's breast. Blood sprayed out.

The marquis ran for the door. 'I will catch him and I will kill him, and then you shall do as you are bid.'

Viviane cradled Luna in her arms, sobbing.

A gleam of something gold caught her eye.

She reached out one shaking hand.

On the floor lay a severed finger, encircled by a fleur-de-lis ring.

Part II

Blue Murder
May 1789 – September 1792

Blue Murder: To shout blue murder.
Indicative . . . of terror or alarm . . .
It appears to be a play on the French
exclamation *morbleu*.
The Reverend Ebenezer Cobham Brewer
Dictionary of Phrase and Fable (1898)

10

Fretted
28 April – 5 May 1789

The Palace of Versailles was a gilded cage, and Viviane a pinioned bird within.

She stood silently, braced against the weight of her immense hooped skirts, bruised in spirit and in flesh. The vestibule was crowded with people. Most were, like her, bedecked in gaudy court dress. Some wore shabby homespuns, hired swords buckled around their waists.

Viviane could not meet anyone's eyes. It felt as if her misery was an open sore that all must see and mock.

Her wedding ring fretted her finger.

Her husband, the Duc de Savageaux, stood beside her, swinging his quizzing glass from one languid hand. He wore orange velvet embroidered with gold at the cuffs, lace at his throat and wrists. His red heels were so high and his white wig so tall, he towered above the crush of people. His lined face was heavily painted, with reddened lips, rouged cheeks and black patches affixed to his temple and cheekbone.

Viviane's father was as magnificent as always in a long, gold-embroidered red coat and matching waistcoat, with a daring red velvet patch in the shape of a heart glued near the corner of his thin mouth.

Clothilde looked sulky and bored despite her exquisite gown of embroidered silk. Madame de Ravoisier just looked hot. Her round face was flushed and perspiring, and she fanned herself frantically. Her wig today was pale lavender, to match her vast satin dress.

The crowd began to stir. 'The king! The queen! They're coming.'

A billowing wave of bows and curtsies.

Viviane saw only a glimpse. The king, stout and ungainly, with a bulbous red nose and grey powdered hair in thick artificial curls on either side of his broad face. The queen, pale under her rouge, red-rimmed eyes downcast, tall white ostrich plumes nodding from her coiffure. Louis-Charles, the youngest of the royal children, marched at her side. He was a bright-eyed four-year-old, with ash-blond ringlets and a tiny sword by his side. Unlike his parents, he looked about him with curiosity and occasionally waved his pudgy hand at the crowd.

Behind the king and queen walked the eleven-year-old princess, Marie-Thérèse, looking like a sullen-faced china doll with long powdered curls, round blue eyes and bee-stung lips. She was dressed, like her mother, *à la grand panier*, her velvet court dress extending a foot to either side of her tiny waist. It must have weighed almost as much as she did. Viviane felt a pang of pity for the little girl, bound as tightly by the rigorous etiquette of the court as she was by her stiffly boned stays.

Another girl paraded alongside the princess, dressed as richly. She was the daughter of a chambermaid. After her mother died, the girl had been adopted by the queen. She slept in the same room as Marie-Thérèse, ate her meals with her, and was taught the same lessons.

Clothilde whispered behind her fan, 'They say the little mademoiselle is the baseborn daughter of the king and that is why she is honoured so.'

Madame de Ravoisier snorted with derision. 'Well, I have it on the very best authority that none of the children are the king's! All the court knows he has no interest in bed sport.'

Clothilde giggled. 'Only in playing with locks and keys.' She turned to Viviane. 'Did you know he had a forge installed in the palace grounds? With anvils and hammers and everything!'

'At least with a lock, he knows where to find the keyhole,' Madame de Ravoisier said with a loud laugh.

Clothilde rapped her arm with her folded fan. 'Madame! I am shocked.'

Viviane did not speak. Gossip and scandal was all she heard at Versailles. Some said Marie-Antoinette had taken a Swedish count named Axel von Fersen as her lover, and that he was the father of her youngest son, Louis-Charles. Others said that it was the king's dissipated youngest brother, the Comte d'Artois, who warmed her bed. Even more scandalous was the suggestion, repeated everywhere, that Marie-Antoinette's lovers were her closest friends, the Duchesse de Polignac and the Princesse de Lamballe. Scurrilous pamphlets with titles like *The Royal Orgy* poured out of Paris, filled with images of the queen lifting her skirts for her lovers. In one pamphlet, a knight, a bishop, a baron and a marquis took turns having bed sport with the queen while the court looked on.

It seemed impossible to Viviane. Marie-Antoinette was never alone, not even when she slept, for one of her ladies-in-waiting was always present, in case the queen woke thirsty or bored. Living at Versailles was like being under the constant glare of a thousand chandeliers. No matter where you went, no matter how hard you tried to find a moment to be alone, a crowd of people would soon be tramping past, giggling and gossiping and quizzing your every step.

No wonder the queen looked so tense and white, Viviane thought.

Though the queen had other sorrows to contend with. Her eldest son, Louis-Joséph, the seven-year-old dauphin, was not part of the procession. He was ill, and so kept at Château de Meudon, some five miles away, where the air was thought to be sweeter. Marie-Antoinette had spent most of the past few months there with him, but had returned to Versailles in preparation for the meeting of the Estates General in a fortnight.

A thin young man in a worn black coat and broken-down shoes pushed his way through the throng. His shaggy dark hair hung about his haggard face, uncombed and unpowdered. His eyes burned with fervour.

'Your Majesty!' he cried. 'The Third Estate d-d-demands that we be . . . be . . . be . . .' His mouth contorted as he tried to force out the words. '. . . permitted to . . . v-v-vote by head!'

He took a deep breath. 'Else the mee . . . meeting of the . . . Estates General will be n-n-nothing but a . . . a farce. A charade. A m-m-mockery!'

He shouted the words at the king's back, for Louis did not even pause or turn to look at him, but walked on as if the man was invisible and his words soundless.

'Ignore us at your . . . your own p-p-peril!' the young man shouted. 'The v-v-voice of the Third Estate sh. . . sh. . . *shall* be heard!'

'Not if you are their voice,' the marquis said with a sneer.

The young man stumbled back, his jutting cheekbones hectic with angry colour. He glared around at the watching courtiers, muttered something unintelligible and turned abruptly to leave, brushing against the Duc de Savageaux's arm.

'Must we rub elbows with the *canaille*?' the duke sighed, withdrawing a laced-edge handkerchief from his pocket and dusting his sleeve. 'Really, Versailles has grown to be such a bore. César, I think I shall go to Vincennes for the day and watch the horse races.'

'That should be amusing,' Clothilde replied eagerly. 'I hear the Duc d'Orléans is racing against the Comte d'Artois. The stakes will be high.'

'Oh, I think not,' the marquis replied. He clamped his fingers about her arm. 'You would be fatigued by the heat and the noise, my dear, and we do not wish that. You have other, more pressing duties to perform.'

Clothilde tried hard to suppress her distaste. 'But it is so boring here,' she faltered.

'I am sure we shall find another way to amuse ourselves,' the marquis said.

She shrank back a little, and tried to protest again.

'I have made my decision,' her husband answered coldly. 'Your only concern must be providing me with an heir, madame.'

'Yes, monsieur,' she answered in a low voice, staring at the floor.

'Perhaps we should stay at Versailles too, my dear,' the duke said, smiling.

'I'd rather not,' Viviane answered clearly. 'Much as I hate the races.'

*

The racecourse was as dirty, crowded and noisy as Viviane had feared.

Much of the court had flocked to Vincennes, where they could gamble as much as they liked without incurring the king's displeasure. Many stared at Viviane and whispered to each other behind their fans.

'Must you always look so sour?' her husband said. 'Your face is enough to turn the milk.'

Viviane did not answer.

He took her elbow in his hand, squeezing it cruelly. She tried to endure in silence. Her skin would show his dark fingerprints later. She had many such marks under her clothes, where no-one could see.

'Smile,' he whispered. 'Or I shall make you weep later.'

She did not smile.

At last the day was over, and Viviane could take refuge in the duke's carriage. They were to spend the night at his Parisian residence, a luxurious townhouse on the Place Royale in Le Marais. It was not such a fashionable address as it had once been, but the de Gagnon family had owned a house there since the early 1600s.

They drove into the city as twilight began to fall. Narrow alleyways ran between crooked buildings stained with soot. Open sewers seeped down to the river, where emaciated children in rags dug through the filth. Pigs rooted through piles of refuse. Viviane pressed her hand over her nose, trying to block the smell.

The carriage turned into the Rue Saint-Antoine, and she saw the great hulk of the Bastille looming against the tarnished sky. She became aware of a swelling noise, like the rumble of a gigantic threshing machine. Shouts and screams, then a sudden explosion.

'What is it, what's happening?' Viviane dragged down the window and looked out.

Over the rooftops she could see the glare of red fire. The air was acrid with smoke. People ran along the road, carrying makeshift weapons.

The duke thrust his head out the window. '*Sacré diable!* It's a riot.'

Further down the road, hundreds of people struggled against blue-clad soldiers. Many carried fiery torches, the flames glinting in the shards of broken glass in the gutter. Piles of broken furniture and bolts of brocade wallpaper burned on street corners. Straw effigies of men in silk coats were hoisted high on pikes and set on fire.

'Down with the rich! Down with the aristos!'

Some men saw the duke's coach and ran towards it, banging on its lacquered sides with their wooden staves. One thrust his grinning face in the window. He had a pistol clenched in his red-knuckled hand.

'Help a poor working man!' he cried. 'I've got a family to feed.'

With an expression of distaste, the duke drew out his purse and pressed a few sous into the grimy hand.

'That's not enough. My family are starving.' He leant forward and seized the duke's purse. 'Give me your watch too! And those pretty jewels.'

'This is an outrage! To be robbed blind on the streets of Paris, in my own carriage.' The duke unfastened his watch and chain and held it out at arm's length. The man snatched it.

Viviane shrank back. Quickly she slipped off the rose-enamelled ring David had given her and thrust it into her pocket.

Then she said, in a clear voice, 'Here is my wedding ring. You are welcome to it. I hope you can sell it and feed your little ones.'

She handed the heavy golden ring to the man, who took it eagerly. The duke was tense with fury, but Viviane did not care. She wished she could give away all that he had given her, the trappings of her ensnarement.

Other men were jostling the coach, rattling the windows, banging on the roof with sticks.

'*Vive le Tiers!*' they shouted. 'Long live the Third Estate!'

'Toast the Third Estate with us!' A woman thrust a dusty bottle of wine in through the coach window.

The duke refused angrily, but Viviane leant forward and took the wine bottle. She lifted it high, cried, '*Vive le Tiers!*' then drank a mouthful.

The crowd roared with appreciation. 'Bless your pretty face,' the woman said, taking the bottle back and draining it dry.

Laughing and shouting, the crowd surged on.

'Your father told me you had a taste for low company.' The duke's voice was cold and contemptuous. 'You will not drink a glass of wine with me, but are happy to do so with a filthy woman from the gutter.'

'Indeed,' Viviane replied, meeting his gaze coolly.

The duke was white lipped with anger. He rapped on the roof of the carriage with his cane, leaning out the window to shout at the coachman. 'Get us away from here, now!'

But the carriage could not move, surrounded as it was on all sides by shouting, jostling people. Viviane heard the cry '*Vive le Tiers!*' repeated again and again.

Gunfire rang out. The crowd howled in anger. Viviane craned her neck to see. The Garde Française had their rifles raised, smoke billowing above their cocked hats. Stones and tiles and refuse rained down on their heads from the windows and rooftops of the buildings nearby. Then a cannon fired. A young man was hurled backwards. He crashed into the ground. Blood snaked away from his skull.

Viviane gasped. She had never seen anyone killed before. She pressed both hands to her mouth.

'Away! Away!' the duke commanded, rapping on the roof of his carriage with his cane. The coachman turned into a narrow side street, the wheels clattering over cobblestones. People ran alongside the coach, shouting, but the coachman cracked his whip and they fell back.

At last the carriage made it safely to the duke's townhouse. The sound of shouting and screaming and smashing continued long into the night, interrupted by bursts of gunfire. Viviane could not sleep. She paced the floor of her room, trying to steady her breath, her hands clenched. Tears slid down her face.

She thought of the young man flying backwards through the air. His body, limp and broken. A woman would be weeping for him tonight. His mother, or his sister, or his sweetheart.

Viviane could not stop crying. It was as if the explosion had cracked the glass box which had encased her so long.

'David,' she whispered. 'Oh, David.'

*

'Your lover is dead,' her father had told her. 'The ice broke beneath him and he drowned.'

Viviane had not been able to speak.

She saw it all in her mind's eye. David running. The hunt galloping after him, horses blowing steam into the night air, dogs yelping. David driven on to the frozen stream. Stumbling. The ice cracking. Falling. Struggling to keep his head above black water. His strength failing. His body sinking away. Her father and the duke watching from their horses' backs, laughing. Doing nothing to save him.

She had laid her head back down on Luna's bloodstained fur.

'You will be married as soon as the banns have been read,' her father had told her.

Viviane did what she was told.

She did not know if Luna had survived. She had sewn the wound closed with her embroidery silks, but it had been deep. Her father had taken her away the very next day, galloping through the snow in his great golden carriage, the duke watching her with hot, possessive eyes.

Viviane had begged Pierrick to write to her, and tell her how Luna fared.

She had received no letter.

She had buried David's severed finger in the garden, under the statue of the Lover. She kept his fleur-de-lis ring sewn inside her chemise, over her heart.

It was warm to touch.

A weary lassitude weighted her limbs.

'You will get up,' her husband said to her, 'and you will dress as befits a duchess, and you will say all that you ought, and try not to disgrace my name.'

Viviane lay in bed. She hurt all over.

The duke raised his hand. She flinched back.

'Get up,' he repeated.

Viviane obeyed.

It was the 4th of May, and Viviane was to be part of the procession that would lead through the streets of Versailles to mark the opening of the Estates General.

Her maid Yvette was waiting with curling tongs and pots of pomade and powder. Viviane submitted to being swathed in a powdering gown, and her hair roughly rubbed with scented pomade and then set in stiff curls. Yvette held the hot tongs too close to her scalp, so that Viviane cried out with pain, and the air filled with the smell of scorched hair.

'Please be careful,' Viviane said, wondering that a Parisian maid should be so ham-fisted.

Yvette huffed out an angry breath, and then dug the hairpins in deep as she pinned up Viviane's curls. She then pumped so much powder onto Viviane's hair that Viviane could not help coughing, even though she had hidden her face in a cone of thick paper.

As Yvette flounced away, Viviane wondered if the pretty young maid-servant had been, perhaps, her husband's mistress. She could think of no other reason for her petulance. Viviane wished she could tell Yvette that she was welcome to the duke's attentions.

The maid returned with vast panniers, and tied them about Viviane's waist. Then Viviane's corset was tightened with such ruthless strength all the breath was crushed from her lungs. Even as she opened her mouth to protest, she was smothered in stiff heavy folds of gold-embroidered red brocade. The skirt was so wide Viviane would have to turn sideways to walk through a door. Her feet were shoved into matching shoes, tight and pointed with perilously high red heels, and ostrich plumes were jammed into her towering coiffure. Thick bands of rubies were fastened tight about her wrists and neck, and dangled from her ears, and glittered from her fingers.

'Now you look like a duchess, madame,' Yvette said with thinly disguised malice.

'I'd much rather not,' Viviane flashed back.

Her maid made a disbelieving snort, and snapped open a chicken-skin fan for Viviane to carry.

The royal couple walked at the head of the parade, with the king in cloth-of-gold and the queen dressed in silver-embroidered silk, the famous Sancy diamond in her hair. Walking beside her mother was Marie-Thérèse, her china-doll face set impassively. Behind glided the queen's favourites, the Princesse de Lamballe and the Duchesse de Polignac, their silk dresses rustling over the cobblestones, their wide-brimmed hats laden with feathers and ribbons. Both were fair with blue eyes, but they could not have been more different. The princess was slender and delicate, with a sweet face and sorrowful eyes. The duchess's colouring was far more vivid, and her step more vigorous. She looked around at the crowd with great interest, and laughed and waved as they cheered the royal party.

Behind walked the deputies of the Estates General. The clergy in long soutanes. The nobility in black silk coats and white satin breeches, cloaks lined with gold flung over their shoulders, white plumed hats on their powdered wigs, ornately wrought swords at their hips. The commoners at the back, in plain black wool.

'*Vive le Tiers! Vive le Tiers!*' the crowd shouted. The sound made Viviane flinch, reminding her of the riot in Paris.

The cheers for the Third Estate were punctuated with loud shouts for the king's cousin, the Duc d'Orléans, who had caused a stir by choosing to walk with the commoners. He was taller than the other men by more than a head. He waved his plumed hat at the crowd, laughing, as they shouted, '*Vive Duc d'Orléans!*'

The ovations were much louder for him than they were for the king and queen. Indeed, one woman surged towards the queen and shouted the words right into her face, causing the queen to stumble. The Princesse de Lamballe hurried to support her, her pale skin flushing, while the Duchesse de Polignac cried aloud in indignation.

'Why do the crowds cheer the duke so?' Viviane asked Clothilde, who was walking beside her.

Clothilde looked at her in surprise. 'Good Lord, she speaks!'

Viviane flushed. 'I speak if I must,' she answered stiffly. 'I am new here at Versailles. I know no-one else to ask.'

'Why, thank you for the compliment!' Clothilde answered. 'So glad to know my new step-daughter speaks to me only because she has no-one else with whom to converse.'

Viviane pressed her lips together, refusing to be drawn into bickering.

After a moment Clothilde said, 'Well, I suppose stupid questions are better than the stony silence with which you have greeted me so far.'

She gave an exaggerated sigh, and began to explain in slow loud tones, as if Viviane was a dim-witted child. 'The Duc d'Orléans was once a close friend of the queen's, but she made the mistake of mocking him when he boasted of his victories against the English in the American war. The Duc d'Orléans is very proud, and never forgave her. Then he spoke out against the king in Parlement, something no prince of the blood has ever done before. The king was furious. He banished the duke to his country estate. The people felt that Orléans had become their champion, and so they began to cheer him. He finds their adulation intoxicating, as you can see. And he enjoys stirring up trouble.'

'But does he wish for reform?' Viviane asked.

Clothilde glanced at her. 'He wishes for power.'

Just then the procession passed the royal stables. The king and queen looked up and smiled, waving their hands to a velvet-clad child lying on a sofa on one of the balconies. He was painfully thin and white, with sores about his mouth. The sight of him smote Viviane's heart. The young dauphin did not look as if he had much longer to live.

'Poor little boy,' she murmured.

'It is hard for the queen,' Clothilde replied. 'She lost her baby daughter not so long ago, and now the dauphin is dying.'

It was awful to see the dauphin so sick. All of France had celebrated his birth, which had occurred a few weeks after Viviane and Pierrick's fourteenth birthdays. There had been fireworks in Paris. Pierrick and Viviane had wanted to go, but of course had not been permitted. So Pierrick had made his own fireworks. He had discovered the recipe in an old book, and had experimented in secret for days. Charcoal was easy enough to get, and he had extracted saltpetre from the contents of the château's chamber-pots, and stolen some sulphur from the weavers' cottages, who used soda ash to bleach the linen white. He had also ground up the seeds of a low-growing plant called clubmoss or wolf's foot, which sent out spurts of fire when shaken through the flame of a brimstone match. For a few mad hours, Pierrick and Viviane had set the dark sky ablaze. Pierrick had burned off his eyebrows and Viviane had scorched her dress, and they had both been whipped, but it had been worth it.

The procession crossed the Place d'Armes, and finished at the church of Saint-Louis, where Monseigneur de La Fare, bishop of Nancy, was to say the Mass. He took the chance to deliver a long and furious tirade against the royal court, and the queen in particular, calling her mock farmyard at the Hameau 'a puerile imitation of nature' and castigating her folly and extravagance. The king appeared to have fallen asleep. The queen sat motionless, her lips pressed together tightly. When he had finished, the audience broke into spontaneous applause, something Viviane had never heard happen in a church before.

The next day more than a thousand people crammed into the Salle des Menus-Plaisirs, a great vaulted hall lined with marble pillars where the meeting of the Estates General was to be held. As the king and queen entered the hall, the deputies of the Third Estate remained on their feet, refusing to kneel. The king paused, nonplussed, then – after a long awkward moment – proceeded to his throne at the far end of the hall. He gestured to his wife to be seated also. Her head held proudly high, Marie-Antoinette curtsied deeply before him, acknowledging his sovereignty as the Third Estate had refused to do. Many of the nobles applauded and called out '*Vive la Reine!*'

The deputies of the Third Estate maintained an icy silence.

It was hard to believe. Royal etiquette demanded that the king's throne be bowed to, even when he did not sit there. The monarchy had ruled in France for over thirteen hundred years. Never before had the French people refused to bow to their king.

Viviane felt a sickening twist of fear in the pit of her stomach.

11

Death Mask
4–27 June 1789

A month later the dauphin died.

The king and queen stayed in seclusion for the next few days, grieving together.

On the 7th of June, all those who had been presented at court were permitted to express their condolences. Dressed in a black mantle, Viviane joined the long queue filing through the gallery, offering their condolences to the king and queen. Marie-Antoinette's face was pale as a death mask. She seemed not to see the gloomy procession passing before her. Her youngest child, Louis-Charles, was honoured as the new dauphin. He was only four years old. Looking troubled and unsure, he clutched the hilt of his little sword. His sister Marie-Thérèse stood silently, but her sensitive lips trembled.

'I am so sorry.' Viviane curtsied to the queen. 'Please receive my sincere regrets.'

Her voice quivered with emotion. The queen seemed to see her for the first time. 'Thank you,' she murmured.

A commotion occurred when some deputies of the Third Estate arrived, once again asking for an audience with the king.

'Are there no fathers amongst you?' the king cried out.

'Is the State not as sick as your son was?' one deputy answered contemptuously.

Once, the death of the dauphin would have plunged the whole country into mourning, but the business of the Estates General was too urgent to be set aside. Within two weeks, the Third Estate had declared itself a National Assembly and began to talk about creating a constitution to limit the powers of the king and his nobles.

The Duc de Savageaux was white-lipped with fury. He strode about their apartment, his hand clenched on the handle of his riding crop, hissing imprecations against those damned impertinent lawyers and bureaucrats, who dared try to curb their betters. He lashed out and smashed a priceless Sèvres vase, then strode from the room. He would go hunting with the king, Viviane knew, and take his vicious temper out on the wild creatures of the forest.

The duke had once been at the centre of the court, along with Viviane's father. They had been the closest friends of Louis XV, the present king's grandfather, a hard-drinking, hard-riding gambler famous for his many young and beautiful mistresses. When Louis XV had died and his young grandson had inherited the throne, the duke and the marquis had found themselves out of favour. Louis XVI was a simple devout man who did not like to drink or gamble.

The king, however, loved to hunt. So Viviane's husband and father never missed a day. Their fearlessness in the saddle and ruthlessness in the kill endeared them to the king. Perhaps they reminded Louis of his dissolute but charming grandfather.

Viviane hated blood sports. Her sympathies were always for the hunted. Yet now, in Versailles, she was grateful for it. Hunting took her husband away from her for many hours of the day. It left Viviane free to walk in the gardens or sit in the shade of a tree and read. She pored over the daily accounts of the Estates General, fascinated and fearful at the same time, wondering that the commoners dared to so challenge the king's authority and yet secretly cheering them on. It made her feel closer to David. He too had believed in the right of all humans to be free.

One day Viviane did not have the strength to get up out of bed and go through the long and tedious ceremony of dressing and having her hair done. She dismissed her maid Yvette, and stayed in bed and read. Rain drizzled against the window.

When Viviane had finished her book, she lay quietly for a while, dull and dispirited. Boredom eventually drove her to rise and walk about her room and stare out the window. She could not dress herself in court attire or powder her own hair. So she found an old muslin dress in her trunk, and combed her own curls and tied them back with a riband, and threw a warm shawl Briaca had once knitted for her about her shoulders.

Viviane intended only to go and find a new book to read, but as she made her way through the crowded halls of Versailles, she found to her amazement that she was now, miraculously, invisible. No-one recognised the Duchesse de Savageaux in the simply-dressed young woman with loose dark curls. She thought to test the limits of this new invisibility and went out into the courtyard, and then through the golden gates and into the town. No-one stopped her. No-one noticed her at all.

Footsteps quickening, Viviane set out to explore. Rain came and went in gusts, and she drew the shawl over her head.

A commotion in the distance caught her attention. Viviane turned that way, curious. She saw a group of men, in the dark coats of the commoners, jostling about a door that was guarded by stiff-backed soldiers in the king's colours.

'Th-this is an . . . an . . . outrage!' someone cried. Viviane recognised the stammering voice of the young man who had accosted the king in the palace. She went a little closer.

'Who ordered the doors locked?' demanded a young man with greenish eyes and a grey powdered wig.

'Orders of the king,' one of the soldiers said. 'Repairs need to be made to the room.'

'What r-r-rubbish! The room does not . . . not need to be repaired. He is just trying to stop us from m-m-meeting, damn him!'

The soldier raised his bayonet. 'Speak more respectfully of His Majesty or I shall run you through!'

'Hush, Camille! There is no need to be so intemperate.' The green-eyed young man drew his shabby friend away.

'But, Maximilian, you know it is noth . . . nothing but a ruse to shut us d-d-down!'

'Yes, I know. But we shall achieve nothing if we have to spend the night in gaol. Try and think before you speak, Camille!'

It was now raining hard. The deputies milled about, growing damp and irritable. Viviane ducked into the shelter of a nearby doorway.

'What do you suggest we do then, Monsieur Robespierre?' another man asked.

'We must not allow ourselves to be shut down. Let us find somewhere else to meet,' Robespierre said.

'But w-w-where?' Camille stammered.

'The royal tennis court is nearby, Monsieur Desmoulins,' a neat little man declared. 'It's not in use, and it has a roof. We shall at least be dry.'

'An excellent plan, thank you, Doctor Guillotin,' Robespierre answered. 'Will you show us the way?'

'And be quick about it!' Desmoulins cried. 'I only have one c-c-coat and it's getting so . . . soaked!'

The crowd of deputies hurried along the wet street. After a moment Viviane followed them. She was interested to see what would happen next. A few other onlookers came too, crowding into the indoor tennis court after the deputies. It had a smooth wooden floor and high vaulted ceiling, with rows of chairs for spectators. Viviane took a seat near the door, lowering her damp shawl from her hair and shaking out the drenched hem of her skirt.

'M-m-may I sit here?'

She looked up and saw Camille Desmoulins, his hair wilder than ever from the wind and the rain. Viviane nodded, and drew her skirts aside so he had room to sit.

He pulled off one shoe with a wry twist of his mouth. 'My feet are d-d-damned damp,' he confided to her. 'Holes in the soles.'

Viviane was startled at his familiarity, but then realised that she did not look at all like a duchess in her simple muslin frock and old shawl. It was a relief to be treated just like an ordinary girl, and so instinctively she slipped into the accent of the lower orders.

'It's raining ropes,' she said. 'Not a good day to be locked out.'

'That's wh-why they did it. Damned aristos.'

Viviane shifted uncomfortably in her seat.

'I was m-meant to be here as a ... as a deputy,' Camille told her, 'b-b-but, well, I have been ill and had to pull out. I would not miss this for anything, though! We are g-g-going to change the world!'

Camille certainly looked as if he had been ill, with his sunken, feverish eyes and pallid skin. He pulled out a wooden writing box and balanced it on his knees, preparing to take notes with a threadbare quill and an almost empty inkpot.

'I'm a writer,' he explained, with only the slightest stumble in his speech. 'I. . . I intend to record the g-g-glorious events for posterity.'

'What have you written?' she asked.

'I've written a p-p-pamphlet called *Le France Libre*, but no-one will publish it. They are all too afraid!' He spoke scornfully.

'I'm sorry,' she said sincerely. 'That's a shame.'

He gave her a swift grin, showing crooked teeth.

The atmosphere was tense and feverish. Many expected the king to order the soldiers to fire upon them.

'We shall stand firm!' one man cried.

'The king must be shown that we are serious!' shouted another.

'How dare he lock us out of our hall? Does he think we shall all just doff our hats and go meekly away?'

'We must prove that we mean what we say.'

'But how?'

Camille leaned closer to Viviane so he could whisper the men's names and backgrounds to her. He pointed out Isaac Le Chapelier, a radical lawyer from Bretagne who had founded a group called the Breton Club, and his friend Antoine Barnave, who had drawn up the club's manifesto and rule book. The ascetic-looking man in the severe black soutane was the Calvinist preacher, Jean-Paul Saint-Étienne.

'And you must know Monsieur Robespierre,' Camille said with a worshipful air. 'He is a man to watch, mark my words!'

'How do you know him?' Viviane asked.

'We met at school. His family are very poor, but he won a scholarship. He is the most brilliant man I have ever met, if rather particular in his ways. So poor he can scarcely buy bread, but he still pays the barber to shave him and powder his wig for him each day!' Camille shook his head in wonder.

'And that man? The one huge and shaggy as a bear?' Viviane asked.

'That is the Comte de Mirabeau.'

'Ah, yes. I've heard of him.'

The young man grinned. 'So has all of France.'

The comte had been thrown into prison four times, thanks to blank *lettres du cachet* employed by his father, and now worked against his own class, rousing the commoners to fever pitch with his passionate speeches.

'We must refuse to disperse, no matter what comes,' Mirabeau shouted now. 'We must all agree to stand together and not be disbanded until we have a constitution that is fair for all Frenchmen, regardless of their birth or wealth.'

'Let us sign an oath to that effect,' cried another man. He was a lawyer named Mounier, Camille whispered, famous for his part in the Day of the Tiles in which the people of Grenoble had risen up and pelted the king's soldiers with roof tiles and cobblestones.

The men gathered around as the Abbé Sieyès hastily scribbled on a scroll of paper, many interjecting suggestions. At last he had an oath for them to swear, declaring their intention to establish a new constitution. One by one, the deputies read the vow aloud and then signed their name to the paper.

Then a man stood up, his face defiant. 'I'm sorry, but I cannot sign this oath,' he declared. 'My constituents did not send me here to Versailles to insult the king!'

A roar rose up from the other deputies. Many leapt to their feet and shook their fists.

'Come on now, monsieur,' Mirabeau cried. 'We all need to stand together!'

'I cannot support any decree not sanctioned by the king,' the man replied obstinately.

'It is not up to you,' someone cried. 'You are part of the Third Estate, you must submit to the general view.'

'I cannot take a sacred oath against my conscience.'

Another great growl of indignation.

'What is your name?' Robespierre asked in a low, silky voice somehow laden with menace.

The man replied stoutly, 'Joseph Martin-Dauch, monsieur, from Castelnaudary.'

'We shall remember your name, Monsieur Martin-Dauch.' Robespierre took a small notebook from his coat pocket and wrote it down.

'Come on, my friend, sign the oath,' Mounier urged, pressing the quill into Martin-Dauch's hand. 'Do not be the only one to fail us.'

'And if a house be divided against itself, that house cannot stand,' Saint-Étienne intoned.

'I cannot.' His jaw set, Martin-Dauch scribbled 'opponent' next to his name.

Shouts of anger and disapproval reverberated through the room.

'Get him out of here!'

'Death! Death to the objector.'

Pale-faced, Martin-Dauch was hustled out the back door and into the street.

All five-hundred-and-seventy-seven remaining deputies signed their name to the oath.

For the next few days, the palace and town of Versailles were in turmoil.

The king declared the meeting of the National Assembly illegal. In response, crowds of angry people gathered in the streets, shouting, '*Vive le Tiers!*'

The streets resounded with the stamp of marching soldiers. All through the royal apartments, small groups of courtiers huddled, agitated and afraid.

On the 24th of June, numerous members of the clergy left the First Estate and joined the National Assembly. The Duc d'Orléans followed suit the following day, taking close to fifty liberal-minded noblemen with him.

The queen was white with anger, the king miserable and bewildered at his cousin's betrayal. The crowds were ecstatic, calling 'Vive d'Orléans!'

Some even began to shout, 'Vive le Roi!' as the duke rode along the streets of Versailles, waving his gloved hand, the sun glittering on the diamonds in his hat.

Two days later, Louis gave in and agreed to allow the three estates to meet together. He was greeted with cheers and clapping. The royal couple stood on the balcony, waving to the crowd. Marie-Antoinette lifted the dauphin into her arms, and he smiled and waved his chubby hand, to the delight of the throng.

It seemed as if all would be well.

12

The Devil's Thimble
6 June 1789

The gardens at Versailles were vast and regimented.

Marble statues of disdainful gods and goddesses, framed by tall yew hedges. Trees clipped into cones and spheres. Raked gravel paths. Fountains that magically began to spout as the king walked by, only to die away once he had passed. Viviane had been awed and amazed by this, as she was meant to be, until Clothilde had told her servants were posted everywhere in the garden, their only job to blow a whistle so that the gardeners knew when the king approached and could turn the mechanisms on and off.

Viviane could not help thinking of David as she walked down the marble steps, her heavy skirts dragging against the gravel. She wondered what the garden at Belisima looked like now. Surely the rose garden would be in full and heady bloom? She imagined running through the maze in a light muslin dress, laughing, Luna leaping at her heels. She would find her way through all the twists and turns to the inner garden, where David waited for her, smiling. She would spring into his arms and he would clasp her close, his hands whole and unscarred. She would feel his heart beating fast under her cheek. He would lift her face so he could kiss her . . .

If only she had been brave enough to flee with him when she had had the chance! David would still be alive. She would not carry the awful burden of his death on her soul. She would not be trapped in a loveless marriage with a man who took pleasure in her pain. She was as fettered as the falcons in their hoods and jesses in the royal mews. Just like them, if she tried to spring free, she would be dragged back down to earth.

Her bitter thoughts were interrupted by the sound of a girl's voice. 'Oh you naughty dog, look what you've done!'

Viviane looked up.

The princess Marie-Thérèse was kneeling on the lawn, holding tightly to one end of a piece of cloth. A small dog had gripped the other end with its sharp teeth, and was trying to drag it from her hand, growling, even as its stumpy tail wagged furiously. Louis-Charles, the little dauphin, was sobbing in the arms of the royal governess, the Duchesse de Polignac. She was trying without success to comfort the prince, save the princess's sewing, and stop the puppy from trampling all over her silk skirt with its muddy paws.

Viviane ran forward to help. She bobbed a quick curtsey, then caught up a stick from the nearby garden bed and waved it in front of the dog's nose. 'Here, puppy!' she called, 'Fetch this.' Then she flung the stick away from her. The puppy let go of the cloth and romped away after the stick.

'It's ruined,' the princess cried, snatching up the cloth. 'And I spent so long on it.'

'Let me see.' Viviane took the cloth from her hands and smoothed it out. It was not badly torn. 'Never fear, Madame Royale. A tiny stitch or two, and you will never know a puppy had been playing with it.'

Just then, the puppy bounded back, the stick in his mouth. Louis-Charles cowered into the duchess's arms, his tears breaking out afresh.

'He is afraid of dogs,' the Duchesse de Polignac said apologetically. 'I usually take such care to keep them away from him.'

'There is no need to be afraid,' Viviane said soothingly to the little prince. 'See, he just wants to play.' She threw the stick with all her strength into the bushes, and the puppy sprang after it, burrowing into the leaves till nothing was left in sight but the curly end of his tail. The dauphin sneaked a look between his pudgy fingers, then gave a watery smile at the comical sight.

'Would you like me to mend your sampler for you, madame?' Viviane said to Marie-Thérèse. 'Indeed, I'm afraid my own puppy often used to run off with my sewing and so I was always trying to repair the damage before my great-aunt saw.'

The princess nodded, her face grave.

'May I sit, madame?' Viviane indicated the rug spread on the grass.

'You may.'

Viviane sat down on the ground, then spread the sampler over her lap. She took up the princess's sewing basket, rummaging inside for a needle and threading it deftly. She then found the silver thimble and slipped it on to her forefinger.

'Did you know the Devil invented the thimble?' she said.

The princess's eyes rounded. 'That is not true.'

'It is, according to the tale my wet-nurse used to tell me.'

'Why would the Devil invent a thimble?' Marie-Thérèse demanded.

'Well, long ago in Bretagne, all the knights had ridden away to fight in the Crusades and the womenfolk were left alone. Lady Melita was one of them. She missed her husband with all her heart. But she was determined not to grieve. "We must not sit idle," she told her ladies. "Let us find some work to do." So the ladies opened their chests and brought out cloth of the finest wool and silk, and they began to sew beautiful tapestries and cushions and curtains, and warm clothes for the poor folk, and thick quilts for the old.'

As Viviane spoke she was repairing the torn sampler with the finest and most fairy-like of stitches. The princess's solemn eyes never left her face.

'Now Old Nick saw this from his dark abode. All this useful and beautiful work did not suit his wicked plans. For you know the Devil likes idle hands. "I must put an end to this," said Old Nick to himself. "And an end there shall be." He called on one of his most mischievous imps, who cried, "Master, I will twist and turn their needles so their fingers are pricked with every stitch. They will be stung so sore they shall never sew again."'

The dauphin had lifted his face from the duchess's shoulder and turned to face her, one finger in his mouth. At that moment, the puppy gambolled back again, the chewed-up stick hanging out of the corner of its mouth. Viviane laid down her sewing so she could once again throw the stick, and off the dog ran once more. The dauphin watched anxiously, but did not weep.

Viviane took up her cloth and her tale. 'You may be sure that naughty imp spent a busy night. Every single needle in the land was cursed. And what squeals and squeaks were heard the next day! Poor dames! The needles would poke and prick no matter what they did. Soon all the ladies but one had laid aside their work.'

'Lady Melita?' Marie-Thérèse whispered.

'Yes, Lady Melita. No matter how her poor fingertips were stung, she kept on sewing, for she was determined that she would not sit idle while her beloved husband was fighting so far from home. "I must put an end to this," said Old Nick to himself. "And an end there shall be." And so he snatched up a shell from the seashore, and he spat in it, so that it was poisoned. Then he dressed himself like a pilgrim and, staff in hand, went to ask for charity at Lady Melita's castle gate.'

The children's eyes rounded with fear and amazement. They wriggled a little closer. Viviane lowered her voice, leaning forward a little. 'Melita's kind heart was moved. She ran down to the gate and, taking the Devil by the hand, said, "Come in, come in. Pilgrims are always welcome here; they are heaven-sent." So Old Nick entered the castle, and ate and ate and ate. He ate till all the sacks and chests were empty. And he drank even more. He drank till every bottle and barrel in the castle was drained dry.' Viviane looked up and smiled at the princess. 'You must know that sobriety is not the Devil's special virtue.'

A faint smile curved the princess's pale cheek. The duchess laughed, and settled the dauphin more comfortably in her lap.

'Lady Melita said not a word, but took up her sewing. Soon her fingertips were beaded with blood, and she had to take care not to stain her cloth. Old Nick took out the shell from his pocket and gave it to her.

"To protect your finger from the prick of the needle," he said with a secret smile.

'Melita took the shell and kissed it, then slipped it on to her finger. She found she could sew without any pain, and her stitches flew ever faster. Old Nick grinned to himself and slipped away, for he thought she would soon drop dead from the poison. But he was wrong. The poison did not hurt her, for no harm can come to the innocent. She sewed with such tiny delicate stitches, and created such rare beauty, that soon her fame spread far and wide, and all the other ladies wanted a thimble too. No-one realised that it had been invented by the Devil.'

For a moment, Marie-Thérèse considered her solemnly, but then a real smile broke out on her face, transforming it. 'I like that,' she said. 'I will think of that story every time I put my thimble on now.'

Viviane gave her back the mended cloth. '*Voilà!* All fixed now.' She put away the needle and thimble, then stood as the puppy pranced up again. She lifted him into her arms and bobbed a swift curtsey.

'If you will excuse me, Mesdames, I shall go and find where this puppy belongs.'

'That was a charming tale, madame,' the duchess said. 'I thank you for coming to my rescue.'

The puppy was wriggling and squirming, wanting to be free. Louis-Charles stared at it in frightened fascination, then, when the puppy yapped, flinched back.

'Would you like to pat the puppy, Monseigneur?' Viviane asked. 'He is so soft, and I promise you he will not bite.'

After a moment, the little boy nodded. Viviane knelt so he could pat the dog, who whined and licked his hand. The dauphin laughed.

'What is that creature doing here? Gabrielle, I thought my instructions were clear. You know he is afraid of dogs!'

The queen hurried towards them, looking worried and upset. It had been a difficult week, Viviane knew, with the price of bread rising day by day and causing riots and the looting of bakeries. Aristocrats were being accused of hoarding flour in some kind of sinister plot to starve the poor to death. Crowds gathered every day at the gilded gates of Versailles, throwing stones and rubbish, shouting 'Death to the rich! Death to all aristocrats! Death to hoarders!' Viviane had not dared go into town, for fear of being caught up in the mob.

She jumped up and swept a deep curtsey, the dog still in her arms. 'Your Majesty! I beg pardon . . .'

The Duchesse de Polignac rose to her feet, laughing. '*Ma cherie*, you malign me! Would I allow your darling *chou d'amour* to be frightened by a dog? It is a stray, wandered in from the streets, no doubt. This sweet girl was just whisking it away for me. And she told the children the most enchanting story. Even your little dauphin was entranced and forgot to fear the dog.'

'Is that so?' Marie-Antoinette's face softened and she smiled at Viviane. 'What story did you tell, to work such a miracle, madame?'

'It was just a story my wet-nurse used to tell me, Madame la Reine,' Viviane said, colour mounting her cheeks. 'I used to like it when I was small.'

'It was about how the Devil invented the thimble,' Marie-Thérèse told her mother. 'I liked it. I like her. I want her to come and tell me another story.'

'Very well, *ma Mousseline la Sérieuse*,' the queen said with a laugh. It was not a term Viviane had ever heard before, but somehow it suited the princess. She was as pretty and delicate as muslin, but so serious and grave in her ways that no-one could ever think her frivolous.

The queen took her son into her arms, kissing his soft curls. She looked at Viviane with keen interest. 'You are the young Duchesse of Savageaux, are you not?' she asked. 'I heard of your marriage. It is hard to be married to a man you have never met. I remember well my own trepidation when I came here to France. And at least my bridegroom was not old enough to be my father. Or indeed, my grandfather.'

Viviane's eyes stung. She dropped her gaze, not wanting anyone to see her distress.

The queen seemed to come to some kind of decision.

'We are going to the Petit Trianon this afternoon. I must have an afternoon away from court. Would you care to accompany us?'

'I would be honoured, madame,' Viviane answered, with a deep curtsey. 'I love gardens, and the fame of yours has spread far and wide.'

The queen smiled. 'Come dressed simply in muslin, as you are now, and remember, no curtseys or bows are allowed at Petit Trianon. And think of another story! I should like to hear one. As long as it has a happy ending.'

13

The Fall
11–14 July 1789

'Versailles is intolerably tedious,' the Duc de Savageaux said.

'Indeed,' the Marquis de Valaine answered, yawning behind his fan. 'All these earnest fellows thumping their pulpits.'

'Let's go to Paris,' the duke suggested. 'At least at the Palais-Royal, we can gamble to our heart's content.'

Neither men thought to consult their wives. Viviane and Clothilde were expected to do as they were told.

As their carriage rattled into Paris, Viviane was surprised to find soldiers tramping the streets, guarding toll booths, and rolling heavy cannons into place at the city gates. They were not wearing the familiar 'king's blue' coats of the Garde Française.

'Why are there so many soldiers?' Clothilde asked, her voice shrill with alarm.

'No need to fret, my dear, the king just wishes to keep the peace,' the marquis replied.

'His Majesty has given secret orders for twenty thousand soldiers to gather around Paris and Versailles,' the duke said. 'For the people's protection, of course.'

'Of course,' Viviane said bitterly. 'Not because he wants to seize back control.'

Her father raised his thin brows. 'Viviane, you speak of His Majesty the King. He does not need to *seize back control*.' He repeated her words with ironic emphasis. 'The king controls all. He is the supreme ruler. One king, one law, one faith.'

'Times are changing,' Viviane said.

'Not if we can help it,' the duke said. He made an elegant gesture out the coach window at the soldiers marching, muskets over their shoulders. 'And not if the king can keep those unruly Parisian mobs under control. A few sharp lessons, and they'll slink back to their slums.'

'The Comte de Mirabeau said French soldiers are not automata, they will not fire on French citizens,' Viviane said hotly.

'How do you know that?' her father asked.

Viviane flushed. She could not admit Camille Desmoulins had told her. She had seen the fiery young revolutionary a few times since that day in the royal tennis court. He was thinner and more dishevelled and more passionate than ever. Viviane found his talk fascinating. He reminded her of David in so many ways – his dark unruly hair, his vehement conviction, his refusal to bow his head and bend his knee.

'It is reported widely,' she answered. 'Strangely enough, I read the newspapers too.'

'It is unbecoming,' her father said sharply. 'A woman should not know anything about politics, let alone have the temerity to voice an opinion.'

Viviane clenched her jaw and did not answer.

The duke shrugged his velvet-clad shoulders. 'Well, she is right, no matter how unbecoming it is in her. That is why we do not see the Garde Française out in force, here in Paris, where they have so many friends and relatives. It is the Swiss and German mercenaries that the king has ordered to guard the city.'

Viviane gazed out the window at swarms of begging children with dirty faces and ragged women with bare feet and arms hanging out scraps of

133

clothing on drooping lines, and felt no comfort at all at the idea of well-fed foreign mercenaries marching through these narrow filthy streets.

The following day was Sunday.

The marquis and the duke took their young wives to promenade around the Palais-Royal. Owned by the Duc d'Orléans, the colonnades around the inner courtyard of the palace had been transformed into a shopping arcade filled with shops, theatres, cafés, bookshops, hair salons, museums and bars. People of all kinds meandered through the gardens, and browsed in the bookstores and museums.

Men in tattered coats rubbed shoulders with rakes with rouged cheeks and black patches glued beside their reddened lips.

Women in cheap satin and broken feathers beckoned from doorways, while young ladies in white muslin with sky-blue bows promenaded with their governesses.

Young men in worn black suits sold newspapers and pamphlets, shouting out lewd headlines in hoarse voices, while a blind girl with the voice of an angel sang for coins flung into a wooden bowl at her feet.

Viviane was wide-eyed and amazed, turning her head in all directions as she tried to take it all in. She had never seen such a place. It seemed as if all of Paris was here, enjoying the sunshine.

It was not long before the marquis grew bored, however, and he and the duke went to find livelier company at one of the gambling dens. Viviane and Clothilde were left in the care of their footmen, two tall strapping young men with white powdered wigs and spotless livery.

They sat for a while in one of the cafés, drinking coffee, and watched the crowd go by. Some boys nearby were running about and setting off firecrackers under people's feet, to the accompaniment of much screaming and laughter.

'They buy them cheaply here,' Clothilde said. 'I heard the sky over the Palais-Royal was ablaze with fireworks the night the king agreed the three estates should join together.'

'Yet all the time the king was giving secret orders for soldiers to converge on Paris,' Viviane said.

'Well, what do you expect? He can't take all these threats to his power lying down.'

'Does he think the commoners are idiots with no eyes in their heads? A child could see what was going on. He hopes to force the Third Estate to back down.'

'Of course. Then life can return to normal, without all these histrionics.' Clothilde took a sip of coffee, then made a face of distaste and put her cup down.

'I don't think the commoners will submit,' Viviane replied, thinking of the young men she had seen, afire with zeal, determined to break the template of French society and make it anew.

Clothilde laughed. 'They'll soon back down before the blast of a musket.'

'I'm not so sure . . .' Viviane began, but Clothilde was pulling on her gloves.

'I want some new ostrich plumes, and some blue satin ribbon. I just adore the bows you have on your brocade shoes. Come and help me choose some.'

'I'd rather look at the books,' Viviane said.

Her stepmother shrugged. 'As you please.' She glanced up at the clock on the pediment, held aloft by two stone angels. It was almost three o'clock. 'I will meet you back here in an hour.'

Off she swept, followed by her footman, his arms laden with all the furbelows the marquise had already bought. Viviane wandered over to the dusty old books piled high on tables and shelves in the bookstore, her footman keeping a discreet few steps away.

Viviane was turning over the pages of an age-spotted book when a sudden roar of applause caught her attention.

She looked up. A crowd had gathered around the Café Foy, where an orator was standing on a table in the shade of an ancient chestnut tree. He held high a sheaf of paper, shaking it excitedly. Curious, Viviane went a little closer.

'Have you heard the n-n-news?' a familiar stammering voice cried. It was Camille Desmoulins, more dishevelled and ardent than ever. 'The king has f-f-forced Monsieur Necker to resign. Our only hope of rescuing our nation from bank . . . bankruptcy! We patriots will be next. They shall ma-ma-massacre us in the street as they once massacred the Huguenots.'

There was a great roar of anger and disapproval. Everyone was shouting and shaking their fists.

'Make the king bring back Monsieur Necker!'

'Does he think we're fools?'

'Nothing will ever change . . .'

'. . . unless we make it change!'

'To arms! To arms!' Camille cried, pulling a pistol from his pocket and raising it high. 'We must fight, else all will be l-l-lost.'

'Let us find guns,' someone in the crowd shouted.

'But the guards . . . the soldiers will shoot us down.'

'We must shoot them first.'

'I would rather d-die than live a slave,' Camille shouted. He reached up and snatched a leaf from the chestnut tree and stuck it in his hat. 'All of you, take a leaf. Green is the c-c-colour of hope. If we wear green cockades in our hats, we will know who is one . . . one of us. Find green ribbons, green scarves, anything to mark out who the true patriots are! To arms, I say.'

'Bravo! Bravo!'

He was lifted high onto men's shoulders and carried away. Viviane shrank back, afraid he would recognise her, but he did not see her as the crowd surged around him.

Men leapt high to grasp leaves from the chestnut branches, or ran to nearby shops, snatching rolls of green silk and ripping them to shreds, tying the scraps to their hats or their buttonholes. A fat lady in a green dress found her clothes being torn from her shoulders.

'Pardon, madame, but I must get you away,' her footman cried. 'This is no place for a lady.'

Shoved and jostled on all sides, her ears ringing with the shouts and screams, Viviane could only agree. She let him lead her away from the tumult and lift her up into the carriage, waiting in the street beyond.

'Thank you,' she said, as he shut the door upon her. 'I am sorry, I do not know your name.'

He bowed his head to her. 'I am Henri Dumont, madame. You were most kind to me in Bretagne, when we first arrived.'

For a moment she did not know what he meant, then he prompted, 'You offered me mulled wine.'

Then she remembered the footmen who had been made to run ahead of her father's carriage all the way from Paris to Bretagne, a distance of some two hundred and fifty miles.

She nodded her head. 'I wish I could have done more.'

'A kind word was more than I expected.'

Viviane wanted to apologise for her father's heartlessness, but it would not be proper. Instead she said, 'What of the others? If I take the carriage, how will they get home?'

She could not bear to say, *My husband, my father, my stepmother . . .*

'I will see you returned to safety, then return to find them, madame,' he said, and withdrew.

As the carriage clattered away from the Palais-Royal, she saw the crowd surging towards the Jardin des Tuileries. Then she heard distant gunfire.

Back at the duke's townhouse, Viviane paced back and forth. She was tense and agitated. That cry: *To arms! To arms!*

Bells rang the alarm. Smoke tinged the air bitter orange.

The duke returned at last, white around the mouth. He ordered the footmen to barricade the doors.

'What's happening?' Viviane cried.

'The king's soldiers are under attack by a mob,' he said shortly. 'But order will be restored soon.'

Yet the bells kept clanging, punctuated with bursts of gunfire and screaming. The duke ordered Henri to go and gather news. The footman hesitated, then said, 'Yes, monsieur, of course. May I change first? Out of my livery? I would not wish to get dirty.' He gestured to his white satin breeches.

The duke jerked a nod in response, and Henri withdrew. Viviane knew it was not concern for his livery, but for his life, that caused the footman to break the rules of etiquette that required a servant to wear his master's uniform at all times.

Henri returned long after nightfall. He was ruffled and dirty, with his old woollen jacket torn at the shoulder. He wore a green ribbon tied around his arm.

'Paris is lost,' he gasped.

The duke stared at him. 'Whatever can you mean?'

'Monsieur, the Garde Française have joined forces with the mob. They fired against the German soldiers.'

'The king's guards fired against the king's mercenaries? You must be mistaken.'

'I am not mistaken, monsieur. I saw it with my own eyes. The German soldiers were surrounded by the mob, using whatever weapons they could lay their hands on. Chairs, cobblestones, smashed statues, broomsticks. The horses could not run the mob down, there were too many of them. The Germans lay about them with their sabres, killing many. Then the Garde Française arrived, guns at the ready. Everyone thought they meant to join forces with the Germans, but they would not shoot their fellow Frenchmen. The Germans were driven back. They have abandoned Paris, they have retreated all the way to Pont de Sèvres.' Henri's eyes were wild, his hands shaking.

'What of the mob?' Viviane demanded. 'What is happening now?'

'They are raiding the gunsmiths and the armouries,' Henri answered. 'Anyone who resists is being knocked down, assaulted. They are tearing down the toll booths, madame, they are knocking down the city walls!'

Viviane nodded in understanding. She knew how much the people of Paris hated the wall of the Ferme Générale, which had been built over the past few years to ensure that tax was paid on every single item that was taken in and out of the city. Fifteen feet high and almost seven leagues long, it encircled nearly all of Paris, making all those who lived within prisoners.

'This is an outrage,' the duke cried. 'The king's guard should all be shot.'

'It is the king's mercenaries who are being shot,' Henri replied, then added quickly, *monsieur le duc.*'

The duke called for his carriage. He must go back to Versailles, he said, and inform the king.

'You will never get out, monsieur,' Henri said. 'The city has been taken over. They have formed a new National Guard, and are arming themselves even now. You'll be killed.'

'I am the Duc de Savageaux. Who will dare touch me?' he said contemptuously.

Henri bowed and said no more, and soon the duke drove off into the night.

It was difficult to rest. The sky was lit up with a reddish glare. Throngs of people ran through the streets, looting shops, stealing sacks of grain and wheels of cheese and bottles of wine, brandishing stolen muskets and pistols. The duke had ordered all the doors barricaded with furniture, and shots fired over the heads of anyone who tried to break in. At dawn, every bell in the city was rung with a great clangour. Guns boomed. Drums rumbled. The streets were full of the clatter of running feet.

Yvette failed to bring Viviane her coffee and *pain au chocolat* for breakfast. Tying a wrapper over her nightgown, she went down to the servants' quarters. There seemed fewer than usual. Yvette and Henri were hunched over the newspapers, their faces white and frightened. They looked up as Viviane came in, and rose to bow and curtsey, but she thought she saw hostility in their faces. She wanted to tell them that she was a duchess against her will, that she did not believe she was born better than any of them, but thought miserably no-one would believe her.

'Pardon, madame,' Henri said. 'We did not know you were awake. Go back to bed, and Yvette will bring you something to eat.'

But when it came, her coffee was cold and bitter, and the bread was stale.

Looking out into the street from behind her shutter, Viviane saw that many of those marching in the streets were now wearing a cockade of red and blue ribbons, the medieval colours of Paris. They were laughing and singing and dragging cannons. Women and children as well as men, many with nothing more than a rolling-pin or broomstick as a weapon.

Viviane quickly unfastened the blue ribbon from her favourite shoes and fashioned it into a rosette. She dressed herself in her oldest gown, borrowed some sabots from Yvette's room, and slipped out into the streets, the rosette pinned to her cap.

Viviane had to know what was happening. She could not bear to be confined within the duke's palace any longer.

She knew it was stupid. The streets were dangerous, unpredictable.

Yet it was more like a festival than a riot. People were dancing along, arm-in-arm, waving wine bottles and slurring the words to old marching songs:

> Three young drummers were coming back from war.
> Three young drummers were coming back from war.
> And ri, and ran, rap-at-ap-lan,
> Were coming back from war.

'We're off to the Bastille!' a woman shouted to Viviane. 'To get us some gunpowder.'

'We're going to join the National Guard,' another said, laughing.

'Drink!' another cried, shoving a bottle in her face. 'To the Third Estate!'

Viviane drank obediently, and almost choked on the roughness of the wine.

'Why are the cockades now blue and red?' Viviane dared to ask, instinctively mimicking the woman's Parisian accent. 'Yesterday they were green.'

The woman spat on the ground. 'Green is the colour of the Comte d'Artois, the king's brother and our enemy. It was he who persuaded the king to sack Monsieur Necker! He plots with the queen to grind us down into the dirt. No, we are free Parisians! Red and blue are our colours.'

'Red for blood,' a wild-eyed woman slurred, 'and blue for freedom!'

'To the Bastille!' someone shouted.

The shout was taken up by a hundred voices. 'To the Bastille!'

They began to sing again. Viviane sang with them. Soon the crowd marched into the forecourt before the Bastille. It stood dark and silent, its drawbridge raised, cannon pointing their dark muzzles towards the crowd. Viviane felt a sudden qualm. She had better return, she thought, before anyone realised she was gone.

But one of the women slung a heavy arm across her shoulders. 'Down with the Bastille!' she screamed, took a long swig of wine, then passed the bottle to Viviane.

Viviane drank deeply, laughing a little as the women all began to sing again. She felt alive, as she had not done for months. She was like a starling in a vast swirling murmuration, moving as if with a single mind, the moment sharpened by the presence of the silently hovering hawk.

It was well after noon, and the sun beat down from a cloudless sky. Carts filled with burning straw and dung were drawn up near the gatehouse, to hide the movements of the attackers. As the heat intensified, so did the anger of the crowd. 'Give us the Bastille!' they screamed.

Some men had climbed onto the roof of a nearby shop, then scrambled onto the gatehouse. They sawed away at the chains holding up the drawbridge. Suddenly the chains snapped. The drawbridge crashed down. People trapped beneath screamed in pain, but the crowd surged forward, over the bridge and into the fortress.

A sudden loud explosion of cannon fire. Then the rumble of muskets.

'They dare shoot at us?' one of the women cried. 'We're unarmed!'

Caught up in the rage of the moment, she ran forward, brandishing her rolling-pin.

For a while, all was chaos. Smoke rolled across the courtyard, making Viviane cough. Then a great roar resounded.

A white handkerchief waved from one of the tower windows.

Moments later, a gate swung open. A man, his face contorted with rage, rushed forward and slashed with his sword at the guard opening the gate. The guard's hand was chopped off. Blood sprayed out. With a howl, the hand was impaled on a pike and paraded high, still holding the heavy iron key.

Cold rushed over her. Viviane swayed. People hurried past. Pushing and shoving. Shouting and screaming. She groped her way free. Her stomach roiled. She reached a wall, leant against it, retched. When her stomach was empty, she wiped her mouth with the back of her hand and stumbled away.

Viviane remembered her father's rapier, hissing down. David's cry of pain. His maimed hand, running with blood. His severed finger, still encircled with gold.

Somehow she got herself back to the duke's townhouse.

She had left the garden door unfastened. She crept through and locked it behind her, standing with her back pressed against it, her breast heaving. It was hard to catch a breath.

The mood of the crowd had changed so quickly. One moment Viviane had been singing with the other women, the next guns were firing and swords slashing.

No-one had noticed she was gone. Viviane made it safely to her room. She rang for hot water. When at last it came, she washed herself free of the smoke and the grime and splatters of blood. She dressed herself in her nightgown and crawled into bed.

But it was impossible to sleep.

Outside, the mob paraded the streets of Paris, the severed heads of the city mayor and the governor of the Bastille hoisted high on pikes.

14

The Great Fear
15 July – 1 October 1789

Flames leapt high. The château windows glared orange. Smoke choked her. Heat like a brass cymbal.

Maugan, the mole-catcher, reaching out for her. Dead moles, pale hands dangling.

A storm is coming . . . heads shall roll . . .

Dice rattling. Falling to the ground. Trying to catch them. Cloven hooves under the filthy tattered cloak.

Screaming. Screaming with all her might.

Soundless.

Orange flames leaping to devour her . . .

Viviane woke with a wild cry.

Damp sheets wrapped about her throat, strangling her. It was hot. The air smelled of smoke. The light striking in through a crack in her curtains had a strange copper tint. A low ominous rumble from the city beyond her windows. Viviane tore the sheets away from her neck and lay, panting, heart thudding painfully.

It was just a dream, she told herself.

But yesterday was not a dream. The fall of the Bastille was not a dream.

Her head ached, and her limbs throbbed. Her mouth tasted foul. The rough wine and the smell of gunpowder and the blood. Sickness rose in her throat again.

After a long time, Viviane managed to get up. She put on an old gown she could fasten herself, and went to put on her shoes. The ribbons were missing. She had used them yesterday, to fashion herself a blue rosette. She could not find the rosette now. It must have been torn from her hair. Viviane found some other ribbons and laced her shoes. Her feet were sore and blistered. Her hands trembled.

Viviane went slowly through the vast echoing house. The servants would not meet her gaze. Outside, the streets surged with people, drunk and rowdy. She tried to settle to read or sew, but her nerves quivered with every shout or scream.

Then a boy came with a message from her father.

Her husband was dead. Killed by the mob as he tried to leave Paris.

She was a widow.

Viviane remembered her nightmare. Fire flaring orange from the windows of the tower. An omen of death for the lord of the château.

Her stomach twisted. She did not know if it was horror or relief.

The next few days were taken up with ordering mourning clothes and discussing matters of business with her husband's lawyer. Viviane was her husband's heir, but the Duc de Savageaux had been deep in debt and the lawyer felt it expedient to sell all his properties and repay the money owed. Viviane was left with nothing but the château at Belisima-sur-le-lac, which had been her dowry and remained hers under Breton law.

The duke's body was to be buried in his family crypt in Paris. Viviane was not permitted to go, of course. She sat with her stepmother and great-aunt in the hot gloomy drawing-room, draped in black, listening to the monotonous ticking of the ormolu clock on the mantelpiece. Madame de Ravoisier fanned herself vigorously, her round face red as a plum.

144

'How very boring for you,' Clothilde said. 'A whole year in mourning clothes.'

Viviane gave a little shrug.

'You must be sorry now you did not make more of an effort to win his affections. Why, he'd still be alive and you'd not be a dowager.'

Viviane stared at her in amazement. 'How is it my fault? I was not the one who dragged him out of his coach and stabbed him to death.'

'If you had begged him not to go . . .'

'He still would have gone,' Viviane said wearily. 'He believed no-one would dare touch him.'

'And no-one should have dared! He was the Duc de Savageaux,' Madame de Ravoisier cried.

'And yet he bled to death like any other man.'

Clothilde raised her thickly pencilled brows. 'How heartless.'

Viviane shrugged. 'I do not mean to be. It's a lesson for us all, though, isn't it? If we are pricked, we all bleed.' Thinking of Shakespeare made her think of David, and a tremor rocked her. She clenched her hands, trying to steady herself. If only you had not died, Davy *bach*, she thought. If only I had fled with you when I could.

'Well, you hated Monsieur le Duc and now he is dead,' Clothilde pointed out.

Viviane did not speak. It was true.

'Well, I suppose it is some consolation that you inherit this house, and the château in the Loire, and all the jewels . . .'

'I don't want them,' Viviane said. She hesitated, then said, 'Besides, you know all must be sold?'

'Sold? But why?' Madame de Ravoisier was horrified.

'Monsieur le Duc was deep in debt.'

Clothilde gave a shrill giggle. 'Surely no-one expects you to pay them? They are tradesmen's bills! I suppose the duke had debts of honour, of course. Most probably to my husband the marquis! Those should be paid, of course. And I suppose you do not much care if you need to sell this old place – nobody lives in this part of town anymore, anyway. But the château! It is very fine. One simply must have somewhere to retreat to in summer – court is intolerable then . . .'

As Clothilde rattled on, Viviane stared at her in consternation. It seemed a dreadful thing that her stepmother thought that gambling debts owed to rich noblemen must be repaid, while money owed to poor, hard-working tradesmen was to be left outstanding.

At last her father and the other male friends of the duke returned from the funeral. The Marquis was dressed in black silk, his face pale and drawn under his tall white wig. He gave her his condolences, his voice cracking in the first sign of emotion she had ever seen in him.

'You shall return to Versailles with us now,' he said.

'May I not return to Belisima?' she begged. 'To . . . to mourn in private?'

No,' he answered shortly. 'You will return to Versailles and do your best to make yourself known to the queen. You will need a position at court to support yourself.'

'I have the income from Belisima,' she replied, trying to hold herself firm.

He regarded her coldly. 'Do not start thinking yourself a rich widow, able to choose your own way. Life at Versailles is expensive. Your pitiful little estate in Bretagne will come nowhere near paying your costs.'

'But if I am living at Belisima . . .' She began to argue.

'Do not think to defy me,' he answered silkily. 'You shall stay at Versailles, ingratiate yourself with the queen, and hope to win some other rich nobleman as your husband.'

'But I don't want to.' Her voice shook.

'Your wishes are of no consequence to me. You are of noble blood, you owe a duty to your name and your lineage, and to me, your father. Remember what I am prepared to do if you dare disobey me!'

She could see no way free. The tiny rush of hope she had felt on news of her husband's death was nothing but an illusion. Her shoulders slumped.

'Yes, monsieur,' she answered in a low voice.

Viviane took very little with her. Only her clothes, and the miniature painting of her mother. David's signet ring and the rose ring he had given her were hidden inside her bodice, as always.

It was difficult to tell the servants they had been dismissed. Many had been in the Duc de Savageaux's service for years. Viviane gave them as much money as she could, but it was not enough. Her maid Yvette cursed and spat at her. Viviane could only hope she had somewhere to go.

As they left the stinking streets of Paris behind them, Viviane ventured to ask her father what had been happening in Versailles.

'The rats are leaving the sinking ship,' her father replied tersely. 'The Comte d'Artois, the Polignacs, all have fled. Even your fat fool of a great-aunt has gone!'

Viviane could scarcely believe it. Madame de Ravoisier hated to travel and hated foreign places. She must be frightened indeed to have fled France.

'I tried to convince the king that he too should flee, but he cannot believe the people of France wish him harm,' the marquis continued. 'He came to Paris today, and let them lead him around like a tame bear on a chain, with that damned cockade in his hat. It was humiliating!'

Viviane tried to imagine it. The king as a dancing bear, a ring in his nose, a silk rose in his hat. She had to choke back a hysterical giggle.

The carriage rolled into Versailles as the church bells were ringing the eleventh hour. The king's coach had led the way. As Viviane was being handed down, she saw the royal children rushing to meet their father.

'I knew he would be safe!' the dauphin crowed. 'My father is so good no-one could hurt him.'

Marie-Thérèse did not speak, just buried her face in her father's waistcoat. The queen wept silently. As Louis went to her, Viviane saw that the king indeed wore a cockade in his hat. It was blue at its heart, rimmed with white, and then red. It gave her a little spurt of hope. White was the colour of the royal Bourbon family.

'Look at that loathsome thing,' her father muttered. 'Made in the colours of the d'Orléans family. I'd wager the duke had something to do with that. I heard the crowd shouting *Vive le Roi d'Orléans* as I rode through Paris this afternoon. He plots to overthrow the king and take the crown himself, though there's half a dozen between him and the throne.'

The next few days were uneasy. News came of riots in the countryside, uprisings in every town. The violence spread. Foulon de Doué, the man appointed by the king to replace Necker, had fled Paris after the storming of the Bastille. He was found by local peasants, and forced to walk back to the city barefoot. A bundle of hay was tied to his back, and the sweat pouring down his face was wiped away with nettles.

He was hanged from a lamp-post in the Place de Grève, the square where the most notorious murderers, heretics and rebels were executed. The rope around his neck broke three times and so the mob hacked off his head, shoved his mouth full of straw – in retaliation for the rumour he had once said, 'If the people are hungry, let them eat grass' – and paraded his bloody remains around Paris on pikes. His son-in-law soon suffered the same rough justice.

The palace of Versailles was eerily quiet.

The queen stayed at the Petit Trianon with her children, and many courtiers left for Switzerland or Italy.

Viviane had nothing to do. The men were all busy with the National Assembly, which met most days to discuss and debate and argue over the future of France. The king had recalled Monsieur Necker once more, at the insistence of the people, and he arrived back in Versailles to a rapturous reception in late July. He looked haggard after his long journey from Geneva, and told the king bluntly that he feared there was little he could do with unemployment and bread prices soaring.

A kind of madness had swept the country. Gangs of brigands were thought to be hiding out in the forests, ready to rob and plunder and murder. Aristocrats were said to be hiding all the grain so that the peasants died of hunger. Monasteries were sacked, and the monks driven out into the countryside, their pantries and cellars emptied. A cloud of dust on the horizon caused one town to ring the alarm bells, the men all rushing out, armed with scythes and pitchforks, only to discover it was nothing but a herd of cows being driven along the road.

One sultry-hot day, Viviane was carrying a basket of supplies out to the beggars who thronged about the palace gate when she heard a sudden joyous bark. She looked up and saw Luna streaking towards her, red ears flapping. She dropped her basket as the excited dog leapt up to wash Viviane's face with her tongue.

'Luna, oh, Luna! What are you doing here?'

Then she saw Pierrick limping towards her, one arm in a makeshift sling, his head bound in bandages.

She hurried towards him. 'What is it? What has happened?'

Then she saw his face, bruised and sombre, and her stomach sank like a stone.

'Belisima?'

He shook his head. 'I'm so sorry, mamzelle. They burned it.'

'But who? Why?' She felt dazed, uncomprehending.

'Why do the men of this world burn anything?' he answered unhappily.

Pierrick had been woken in the middle of the night, roused by something. A sound or a smell. Something wrong. Dressed only in his nightshirt, he ran out into the corridor. A taint of smoke, a glimmer of red light through the window. He raced out to the courtyard. Far above him, a window blazing with flames. A dark figure, dancing and gibbering and shouting nonsense.

'Maugan,' Vivienne said.

Pierrick looked at her in surprise. 'Yes. Though we only found that out later.'

He had rung the alarm bells, roused the servants, organised chains of men passing buckets of water from the lake, but it was too late. Maugan was not alone. A whole gang of local peasants had joined him, robbing the château of its silver and gold, stealing the pigs and hens and cows, burning the estate documents in the banqueting hall.

'There was nothing we could do. The fire spread too fast. He must have carried a torch with him, kindling every room he passed through. I'm so sorry, mamzelle.'

'How much damage?'

'It's bad. I saved what I could, and locked the gates so no-one else could get in. I threw the key into the well. If it had been found on me, I'd have been beaten and the château utterly destroyed.'

Viviane sank down on to a low wall. 'Was anyone hurt?'

There was an odd silence.

She looked up. 'Briaca?'

He tried to master himself, but could not. 'She ran in . . . to try and stop him . . . I tried . . . but I was too late . . .'

Viviane was tearless, breathless. 'She's dead?'

He nodded.

She could not believe it. 'Briaca is dead?'

He nodded. His face worked, and then he was in her arms, sobbing, heedless of who might see. She patted him and soothed him as if he was still the little boy she had once toddled about with, both in their long white gowns and caps. Luna whined, and put up her single front paw on to Viviane's thigh, and she did her best to comfort the dog as well.

She did not weep.

'I'm all alone now,' Pierrick cried. 'I have no-one.'

Viviane held him closer. She wanted so much to tell him that he was her brother. But she dared not. He'd do something mad, like challenge her father, or strike him, or demand restitution. Then Pierrick would be thrown onto the street, with no option but to join the starving hordes begging at the palace gates.

She could not risk it.

A few days later, the National Assembly declared all feudal rights abolished.

Dovecotes to be locked. Any pigeon flying free considered prey.

Rabbit warrens free to all.

Hunting rights abolished, even in the royal forest.

150

Poachers to be released from prison.

Manorial courts suppressed.

Tithes abolished.

The fees of all parish priests and curates stopped.

All privileges of the nobility eradicated.

Then it was announced that no-one in France would ever kneel before anyone again.

All this happened in an atmosphere of feverish exhilaration and dread.

Many of the nobles were among the first to suggest the surrendering of their privileges. Viviane hardly noticed. She was so overcome with grief and despair she rarely rose from her bed.

By the end of August, the National Declaration of the Rights of Man and the Citizen were drawn up and published.

'I notice women aren't granted any rights,' Viviane said bitterly to Pierrick. He had taken up his role as her footman again, though he seemed to spend all his time drinking in the inns and gathering rumours.

He tried to grin. 'Why do women need rights? They have men to take care of them.'

Viviane's chest felt tight. No man in her life had ever cared for her, apart from Pierrick, who was divided from her by a vast chasm of privilege, and David, who was dead. Viviane feared her father and had hated her husband. They had only cared for her lands, which were now worthless. Which meant she was worthless.

'Mamzelle, don't cry,' Pierrick said in alarm. 'I was only joking.'

'I'm not crying,' Viviane said, even though she was.

September was a month of unrest and deprivation.

Despite a rich harvest, bread was scarce. The multitudes of beggars and vagrants were swelled by periwig-makers, silk weavers, jewellers and mantua-makers, their luxury goods no longer in demand as the court emptied of its nobles.

Those who remained were in a fever of self-denial. Duchesses and marquises donated their earrings and rings to the commoners. So many men cut off their silver shoe ornaments that a long chain of interlinked buckles was carried into the Assembly. From that time on, it was seen as dangerous and subversive to wear ostrich feathers in your hair, rings on your fingers, or lace on your fichu. Overnight, women began to wear loose white gowns without frills or ribbons or jewels. Even her father put away his embossed snuffboxes and plush velvets, and wore sensible dark coats, a red-white-and-blue cockade in his hat.

In mid-September, a baker was hanged from a lamp-post in Paris, accused of hoarding his grain for aristocrats. Crowds demonstrated outside the Hôtel de Ville in Paris nearly every day, shouting 'Bread! Bread! Give us bread.'

The king called for reinforcements to guard the palace. More than a thousand soldiers of the elite Royal Flanders regiment marched to Versailles. That night, the king's Garde du Corps welcomed them to the palace with a regimental feast.

A message was brought to Viviane from the queen. With the Princesse de Lamballe and the Duchesse de Polignac both absent from Versailles, and many other court ladies gone to their country estates or fled, Marie-Antoinette was in need of new *dames du palais*. She requested Viviane's service. Viviane had no heart for celebrations, but she could not ignore a royal summons. She rose, allowed herself to be dressed in her heavy black court dress, and went to scratch on the queen's door. In Versailles, one did not knock. One scratched with the fingernail of the littlest left finger, grown long for the purpose.

'Thank you for coming,' Marie-Antoinette said. 'I am fearful of my reception, and it will help to have friends around me.'

'It is my honour,' Viviane replied, rising from her curtsey.

The queen was dressed in white, a turquoise necklace about her neck. She carried the four-year-old dauphin, and held her daughter by the hand.

Marie-Thérèse gazed up at Viviane with solemn eyes. 'Will you tell me another story?' she whispered.

'Of course,' Viviane answered. 'I will come and tell one to you tonight, at bedtime, if your mother the queen will permit.'

The little girl gave one of her grave smiles. 'I would like that.'

'Would you go on ahead with Madame Campan, and make sure it is safe for me to bring my little ones in?' Marie-Antoinette asked. 'I cannot rid myself of the great fear in my heart that there are those who wish us harm.'

Madame Campan, an elegant lady in her late thirties, was the first lady of the chamber, responsible for the queen's dressing and undressing ceremonies. She nodded coolly to Viviane, and led her into the opera hall, along with a few other young ladies.

The opera hall was an oval room with ornate balconies receding upwards and backwards towards the magnificent painted ceiling of Apollo giving crowns to the nine muses. The stalls had been raised on pulleys, transforming the auditorium into a great banqueting-hall. A long trestle table was set with white linen tablecloths, well-polished silver and fine porcelain plates rimmed with gold. Mirrors lined the back of the theatre, reflecting the chandeliers so the whole room dazzled with light. The soldiers were in a merry mood, singing and laughing and drinking deeply of the wine in their crystal glasses. Their uniforms were blue, over breeches of white, and most wore the tri-coloured cockade pinned to their coats.

'To the king!' one shouted. They all rose and clinked glasses and shouted the ovation.

Madame Campan, Viviane and the other ladies joined in, as a matter of course.

A dwarfish man in the plain black coat of a commoner turned to them. His head seemed too big for his body, and his eyes too large for his head. His dark hair was uncut and greasy, hanging on his neck.

'Why do you cheer for a man who, according to our new declaration, has no more importance than any other?' he sneered.

Madame Campan drew herself up. 'How dare you speak so of His Majesty the King?'

'Soon there will be no king in France,' the man replied. 'All men will be equal.'

Madame Campan stared at him in consternation. Just then the king and queen – not waiting for her signal – entered the hall, smiling. They must have heard the shouts and cheers.

The room resounded with acclaim. '*Vive le Roi! Vive la Reine!*'

One of the soldiers asked the queen if the regiment could meet the dauphin, and rather anxiously she agreed. The soldier lifted the little boy to stand on the table. Louis-Charles acknowledged the cheers and claps with a cheeky smile and a wave of his chubby hand. Many of the soldiers saluted him with their swords.

'We swear our loyalty to you, Your Majesty, and will serve you with honour,' the captain said, his hat pressed against his heart. He then, in a spontaneous gesture, unpinned the cockade on his coat and turned it over to show the pure white lining, the colour of the Bourbons. 'To the king!'

The crowd cheered, then many followed suit, turning their cockades to white. The queen thanked them, her face alight.

As the royal entourage turned to go, Viviane saw the dwarfish man slip out the back door.

15

The Baker, the Baker's Wife and the Baker's Boy
5–6 October 1789

Viviane sat on the sloping lawn of the belvedere, making daisy chains with Marie-Thérèse. The dauphin played nearby with Luna, throwing a ball for her then clapping his hands when she obediently fetched it and dropped it at his feet. The sun sparkled on the lake, and the waterfall foamed down the rock which hid the grotto.

The queen was sitting at a table outside the dainty belvedere, her head bent down over her hands, her eyes swollen and red. A fair-haired man sat with her, holding her hands, murmuring comfort. He was Axel von Fersen, the Swedish count long rumoured to be the queen's lover.

Viviane did not know what had so distressed the queen, but she could guess. Two days after the welcome feast, a journalist named Jean-Paul Marat had published an article called 'L'Orgie des Gardes Français'. The queen was depicted feasting and dancing and drinking gallons of wine, while the soldiers wrenched off their cockades and trampled and spat on them.

The queen must have felt as if she could do nothing right.

Church bells rang the half hour. The queen lifted her head and straightened her shoulders with an effort. 'Come, you must be hungry,' she called to the children. 'Shall we eat our lunch in the grotto today? We can pretend that we are castaways on a desert island, with no-one near for miles and miles.'

She rose and held out her hand, and the dauphin ran to her. The count made his farewells and bowed to the little prince and princess, then withdrew. His handsome face was troubled.

Marie-Antoinette and her son went through the vine-hung entrance of the stone grotto, a series of dimly lit caves carefully constructed to look real. Viviane followed with the princess, the crown of daisies sitting crookedly on her flaxen curls. Madame de Tourzel, the new governess for the royal children, came to join them with her daughter, Pauline. A lovely, laughing girl, Pauline was less than two years younger than Viviane, and the two smiled tentatively at each other.

The small party ate their simple picnic of bread and cold chicken and brie and fig jam, sitting on a rug spread on a stone shelf in the grotto. Marie-Antoinette and Madame de Tourzel whispered together, heads close, and so Viviane began to tell the children a story.

'Madame la Reine!' a frightened voice cried. Somebody was running down the passageway towards them. The queen leapt to her feet, her hand at her throat. The king's sister, Madame Élisabeth, rushed into the dimness of the cave. She was a slim young woman, only twenty-four years old. 'Madame . . . you must come!'

'What is it? What's wrong?' The queen's voice was shrill.

Madame Élisabeth glanced at the wide-eyed children, then beckoned the queen away. White-faced, Marie-Antoinette went with her.

Viviane got to her feet. Hurriedly she began to pack up the picnic basket. Dread coiled in her stomach.

The queen came back into the grotto. She was pale, her lips colourless. 'We must return to the palace. Hurry!'

'What has happened?' Madame de Tourzel asked.

'A mob of women are marching from Versailles. They have sacked the Hôtel de Ville in Paris, and are armed with guns and cannons. They want bread, they say, and also the heads of the men who spat on the cockade.

But it is all lies, no-one spat on the cockade!' The queen wrung her hands in distress.

They hurried back to the palace. The king had been out hunting, along with Viviane's father, but returned in haste, galloping all the way up the Grand Avenue. The court gathered in the Galerie des Glaces. The afternoon light streamed in through the seventeen tall arched windows, and gleamed in the ranks of mirrors opposite. The marble floors rang with the agitated pacing of high-heeled shoes.

No-one knew what to do.

'You should retreat to Rambouillet,' Viviane's father said. He, like most of the other men, was still dressed in riding clothes. 'You must not face an enraged mob, Your Majesty. Think of what they did to poor Foulon de Doué!'

The king's face bunched in distress. 'But I am their king! Surely they will not harm me?'

'At the very least, Madame la Reine should take the children and go,' Count Fersen urged. 'I will gladly escort them.'

'The horses are still hitched to the dauphin's carriage, for his afternoon drive. If you leave now, you will get away safely,' Madame de Tourzel said.

'I cannot leave my husband,' Marie-Antoinette said. 'My place is by his side.'

'I beg you, my liege, leave before it is too late!' Viviane's father urged.

'You must not go, Your Majesty.' Monsieur Necker spoke with great authority. The finance minister was a tall, heavily built man, with thick black brows in stark contrast with his pure white wig. 'The cost of transferring the court to Rambouillet is prohibitive. It will be seen as improvident and cowardly. You need to stay here in Versailles, and agree to the August Decrees, and ratify the Declaration of the Rights of Man and the Citizen. Once they know that you intend to support the constitutional modifications, the populace shall . . .'

'We do not have time for one of your windbag speeches,' Viviane's father interrupted. 'The mob shall be here soon. Your Majesty, let us get you to safety.'

'I would not like to be thought a coward,' Louis said hesitantly.

'It is not cowardly to preserve your well-being for the sake of France,' Viviane's father said.

'If you abscond, you will be acting in accordance with the rabble's worst view of you and doing exactly what your cousin, the Duc d'Orléans, would wish,' Monsieur Necker continued in his ponderous way.

'You think Monsieur le Duc is behind this?' the queen asked, hands clenched.

'I think it is a possibility, madame. His Majesty has yet to sign the August decrees or the Declaration of the Rights of Man and the Citizen. It is widely believed the Duc d'Orléans would gladly sanction these radical proposals, so there has been much discussion about the possibility of creating a constitutional monarchy under the leadership of the duke instead of His Majesty, who so far has resisted the abolition of the feudal system.'

'Do the people of France forget the dauphin?' the queen said wildly.

'Not to mention myself, or my brother and his noisy brats,' the Comte de Provence interjected from his couch by the fireplace. The older of the king's two brothers, he was enormously fat and rarely bestirred once he had settled himself. Viviane had thought him asleep.

'Monsieur le Comte, the people of France think you and your brother more royalist than the king himself,' Monsieur Necker replied dryly. 'I must reiterate, Your Majesty, the necessity of convincing the people of France that you are not averse to the endorsement of the Declaration of the Rights of Man and the Citizen as a precursor to maintaining some measure of control over any constitutional modifications . . .'

'Good lord!' Viviane's father cried. 'If I must listen to this upstart drone on anymore, I swear I shall swoon from sheer boredom. I cannot understand why the *canaille* adore him so much. They have obviously never heard him speak.'

'It is utterly disgraceful!' cried Madame Adélaïde, the king's aunt, banging her stick on the ground. 'Order your soldiers to shoot and kill these upstart rebels! Teach them a lesson they will not soon forget.'

'But they are my people . . . I do not wish to have their blood on my hands,' the king said, his round face troubled.

'Do you wish *your* blood on *their* hands?' his aunt snapped. 'Grow a spine, for God's sake!'

'But the people of France love me, I am their king,' Louis answered.

Madame Adélaïde snorted. 'The boy is a fool. Our grandfather must be rolling in his grave,' she said to her younger sister, Madame Victoire.

'He is not a boy anymore,' Madame Victoire replied in her soft, faded voice. 'Why, he is a father now himself, have you forgotten?'

Madame Adélaïde glared at her. 'My memory is faultless, thank you very much. I mean simply that he acts like a child. He is a man now, and a king! He should behave like one and hang them all.'

The discussion broke down into heated argument, everyone raising their voices to be heard. If the king had made some kind of decision, action could have been taken, but he vacillated between the views of stronger wills than his, and made no decision. The afternoon wore away.

'If I flee now, will I not end up a fugitive king like the English king, Charles Stuart?' Louis said at last, in plaintive tones. 'No, no, far better to stay and reason with these women, and promise them what they want. To flee would be to admit wrongdoing.'

'You shall not flee before a crowd of fishwives!' Madame Adélaïde spat. 'Arrest them! Throw them in an oubliette! Send them to be galley-slaves. I do not care, as long as you begin acting like a king.'

'Your Majesty, I must insist . . .' Monsieur Necker began.

'But the queen! The children!' Madame de Tourzel cried.

Viviane could not bear the hubbub. With Luna at her side, she slipped away through the long sequence of state apartments to the Hercules Room at the far end. It was like being enclosed within an over-gilded jewellery box. Every surface was painted and adorned, enamelled and garlanded. She sat on a chair of crimson damask, settling her heavy black skirts, looking out the window into the dreary autumn evening. Rain had been washing intermittently against the palace, but she could see a faint line of pale gold to the west where the clouds had cleared.

She wished she was far away from here. If only she had run away with David when she could!

Viviane watched the guards close the immense gold gates of the palace. It had been so long since they had been shut, the gates had rusted into place and it took a great deal of exertion to move them.

The sound of drums. The tramping of feet. A low ominous grumble like a thunderstorm. Viviane leapt up, pressing herself to the rain-washed glass. A great crowd of women marched towards the palace, damp, dirty and bedraggled. The leaders were foul-mouthed fishwives, dressed in bloody aprons, their gutting knives and cleavers stuck through their belts. Others looked like ladies of the night, in dishevelled gowns of shiny satin and drooping feathers. Cannons were dragged along by rope, and many of the accompanying men sported muskets slung over their shoulders.

'Bread! Bread!' they shouted. 'Give us bread!'

Viviane turned and ran through the state apartments, bursting into the Galerie des Glaces, her skirts bunched up in her hands. 'They're here!'

Her voice cut through the uproar. Everyone rushed down the state rooms to look out the windows.

The Royal Flanders regiment were lined in the palace courtyard, weapons at the ready. They looked nervous, Viviane thought, her face pressed against the window. They must know the crowd thought they had desecrated the sacred cockade.

'Give us the Austrian whore!' one woman shouted.

Viviane caught her breath, unable to believe anyone could speak of the queen with such flagrant disrespect.

'We'll hang her from the lamp-post!' Another woman held high a ragdoll hanging limply from a broken neck.

The fishwives flapped their bloody pinafores. 'We'll fill our aprons with her entrails and make ourselves cockades!'

'We'll slit her gizzard!'

The queen was pale and trembling. 'We should have fled,' she whispered. 'Oh, my little ones. What have I done?'

'Bread! Bread! Give us bread.' The chant was incessant.

Eventually twelve women were chosen to meet with the king. They were brought up to the Salon de l'Oeil-de-Boeuf, named for its small round window, thought to resemble a bull's eye. The women had been chosen for their cleanliness and decorum. They looked around them in awe, overcome at the opulence of the gilded halls.

Pierrette Chabry, a delicate young flower seller, was so dazed she fainted at the foot of the king. Louis gestured that she be lifted up. One of the ladies-in-waiting burnt some feathers under her nose to rouse her. At last her dark eyelashes fluttered open. She moaned a little.

'What can I do for you?' Louis asked.

'Bread,' she replied tearfully.

Louis called for food and wine, and then ordered bread from the palace kitchens to be distributed amongst the crowd. In awe and gratitude, the women retreated, only to come back fifteen minutes later, truculent and defiant, asking for the king's promise of bread to be given in writing.

One of the guards reported they had heard the fishwives shouting, 'Go back to the palace and tell them we will be there soon to hack off the queen's head.'

'We need to leave here,' Marie-Antoinette cried. 'It's too dangerous . . . my children . . .'

Orders were given for the royal family to escape through the gardens. Viviane began to hastily pack the queen's bags.

Ashen-faced, the guards reported back that the harnesses for the king's carriages had all been cut. There was to be no escape.

The wind had risen. Rain lashed the palace. It soaked the thousands that fumed outside the palace gates. Courtiers paced up and down the Galerie des Glaces, unable to sit still for a minute. The roar of the angry crowd grew louder.

'Where is that damned declaration?' the king said crossly. 'I will sign it, for God's sake, if that will make them all go home.'

No-one went home.

At midnight, the Marquis de Lafayette, the commander-in-chief of the newly formed National Guard, finally arrived. More talk. More arguments. More vacillation.

At two o'clock in the morning, the queen at last went to lie down in her bed. Her ladies-in-waiting slept in chairs and on couches in her ante-chamber. It was cold, the storm lashing the palace with sleet, the crowd outside restless and uncomfortable.

'Why do they not go home?' Madame Campan asked querulously. 'What do they want?'

No-one answered, or met her eye. The answer was too terrible to speak aloud.

Viviane was woken by a great roar. Voices shrieking. Metal clanging.

'Go and see what is happening,' Madame Campan ordered.

Viviane ran to the guard room. It looked over the royal courtyard. Peering out into the rain-lashed darkness, Viviane saw the crowd pushing at the golden gates. Screaming, shouting. The gates broke. The mob clambered through, then ran across the courtyard, smashing down doors, breaking windows.

Viviane ran to the door. A swarm of screaming people raced up the queen's staircase. The Duc d'Orléans urged them on, riding whip in hand, his tall boots splashed with mud, his hat drawn low. With one gloved hand, he pointed out the guard room which led to the queen's apart-ment. Viviane recoiled. It was true. The duke had betrayed the king, his own cousin.

The palace guard fought to keep the mob back, but they were outnum-bered. Knives flashed. Men fell. Blood splattered on the marble.

Viviane burst into the queen's bedchamber without any thought of ceremony.

'They're coming,' she panted. 'You must go. Now!'

The queen scrambled out of bed. Hurriedly her ladies flung a robe around her, but had no time to fasten the ties. Barefoot, the queen ran across the room and pressed something on her wall. A panel sprang open, revealing a secret passage.

'Quick! Quick!' she cried.

The door slammed open. A guard, covered in blood, cried, 'Save the queen, madame!'

Then he was stabbed from behind.

Marie-Antoinette fled down the secret passage, her ladies close behind. Viviane had to coax Luna to come, and so she was last. As she drew the panel shut, she saw half-a-dozen ragged men and women burst into the bedchamber. One paused to hack the head from the fallen guard. The rest attacked the queen's bed with their cleavers and pikes. Holding her breath, Viviane silently closed the secret door.

She hurried along the dark passageway, trying to keep the frightened dog from whining. A howl of anger and frustration from the queen's bedchamber spurred her on. A slit of light showed her the end of the secret passage.

It led to the king's apartment. Confusion was rife. Louis was dressed still in his nightshirt and nightcap. The queen was sobbing for her children. Madame de Tourzel went running to fetch them, while Viviane helped the queen draw on some clothes. No-one knew what to do. It was impossible to escape. The mob raged through the palace, smashing what they could. At last, the king agreed to show himself on the balcony. He had dressed and hastily pinned a tri-coloured cockade to his hat. A cheer rose up from the ragged crowd at the sight of him. 'Vive le Roi! Vive le Roi!'

But these cries were overtaken by the new chant. 'To Paris! To Paris!'

'My friends,' the king said, smiling tremulously, chubby hands spread wide. 'If you so wish it, I shall go with you to Paris, with my dear wife and children. I trust all that is most precious to me to my good and faithful subjects.'

The crowd shouted its approval, but it was impossible not to see the heads of the queen's slaughtered bodyguards, bobbing about on the sharp end of pikes.

'Bring out the queen! Bring out the Austrian whore,' the mob shouted.

The queen went shakily out onto the balcony, her daughter and son clutched close.

'No children, no children!' the mob screamed.

Madame de Tourzel and Viviane helped draw the frightened Children of France away. Marie-Antoinette stood alone. The crowd booed and hissed, but she bowed her head and stood steadfastly. Some of the crowd shouted, 'Vive la Reine! Vive la Reine!'

But those words were drowned beneath the chant, 'To Paris! To Paris!'

Dawn came, grey and cold, and then noon, before the king's carriage at last set out for Paris. The Marquis de Lafayette rode his famous white horse at one door of the royal coach, and the Comte d'Estaing at the other. Behind followed the coaches of the court. Viviane travelled with her father and stepmother, Luna cowering under her skirts, Pierrick running ahead. Everyone was white and silent, shaken by the violence of the night.

The golden poplar trees burned like flames against the grey sky. Damp leaves whirled in the wind. The crowd pressed close around the coaches, in high humour at their success in forcing the king to Paris.

'We've got the baker, the baker's wife and the baker's boy,' they shouted, thrusting the decapitated heads of the bodyguards at the coach windows.

Viviane looked back. The palace of Versailles disappeared behind her.

All she could see now were the grinning faces of the mob, pressing close all around.

16

A Captive King
6 October 1789 – 25 June 1791

The Tuileries was a ramshackle old palace. As the dauphin was carried inside, he wrinkled his nose and said, 'But, Maman-Reine, it's so ugly.'

Marie-Antoinette looked ill with exhaustion. It had taken the royal cavalcade almost seven hours to reach Paris, and then they had been driven in circles through the streets of the city for another three, for the people to taunt and jeer at them. But she straightened her back and said, with a brave attempt to be calm, 'If your great-great-great-grandfather Louis XIV could live here and like it, so can we.'

Viviane helped Madame Tourzel and Pauline settle the children as best they could. Marie-Thérèse had to sleep on a dusty old ottoman, there being no bed for her. The door to Louis-Charles's room did not shut, so Madame Tourzel barricaded herself inside with furniture, and sat up in a chair to guard the little boy as he slept.

The next day, when the dauphin woke, he heard the sound of the mob still shouting in the Tuileries gardens.

In a tone of dismay, he said, 'Is today going to be like yesterday?'

'No, my boy. Today will be better,' the king said, opening his arms to his son.

Louis-Charles climbed up onto his father's lap. 'Papa-Roi, I do not understand. Why are the people of France so angry with you now?'

The king looked sad. 'I have tried to make them happy, but the fact of the matter is, our country is deep in debt and that means people are hungry. Being hungry all the time makes them angry. Do not blame them or think ill of them, for we are all working together to try and fix things.'

'You must be kind and friendly to everyone, *mon chou d'amour*,' the queen said, 'no matter what they say or do to you.'

When Jean Sylvain Bailly, the new mayor of Paris, came to the Tuileries to see how the royal family was settling in, the dauphin spoke to him with great courtesy, then ran to his mother, climbed up on her lap and said, loudly, 'Was that good, Maman-Reine?'

'Yes,' Marie-Antoinette answered, bending so she could brush his fair curls with her lips. 'Very good, my boy.'

Later, when the Spanish ambassador asked her how her husband was feeling, she answered, in a voice choked with sobs, 'Like a captive king.'

Indeed, it felt like imprisonment. The Marquis de Lafayette posted guards on every door and stair, all dressed in their new uniform emblazoned with *Liberté, Égalité, Fraternité*.

No-one in the royal court could go out to walk in the gardens or go to the theatre without being jeered at by crowds of people. So the queen stayed at the Tuileries, furnishing their apartment, busying herself reading and sewing and hearing her children's lessons, and only venturing out for Mass each day.

Viviane had to share a tiny suite of rooms with her father and stepmother, for the marquis wished to stay close to the king in the hope of being rewarded for his faithfulness once the revolution was crushed. Besides, he was crippled with debt and the Parisian townhouse and the château in the Loire Valley were ruinous to run. So the marquis had sacked many of his servants, and closed both his residences, living only upon his courtier's salary and the king's largesse.

Living with her father was an ordeal. His mood was dark and bitter, his tongue cruel. He told Clothilde she was an empty-headed fool, and kicked

Luna every time he saw her, castigating Viviane for allowing a useless crippled animal to live. He railed against Viviane for being a worthless girl, and against Clothilde for being barren and failing to provide him with an heir. His château was entailed, Viviane knew, and would be inherited on his death by a distant cousin whom he hated.

Most of his anger was directed towards Pierrick, however. The marquis expected Pierrick to bow and scrape and fawn on him, as if all noble privileges had not been abolished. The marquis struck him across the face for bringing cold coffee, even though the kitchens were a long way from their quarters, and lashed him again and again on the back with his cane for failing to keep his linens snowy-white, despite soap being hard to come by. Viviane could not bear it. She tried to defend Pierrick, but that only made things worse. It was as if the marquis hated them both. Viviane returned to her dark cupboard of a room only to sleep, and made excuses to send her milk-brother out on errands.

Pierrick spent most of his time in the inns and coffee-houses, collecting gossip and rumours. He told Viviane that the Breton Club had moved to Paris, along with the National Assembly, and had begun meeting at the Jacobins' friary on the Rue Saint-Honoré, not far from the Tuileries.

'They want to unravel everything,' he told her, torn between high excitement and awed dread. 'The monarchy, the church, everything.'

The Jacobins, as they began to be called, exerted their radical influence on the Assembly. First, all property owned by the Catholic Church was confiscated. Then – some months later – religious orders and vows were dismantled. All priests had to swear an oath to the new French government and forswear any loyalty to the Pope in Rome. The streets of Paris were filled with effigies of the Pope being burned, and nuns and monks were attacked and driven out into the streets as beggars. Viviane could only pray that her beloved Abbé was safe.

The following summer, it was announced that hereditary nobility was abolished for all time. Viviane was no longer the Duchesse de Savageaux, much to her secret pleasure. Her father was no longer the

Marquis de Valaine, much to his blatant displeasure. There were no more princes, dukes, comtes, barons or chevaliers.

No mention was made of kings or queens or dauphins, but the implication was clear.

The anniversary of the fall of the Bastille was greeted with hysterical joy by the Parisians. The king and queen and their children spent all day standing on a stage, listening to martial music and watching soldiers march by. The celebrations went on for days.

Six weeks later, Viviane was at last permitted to put aside her mourning clothes and wear colours once again. This meant a white dress, with a sash of red-white-and-blue. No-one, not the queen, not any of her ladies, not the meanest washerwoman, wore anything but the tri-colours of the cockade anymore.

It was a strange existence. The king and queen retained much of the old etiquette of Versailles, with formal ceremonies of rising and dressing and eating and going to bed, even as they wore the revolutionary cockade and endured the rudeness of their revolutionary guard.

January 1st 1791 was the day when all members of the clergy had to decide whether to take the oath of allegiance to the revolutionary government, or not. On that day, Louis-Charles was given a gift of dominoes made of stone and marble gathered from the ruins of the Bastille.

He opened the box eagerly and began to stack the dominoes up into towers. The queen saw that the lid of the box had been engraved with words, and picked it up.

'The stones of the walls which imprisoned so many innocent victims of arbitrary power have been made into a toy for Your Highness, as a token of the love of your people and as a symbol of their strength,' she read, aloud. Her face stiffened. She bent and began to gather up the dominoes, thrusting them back into the box.

Louis-Charles objected loudly, and she said, a voice of fury, 'You shall not play with such a thing. No, *mon chou d'amour*, I am sorry but the dauphin of France must not soil his hands with such filth.'

He wept, but his mother was intractable. She hid the dominoes, and Viviane had to think of some way to distract and comfort the little boy.

Every day, there was some new disturbance. Lafayette and his National Guard were in constant motion, calming a demonstration here and a rally there.

In late February, a riot was caused by the king's elderly aunts. Horrified by the dismantling of the Catholic church, they decided to go on pilgrimage to the Basilica of Saint Peter in Rome, and asked the king for passports. Someone tipped off the Jacobin Club, who protested to the National Assembly. A crowd of women gathered, determined to stop them, but Madame Adélaïde and Madame Victoire escaped in the coach of a friend.

Protestors invaded the gardens of the Tuileries, shouting and demanding the king order his aunts to return. 'Bring the old bags home!' they screamed.

Pierrick thought it was hilarious. He brought Viviane the newspaper with her morning coffee, and showed her the passage which amused him most.

Two Princesses, sedentary by condition, age and taste, are suddenly possessed by a mania for travelling and running about the world, she read. *That is singular, but possible. They are going, so people say, to kiss the Pope's slipper. That is droll, but edifying. The Ladies, and especially Madame Adélaïde, want to exercise the rights of man. That is natural. The fair travellers are followed by a train of eighty persons. That is fine. But they carry away twelve millions. That is very ugly.*

Viviane pushed the paper away. 'It's not true. The king's aunts took little more than a trunk of clothes each. There is not twelve million in the treasury to steal.'

She rested her head in her hands. How she wished she too could flee this cold and gloomy old palace. She longed to fill her lungs with fresh air, and stride out through the forest. If only she could go home! But there was no home left for her.

'They are two old ladies,' she said wearily. 'Why should they not travel to Rome if they want to?'

'That is just what Monsieur Mirabeau said,' Pierrick answered, folding the newspaper up and tossing it on the floor. 'The thing is, if the king's aunts are allowed to leave whenever they like, what is to stop the king?'

It seemed the people of Paris thought the same, because they continued to crowd around the Tuileries, shouting and shaking their makeshift weapons and pressing their dirty faces against the windows, trying to catch a glimpse of the king to make sure he was still there. By the last day of the month, the rowdy mob had grown to such an extent that no-one in the palace dared step outside.

Then young noblemen began to arrive, showing *cartes d'admission* to gain entrance to the palace. They clustered around the king, their faces hard and angry, and showed him the glint of steel hidden in their boots or under their waistcoats.

'We have come to guard and protect you,' one ardent young man cried.

Louis looked distinctly uneasy. 'We don't want any trouble,' he mumbled. 'Wouldn't do to upset them, you know.'

'But we are prepared to die for you!'

'Sire, we are ready to fight our way free of here.'

'We will carry you to safety far from this dreadful place, Your Majesty.'

'The country will rise for you, and overthrow these despots!'

'For each sword in this room, there are hundreds more just waiting for a word from you!'

The young men's voices rose in their passion and sincerity.

The king tried to shush them. 'Now, now, no need to be hasty. We don't want anyone to hear you.'

Viviane had been sitting with the dauphin on the hearth-rug, playing with his lead soldiers. Luna lay beside her, chin resting on her paw. The clamour of the young officers woke her, however, and she opened sleepy eyes, stretched out her three long legs and yawned.

'But, sire . . .'

'We wish to serve you!'

'There are more of us, many more . . .'

'How many?' the queen asked, looking up from her sewing.

'Four hundred or more, Your Highness.'

'There are four hundred thousand people in Paris,' the queen answered. 'Do you intend to fight them all?'

For a moment, the young men looked dashed but their spirit rallied once more.

'If we must!'

'We will gladly shed our blood for our king and queen!'

Their voices rang clearly through the echoing halls of the palace. The king looked anguished, and made a gesture to them to keep their voices down, but the quick clatter of boots sounded on the stone and then guards rushed in, their faces angry and suspicious. A brief scuffle, the overturning of a chair or two, and then a few of the noblemen were caught and disarmed. The others raced away, their poignards in their hands, calling for aid.

'What is all this?' the head guard snapped. 'An attempt to snatch away the king?'

'Just a few hot-headed young fools,' Louis said feebly.

'We are here to serve the king or die!' one of the captured officers declared.

'That can be arranged,' the captain replied dryly, then snapped out swift orders. 'Call the general! Find those chevaliers, and disarm them at once.'

But the officers had barricaded themselves inside an abandoned hall, and were fighting off any attempt to seize them. Layafette soon arrived, looking dusty and weary. He had been quelling a Jacobin uprising in the Faubourg Saint-Antoine, and was not at all pleased at having to face a royalist insurrection within the palace and an angry and violent mob without. For the throngs of people in the Tuileries gardens had heard rumours of what was happening within, and were beating in doors and breaking through windows, fuelled by rumours the royal family were seeking to escape through some kind of secret subterranean passage.

The general ordered the young chevaliers to lay down their weapons and disband.

They refused.

'Your Majesty, I beg you to add your word to mine,' Lafayette said to the king, in terse angry tones. 'Else there'll be bloodshed tonight. I would not like it to be yours or your family's.'

The king did as he was asked, and slowly and reluctantly the officers surrendered their weapons and were arrested. Shoved, pushed, mocked, vilified, they were dragged through the howling mob, who flung stones and dog excrement at them, and tore at their clothes and hair.

'What will happen to them?' the king asked sadly.

'I do not know,' the general replied. 'It is not up to me to pass judgement.'

In the end, the Chevaliers du Poignard – as the young noblemen came to be called – were sent into exile, impoverished and disgraced.

There were no other attempts to free the king.

Spring came at last, and with it the first Easter since the country's priests had been forced to choose between their new government and their ancient religion.

'What am I to do?' the king said in a voice of misery. 'They will make me take Holy Communion with a priest who has abjured the true religion. How can that be right?'

'Let us go back to Saint-Cloud,' the queen said. 'It is so much nicer there. No-one jeering or hissing at us. You can hunt, and regain your health, and the children can run in the gardens and play. And no-one will know if we take communion from a priest who has not abjured.'

The following Monday, the carriages were called for and the king and the queen descended to the courtyard with their entourage. Everyone was cheerful at the prospect of leaving Paris for a few days. Marie-Antoinette, Louis and his sister Madame Élisabeth were handed into their coach. Viviane lifted the dauphin up to his mother, then turned to help Marie-Thérèse.

As always, the Tuileries gardens were crowded with people enjoying the mild spring sunshine. People saw the royal entourage preparing to leave, and began to gather about the coaches angrily.

'The king's trying to escape!' someone shouted.

The mood turned ugly. Hands seized the horses' bridles, causing them to fret and rear. People pressed close about the coaches, banging on the doors, shouting through the windows.

'Calm yourself,' the Marquis de Valaine said in a voice of cold disdain. 'His Majesty simply wishes to visit the country.'

'He goes to our enemies, to bring an army upon us,' one woman shouted.

'They think to betray us!'

'My dear people,' Louis said, putting his head out the coach window, 'it is very odd that I, your king, the one who granted you liberty, should be so rudely denied it myself.'

The only response was a roar of rage. One of the royal attendants was dragged off the coach and beaten.

Louis-Charles cried out in terror, 'Oh, save him, save him!'

The soldiers of the National Guard stood by and did nothing to help. Eventually, the king and queen gave up and returned to the Tuileries.

'You must admit we are no longer free,' Marie-Antoinette exclaimed, as she stepped out of the carriage. Holding her frightened son by his hand, she marched up the palace steps. One of her ladies-in-waiting was crying.

The queen lifted her head proudly. 'This is no time to cry. We must show courage.'

Mid-summer came, and Paris seethed in the choking heat.

Viviane longed for the cool blue waters of the lake at Belisima, the green shadows of the forest, the fresh scent of the garden. She wondered if the roses were blooming amidst the ruins. The thought made her chest ache. David's death weighed heavily on her conscience. She knew what cruelty her father was capable of, and yet she had encouraged David, made friends with him, let him fall in love with her. Her loneliness and grief were her penance.

The king and queen were distracted and agitated. They argued in low voices all the time, and jumped at every noise. Secret messengers came and went, and Viviane heard rumors that the Comte d'Artois was trying to raise an army to invade France and put his brother the king back on the throne.

One afternoon Viviane was walking with the queen and princess and their ladies when Marie-Antoinette drew her daughter aside and whispered something in her ear. The little girl paled, looking up at her mother with darkly dilated eyes. Marie-Antoinette held her tightly, saying something in a low, urgent voice. Afterwards Marie-Thérèse was upset, and did not want to play or listen to a story. She shut herself in her room. Listening quietly at the door, Viviane heard her crying but when she went in, the young princess wiped her face and pretended nothing was wrong.

Viviane helped prepare the queen for bed. Marie-Antoinette was restless and jumpy, moving from the door to the window to her jewellery box, and shrugging off attempts to disrobe her. 'Madame de Gagnon,' she said suddenly. 'I have noticed lately how peaky you are looking. Perhaps you should think of retiring to your country estates for a while.'

Viviane was surprised. 'Your Highness, I have no country estate . . . my château was burned down and my husband's estates sold off to pay his debts.'

The queen looked distressed. 'I am sorry. I did not realise.'

She dismissed Viviane, who went wearily towards her bedroom. As she climbed the stairs, she saw the Princesse de Lamballe being escorted down to a waiting carriage. She wore a velvet travelling cloak, its hood drawn up over her powdered hair. Her men-servants carried several heavy trunks after her.

'It is most odd,' the princess said to one of her attendants, in her soft gentle voice. 'I do not understand why Her Majesty insists I go to Rambouillet. Indeed, I am quite well, apart from a few slight spells of dizziness caused by the heat. She is adamant, however, that I must go tonight, which is not at all convenient . . .'

The princess passed out of the doors and was handed up into her coach, her trunks corded to the roof. The coachman flicked his whip, and the horses trotted off into the darkness.

Viviane went to her own rooms, perturbed. She slept poorly, worrying about the meaning of the queen's odd behaviour, and rose early, hurrying down to the royal apartment, her sense of unease deepening into real alarm.

Surely the king and queen would not have tried to escape?

The French people would never forgive them if they fled to Austria or England, their traditional enemies.

Her step slowed as she approached the queen's rooms. Soldiers were everywhere, searching every hall and antechamber. One of the guards recognised her and seized her arm, shaking her. 'Where have they gone? You had better tell me all you know!'

'Pardon? I do not know what you mean.' Viviane's breath shortened and her chest felt tight. It must be true. The royal family must have somehow escaped. She felt a sudden giddy hope that they would reach a place of safety.

'You know what I mean! Where have they gone?'

'I don't know!'

Luna growled as the man shook her again, and forced her to sit. Viviane picked her up and held her on her lap, although Luna had grown to such a great size it was not easy. She was interrogated for close on an hour, but only shook her head and wept and said she did not know. At last the man let her go.

Viviane hurried up the stairs, her skirts swishing, desperate to know what had happened. But no-one knew. Apparently the royal family had slipped out after midnight, probably in some kind of disguise.

The day passed very slowly, with all the courtiers closest to the king and queen kept under observation. Viviane was not permitted to go to her own rooms. She slept on a pallet in the queen's bedroom with the other ladies of honour. The soldiers were rough with them, not letting them leave the room to go to the privy, or to fetch water to wash their hands, or quench their thirst. They were all questioned again and again, their guards' refusing to believe they did not know where the king and queen had fled.

In the dawn Viviane was woken by the news that the king and queen had been captured during the night. Even though they had been disguised as servants, with the little dauphin dressed as a girl, a postmaster had recognised the king from his portrait on an *assignat*, the new paper currency. He had galloped ahead of the king's coach and aroused the guards at Varennes, who had then detained the royal family. An old man who had once worked at Versailles was dragged from his bed and taken to see the captured party. As soon as he saw the king, he had instinctively crooked his knee. Louis had then admitted that he was indeed the king.

A few days later, the huge travelling coach returned to Paris, dragged by six sweaty and exhausted horses. The king was so stiff he could scarcely climb down from the carriage. He was dressed like a servant, in a sober coat and round hat. The huge crowd stared at him silently. Then Marie-Antoinette stepped down, her son in her arms. She wore a plain black gown like a governess, her greying hair dishevelled, the little boy's face streaked with dirt and tear stains. A roar of hatred rose from ten thousand throats. People lunged towards her, ripping at her hair, her clothes. The queen screamed and flinched, trying to protect the dauphin. Some soldiers of the National Guard wrestled the attackers away, while others dragged the little prince out of his mother's arms. Marie-Antoinette shrieked and fought to get to her son, and the soldiers seized her and carried her, struggling and crying, into the Tuileries Palace.

Viviane, watching from the window above, felt tears thicken her throat. It was awful to see the queen, usually so graceful and dignified, treated so roughly. She ran down the stairs with the other ladies of honour, but was held back by soldiers. The dauphin was handed back to his mother, and she sank to her knees, clutching him close, struggling to hold back tears. Marie-Thérèse had been carried within the palace too. As soon as she was deposited on the ground, the girl ran to her mother, weeping.

Cold-faced and stern, Lafayette ordered the royal family to be escorted to their rooms. Guards were posted at every door and every stair.

The king's flight had failed.

17

Mouth of the Tiger
14 September 1791 – 20 June 1792

The weeks dragged past.

Viviane woke each morning with a leaden weight of misery and despair in the hollow of her stomach, and went to bed each night bone-weary but unable to rest. The people of Paris had not forgiven the king for trying to escape. Every day, angry mobs swarmed about the old palace, shouting crude insults, shaking makeshift weapons, calling for blood.

In mid-September, the king formally accepted the new constitution. He sat in an ordinary low armchair, and read a prepared speech in a low mumble. Halfway through, he glanced up and saw the deputies of the National Assembly had all remained in their seats. Not one had doffed their hats. Louis flushed beetroot-red at the insult. It was as if he had only just realised that he was no longer God's anointed king.

His bewilderment smote Viviane's heart. Louis could no more help being born a king than she could help being a marquis's daughter or Pierrick the illegitimate son of a peasant. She found herself torn between her sympathy for the royal family and her affinity with the ideals of the revolutionaries.

'I agree that things had to change,' Viviane said to Pierrick that evening, as she sat and darned her stockings by the stove in her room. 'There was so much wrong with the way things were. All people should be born free, and have the same rights and opportunities. But all this violence and bloodshed! It seems to be escalating. I'm afraid of what will happen.'

Pierrick was polishing the marquis's shoes. 'The Jacobins are angry that the National Assembly did not insist on the king stepping down altogether. And they're right! The days of kings and queens are over.'

'But who would you replace the king with?' Viviane asked. 'The Jacobins themselves?'

'A republic!' Pierrick cried. 'Ruled by men voted into power, not born into it. A republic devoted to defending the right to liberty of all men and the destruction of despotism.'

His black eyes sparkled with excitement. 'Don't you see? We have a real chance here of building an entirely new system of government.'

'But what of the king, the queen?' Viviane faltered, putting down her needle. 'What would become of them?'

'Maybe fat Louis can become a pig farmer,' Pierrick answered, laughing. 'And the queen can become a washerwoman.'

Now that the king had signed the constitution, the Assembly wanted all to return to normal. Everyone was tired of the strikes, the riots, the violence. It was time for the revolution to end, they said, and for the business of governing the country to begin.

The queen was urged to set her household in order.

'I must write to the Princesse de Lamballe, and request either her return or her resignation,' Marie-Antoinette said, playing restlessly with her quill. 'I am afraid for her, though. She is so loyal. She shall return if I ask her to. I've told her not to come back, that it would be like throwing herself into the mouth of the tiger, but she will think it her duty.'

'Would you like me to write to her?' Viviane asked. She knew the queen struggled with her penmanship.

'If you would. I have so many letters to reply to!' Marie-Antoinette drew an untidy pile of correspondence to her, lifted one and carefully held it over the little candle she used to melt her wax. After a moment she laid the letter down and scrutinised the hidden words that had sprung into being under the heat of the flame.

So Viviane wrote on her behalf, and soon a letter returned from the Princesse de Lamballe, declaring her intention to return at once.

'I wish she would not,' Marie-Antoinette said unhappily. 'She is so much hated, for no other crime than being a friend of mine. Yet I must admit I miss her. Surely the worst is over now?'

The Princesse de Lamballe returned in mid-November. Marie-Antoinette ran forward and flung herself into her friend's arms, weeping. The princess held the queen close, stroking her hair, whispering words of comfort.

'Oh, you should not have come back!' the queen said, dabbing at her eyes with her handkerchief. 'My dearest Marie, it is so awful here. They hate us, and yet will not let us leave.'

'Oh, my poor Toinette, not all hate you, not at all,' the princess replied. She had the faintest trace of an Italian accent, for she had been born in Turin, the daughter of the Principe de Carignano. 'There are many who seek to restore you to your rightful place. This is just an aberration. The people will soon come to their senses, I promise you.'

Marie-Antoinette shook her head dolefully.

'Come, do not weep. I have brought you a gift.' The princess turned and gestured to one of her footmen, who stood silently against the wall holding a basket. The servant brought it to her, and she opened the lid to reveal a red-and-white spaniel.

'Oh, she is too precious!' Marie-Antoinette lifted the spaniel into her arms. The puppy yapped and licked her chin, and the queen laughed.

'See, she is cheering you up already.' The princess nodded to the footman, who retreated back to the wall. He was wearing the Lamballe colours. Viviane wondered if the princess knew that the wearing of livery had been abolished.

'What is her name?' Marie-Antoinette asked, caressing the puppy's long dangling ears.

'Thisbe,' Marie de Lamballe answered.

'Oh, no, that is not a good name. Is Thisbe not the girl who killed herself and her blood dyed mulberries red? I shall call her Mignon. She may sleep under my bed and guard me, and warn me of assassins,' the queen said, laughing even as she again dabbed at her eyes.

'Maman-Reine, may I pat the puppy, please?' Louis-Charles ran forward, his blue eyes glowing. Marie-Antoinette bent so he could reach the spaniel's soft fur.

'But what is this?' the princess cried. 'Our little *chou d'amour* is no longer afraid of dogs?'

'No, not anymore. It is all due to the young Duchesse de Savageaux, the newest of my ladies.' Marie-Antoinette gestured towards Viviane with a brief flashing smile. 'She has a dog of her own, as you can see, and Louis spends a great deal of time playing with it.'

The Princesse de Lamballe glanced at Viviane with interest. 'I am sorry,' she murmured. 'I do not think . . .'

'I am new at court,' Viviane answered, curtseying.

'And married to the Duc de Savageaux? But was he not . . .'

'Killed? Yes, madame. On the night of the fall of the Bastille.'

'So young to be a widow,' the princess said sadly. 'But sometimes it is better to be a widow than a wife, yes?'

'Yes,' Viviane answered, and the two women shared a moment of silent understanding before the princess turned back to the dauphin.

'If only I had known you were no longer afraid of dogs,' she said, pinching Louis-Charles's cheek. 'I would have brought you a puppy too.'

'Truly? Oh Maman-Reine, may I please have a puppy of my own? Please?'

So the young prince was given a toy spaniel for Christmas. Louis-Charles called her Coco, and carried the pup with him everywhere he went, tucked under his arm or dragged along by a ribbon.

The royal family had now been living in the Tuileries for three years. One of their problems was keeping the prince and princess happy and occupied within the gloomy confines of the old palace. When spring came, the king sought permission for Louis-Charles to have his own plot of garden by the terrace. The little boy – now almost seven – planted seeds and bulbs, and was ecstatic when they first began to flower. Every morning he rose early, and went out to tend his garden in the company of Coco and a chambermaid. He picked a scraggly bunch of flowers and carried it carefully up to his mother's room. He laid it on her pillow, then – stifling his giggles – hid with his puppy behind the curtain.

Marie-Antoinette stretched and sighed theatrically, then opened her eyes. 'My goodness, look at these lovely flowers!' she murmured. 'They are the prettiest flowers I have ever seen. I wonder what fine chevalier has been so kind as to bring them to me?'

Louis-Charles burst out from behind the curtain. 'It's me, Maman-Reine! I brought them!'

Rushing forward, the dauphin flung himself into his mother's arms, and was kissed and caressed and thanked, the toy spaniel yapping at his heels.

He never tired of the surprise.

In February, Axel von Fersen returned to Paris. He had been instrumental in the failed royal escape, but the king – perhaps jealous of the queen's affection for the Swedish count – had not allowed him to travel with their party. Viviane could not help but think the escape might have succeeded if the count – so vigorous and decisive – had been allowed a larger role to play.

Axel was full of plans and schemes for rescuing the royal family, but it seemed impossible. They were too closely guarded.

'Rescue must come from the outside,' the queen said firmly. 'My brother . . . can he not be brought to invade France? What are his scruples? I do not understand his hesitation. He knows what I am suffering!'

'Austria and Prussia have signed a military convention, promising to invade and restore the crown to the king, but there are still those who argue that this is French business, and that this new government seems determined to defend their rights . . .'

'This new government is nothing but a heap of blackguards, madmen and beasts,' the queen said bitterly. 'They could no more command an army than a troop of monkeys! Oh, Axel, I am in despair. I have missed you so much . . .' Glancing around, she saw Viviane sitting in the window seat, Luna curled up on her hem. 'Madame,' she cried, a little wildly. 'Will you leave us? Go and see if Madame de Tourzel needs some help. Perhaps you might play hide-and-seek with the children. They need some exercise.'

'Yes, Your Majesty.' Viviane curtsied and left the room, though she knew the queen was meant never to be left alone.

She hoped the count would be able to console her, just a little.

By April, France was at war.

Beggars were everywhere, pleading for food. Battalions of poorly equipped soldiers marched off to defend the borders.

In late May, the Assembly ordered the deportation of any priest who had not sworn his loyalty to the new French government. A few weeks later, the king used his right to veto any new law, and declared that the rebel priests could stay. He had already vetoed the law that those émigrés who had fled the country during the outbreaks of violence were to be condemned to death, their property confiscated, if they did not return at once. His own brothers were amongst those who would have been so condemned, but his vetoes infuriated the populace.

The 20th of June was the anniversary of the king and queen's failed escape attempt. Thirty thousand people marched upon the Tuileries. Viviane heard them coming long before she saw them. They were singing 'Ça ira, ça ira!' as they marched.

It was a terrifying sight from the palace windows. Men, women and children, filthy and ragged, armed with pikes, scythes, hammers, axes, pitchforks. Crude tricolour banners fluttered above their heads.

'*Vivent les sans-culottes!*' the crowd screamed. Viviane did not know what the term meant. She guessed it signified all those who did not wear the fine satin breeches, or *culottes*, that were the fashion amongst the nobility.

Children hurled cobblestones against the windows, breaking the glass. 'Down with the aristos!' they shrilled.

As the mob reached the palace, they began to smash at the doors with hatchets.

'My God!' The queen started to her feet, one hand pressed against her heart. 'They wish to break in.'

'They will tear us from limb to limb!' one of her ladies-in-waiting cried.

'Just listen to them!' Madame Élisabeth clung to her brother's arm. The king was pale and sweating.

'I must speak with them, try and calm them,' he said, in a shaking voice.

'No, no!' The queen was distraught.

'No, Papa-Roi!' the dauphin flung himself on his father.

'Find the Austrian bitch! Hang her high,' shouted a woman in the crowd.

'Toinette, you must take the children and hide,' Louis instructed.

'No, no, my place is by your side,' Marie-Antoinette cried.

'Madame, it is too dangerous. Your presence will only make them angrier. You must think of your children.' The Princesse de Lamballe caught the queen by the hand. 'Please, Toinette.'

The queen wavered, not knowing what to do.

The Princesse de Lamballe turned to Viviane. 'Madame, help me. We must keep Her Majesty safe.'

Viviane gazed at the queen beseechingly. 'Please, Madame la Reine. For the children's sake.'

Marie-Antoinette cast one last anguished look at her husband, then let herself be hurried from the room. Madame de Tourzel's daughter Pauline held Marie-Thérèse's hand, the young girl sobbing in fright. Viviane carried Louis-Charles, his puppy squirming and yelping in his too-tight grasp. Luna slinked at her heels, tail tucked away tight.

'I shall stay with you, Louis,' Madame Élisabeth cried.

'They may think you are Toinette,' the Princesse de Lamballe protested, her hand on the door.

'Then do not undeceive them, let them believe me the queen,' Madame Élisabeth said bravely, though she was white to her lips.

Viviane looked back, and saw the slight young woman clinging to her brother's coat-tails as he was hustled into a window embrasure, his guards all raising their weapons as the howls of the mob came ever closer.

The queen and her ladies-in-waiting took refuge in the dauphin's room.

'We cannot lock the door,' the Princesse de Lamballe cried. 'What shall we do?'

Viviane looked around wildly. There was no way to escape. The drop from the window was too high and, besides, the courtyard was filled with screaming crowds.

'Let us shut the door and barricade it with the table,' she said. 'Perhaps that will stop them.'

The princess nodded. 'It is the best we can do. Quick, quick! Do it.'

Pauline darted forward and helped Viviane drag the table across the door. The sound of shouting, smashing glass and the drumming of running feet in sabots came closer and closer.

'Let's find that imbecile, the king, and knock some sense into his thick skull!'

'Death to Monsieur and Madame Veto!'

'Where's that Austrian bitch? We'll hang her from the lamp-posts by her own guts!'

Voices right outside the door.

The door-handle was wrenched from side to side. The door rattled, then heaved. Then wood fractured under the steel blades of axes.

Marie-Thérèse stood stiffly against the wall, her face blank, fingers spread. Louis-Charles sobbed and cowered against his mother. It is too cruel, Viviane thought. She is only thirteen, he is only seven. Children should not have to see and hear such things.

No-one should.

Marie-Antoinette sat hunched in an armchair. Her breath came in harsh pants like a hare that has been hunted to exhaustion. Viviane remembered the queen as she had first seen her. Marie-Antoinette had been gorgeously dressed in pink silk, dancing and laughing, the epitome of grace and elegance.

Now she was thin and haunted, her red-gold hair faded to ash-white.

The axe smashed through the wood. The women in the room all tensed, trying not to breathe.

Then the door broke down.

The Princesse de Lamballe stood before the queen, shielding her.

A surge of people. Sharp blades glinting. Sweaty faces contorted with hate. The reek of their hot, half-naked bodies. Hands reached out, pinching, shoving. Foul breath blasting Viviane's face. Foul words scorching her ears.

The ladies-in-waiting all huddled together, trying to hide the queen and her children. The guards stood tense, waiting, keeping the crowd at bay with rifle muzzles.

One brawny-armed woman, dressed in a bloodied apron, her hair hanging in greasy knots, pushed forward with a stained red bonnet and shoved it at Marie-Antoinette.

'Put it on the dear little prince's head,' she sneered. 'Show us what a good patriot he is.'

With trembling hands, Marie-Antoinette fitted the revolutionary cap over her son's bright curls. It was far too big for him, and drooped over his eyes. Louis-Charles tried to push it away and the woman hissed through her blackened teeth. Marie-Antoinette hurriedly straightened it.

Cockades were offered from all sides. Viviane pinned one to her own hair, and then bent to fix one to Marie-Thérèse's long curls. The girl looked up at her with strained eyes, but submitted quietly. Viviane then tied another to Luna's collar, making the crowd laugh and shout ribald comments about bitches in heat.

The ordeal seemed to go on for hours. To Viviane, it was just a blur of cruel laughing faces. She saw an ox's heart impaled on a pike, dripping blood on the placard which read 'the king's heart'. Women dangled tiny dolls with nooses about their necks. One man pranced about with cuckold's horns on his head, naming himself Louis, king of pigs.

At last things began to calm down. Men from the Assembly called for order, and soldiers marched sullenly in. The mob retreated. Silence fell.

'My husband,' Marie-Antoinette whispered. 'Please.'

Cautiously Viviane and Pauline crept out. The corridor was a shambles of broken furniture and smashed china. Blood smeared on the floor. A dead soldier, limbs akimbo. Viviane's legs trembled so much she could hardly stand.

Luna tried to follow her, whining. Viviane turned and put up one hand. 'Stay!' Luna sank to her haunches, eyes dark and fearful, ears low.

Clinging to each other, the two young women tiptoed towards the king's rooms. They found Louis sitting on a chair on top of a table, a red revolutionary bonnet crammed on his large head, an empty wine glass clutched in his hand.

'They wanted me to drink to the health of the nation,' the king said. 'So I did. Then they said that I must revoke my veto. I told them I could not, that I had voted with my conscience. And so they begged my pardon, and drank my health, and went away.'

He looked at the two young women with perplexed eyes. 'I was sure they meant to kill me. Why did they not kill me?'

'You are their king, Sire,' Pauline said in a rush. 'Of course they could not kill you.'

Louis shook his head, the red bonnet waggling.

Viviane could not speak, as confounded as the king.

18

Evil Work
10 August – 3 September 1792

ll night, the bells tolled.

Viviane could not sleep. No-one could. Small groups of people clustered near the windows, peering out into the shadowy gardens. Nothing could be seen. The Paris Commune had locked the gates to the Tuileries. Yet the city could still be heard. A constant low roar, like an ocean gathering itself into a tidal wave.

It had been six long weeks since the mob had invaded the Tuileries. Each day seemed to bring a new crisis. An army had gathered on the border, reinforced by regiments of exiled nobles determined to put the king back on his throne. The Assembly had ordered all French citizens to prepare for war.

Every day, crowds of people milled about the Tuileries Palace, shouting for the king and queen to reveal themselves, to prove they had not again tried to flee. Again and again, Louis and Marie-Antoinette showed their faces at the windows, only to be hissed and jeered. The king had responded by sinking into a strange sort of stupor. He hardly moved or spoke, just sat staring at the wall, shoulders slumped. Even the queen's tears and pleadings did not rouse him.

Louis-Charles had hardly spoken since that awful night. He sat with his father, sucking his thumb till it was red and swollen, the puppy clamped under his arm. Marie-Thérèse was unnaturally silent too. All she had said to Viviane, in a voice of irony far older than her years, 'I thought you said no harm can come to the innocent? I should have known it was just a story.'

Viviane's eyes prickled with tears at the memory.

'Mamzelle!'

At the sound of Pierrick's voice, Viviane rose to her feet and hurried to the door. Her milk-brother was pale and dishevelled.

'Mamzelle, we must get out of here! The Jacobins have occupied the Hôtel de Ville. They've taken over the Paris Commune. It's a coup!'

Viviane felt that familiar sickening twist of fear in the pit of her stomach. 'What does that mean?'

'It doesn't bode well for the king and queen,' Pierrick said. 'Or, indeed, for any of us. We need to get away from here, fast.'

'What shall we do? Oh, I wish we could just go back to Belisima.'

'Why don't we?' Pierrick said.

'But it's nothing but a ruin!'

He shook his head. 'I locked the gates, remember, and threw the key in the well. Half of it was still standing when I left it. And all the land is still there, and the forest. We could plant some vegetables, hunt for rabbits.'

At the word 'rabbits', Luna's tail beat against the floor. She looked up at Viviane and whined.

She smiled faintly. 'Luna would love that. Oh, Pierrick, I want to . . . but what of my father? He will never let me go.'

'Don't tell him. We'll sneak away, dressed as peasants. By the time he notices you're gone, we'll be far away.'

'But he will follow me . . . he'll have me thrown in prison.'

'There are no *lettres de cachet* anymore,' Pierrick said. 'He's not a marquis now, he's just a man. He has no right to throw anyone in prison. That's why we tore the Bastille down.'

Hope flowered painfully in her breast. 'Is it possible?' she whispered. 'Can I really escape?'

'We must try,' Pierrick said sharply. 'They're coming. Can't you hear them?'

The sound of the mob crashed around the dark palace. An orange glare penetrated the windows. Viviane rushed to the windows and looked out.

'It is too late,' she cried. 'They're here.'

Singing a bloodthirsty new anthem, waving pikes, axes, pitchforks and iron bars, the mob surged upon the palace. The Swiss officers fired upon them, but were vastly outnumbered. It was not long before the soldiers had to retreat.

> Arise, children of the Fatherland,
> The day of glory has arrived!
> Against us, tyranny's bloody standard is raised.

The palace doors were battered in by gun hilts and hatchets. Throngs of people rushed in. Gunshots and screams.

> To arms, citizens,
> Form your battalions,
> Let's march, let's march!
> Let an impure blood
> Water our furrows!

The king and the queen were hustled away from the palace, holding their children by the hands. Madame Élisabeth, the king's sister, went with them, and the Princesse de Lamballe and Madame de Tourzel, the royal governess.

With Luna at their heels, Viviane and Pierrick raced upstairs to the apartment she shared with her father and stepmother. It was in wild disorder. Clothes had been thrown onto the floor, and a coffee cup lay smashed. Her father's iron-bound trunk of papers and money was missing. His wig lay discarded on the floor.

'He's gone,' she said blankly. 'He left me.'

'Come on, mamzelle, we need to go!'

She could not believe it. 'My father left me. He knew the mob was coming, and he just left.'

The pain of her abandonment was acute. She had always known her father did not love her. It seemed heartless, though, to leave her to the mercy of the rabble, seemingly without a moment's hesitation.

'Your father always was a sack of shit,' Pierrick said. 'I hope the *sans-culottes* string him up from the nearest lantern. Come on, let's get out of here. Have you any money?'

She looked for her purse and jewel-box, only to find both were missing. She shook her head numbly. 'My father took it all.'

Pierrick caught up an old cloak and flung it around her shoulders. 'We have to get out of here. Come on.'

The glare of fire lit up the night sky, and the air reeked of gunsmoke. It hurt to breathe. Luna whimpered under the bed, and Pierrick fashioned a lead for her from his belt and coaxed her out. Together they ran through the palace.

There was fighting all around. Noblemen with swords, commoners with axes and sledgehammers. Somewhere a woman screamed. The body of a boy lay in a puddle of blood. Viviane recognised the queen's page, only thirteen years old.

A sword had fallen from his grasp. Pierrick seized it.

Maidservants were on their knees, their hands over their faces, a group of blood-splattered men threatening them at the top of the stairs.

Raising high the bloody sword, Pierrick strode towards them, singing the *sans-culottes*' anthem at the top of his voice.

> To arms, citizens,
> Form your battalions,
> Let's march, let's march!

Viviane hurried behind, Luna whining and fighting against her leash. 'It's all right, *mon chouchou*,' she crooned. 'It's all right.'

Pierrick then shouted at the blood-splattered men, 'What are you doing? We don't kill women! You disgrace the nation!'

At his words, the men stepped back. One said roughly to the maid-servants, 'Get up then. The nation pardons you.'

The maidservants scrambled away, weeping. Pierrick saluted the men, crying, '*Vive la Nation!*'

Viviane shakily echoed his words. The men let them pass, laughing even as their weapons dripped blood onto the marble floor.

Singing the *sans-culottes*' bloodthirsty anthem and shouting *Vive la Nation*, Pierrick and Viviane managed to escape the palace, Luna dragged along behind them. Musket shots whined over their heads. The air was full of smoke and the stink of gunpowder. Bodies littered the ground. Many had been hacked apart. Heads were impaled on pikes and carried high, or were kicked back and forth as if they were balls. Women danced around bonfires, the queen's velvet gowns pulled on over their rags.

As she ran, Viviane saw that the hem of her white muslin dress was stained with blood.

'Just a little further,' Pierrick panted, 'and we'll be free.'

Then Viviane saw Camille Desmoulins, standing on the toppled statue of the king, a pistol in his hand. He was urging the crowd on, his face begrimed with smoke, his shirt torn. She was afraid he might recognise her. She caught Pierrick's hand. 'Not that way,' she panted.

They ran towards the Seine, hoping to lose themselves in the crowd.

One man was hacking apart a fallen soldier. He flung a haunch of meat to Luna, and Viviane had to exert all her strength to drag her away. The hood of her cloak fell back. Light from the flaring torches fell full on her face.

'I know her! She's an aristo!' a voice suddenly cried. 'She's the Duchesse de Savageaux. Turned me out on the streets when her husband died, the bitch.'

It was Yvette, the duke's former mistress, filthy and ragged. Her matted blonde hair straggled down her back, and her hands and arms were bloodstained.

Viviane stared at her in dismay.

'She's an aristo, I tell you!' Yvette shouted.

A heavy hand fell on Viviane's shoulder. 'Come with us.'

Viviane let fall Luna's leash. She looked past the man's burly arm to Pierrick. For a moment their eyes met, then he bent, caught up the end of the dog's leash and faded away into the dusk.

Viviane was dragged away.

Her cell was small and bare. A pile of dank straw. An old bucket as a chamber-pot. A slit of a window.

Viviane spent her days pacing the floor, reciting poetry to herself, trying not to let despair overwhelm her. She thought often of her father, fleeing the palace without a thought for her or Pierrick. She wished that she had defied him and gone back to Belisima when she could. The château was hers, inherited from her mother. Her father had no right to take its income for himself, simply because he had gambled his own inheritance away.

She was in La Force prison, she learned from her gaoler. A place for harlots and prostitutes. All day and night, the women shrieked and sang and clanged their tin plates against the bars of their cells. The noise was incessant. Viviane could only press her hands over her ears and try to sleep as the long hours of the night dragged past.

Some days later, Madame de Tourzel and her daughter Pauline were thrust into her prison cell. Clinging together, weeping, they managed to share what little news they had.

'We spent the day in the press-box,' Madame de Tourzel said.

'It was tiny, with wooden bars like a cage,' Pauline said. 'And they did not bring us any food or water. The Princesse de Lamballe fainted.'

'The deputies harangued us all day, shouting.'

'They accused the king of treason,' Pauline said, her eyes wide.

Her mother snorted with derision. 'How can the king commit treason? It is ridiculous!'

'We could hear the screaming.' Pauline shuddered. 'Oh, madame, it was so horrible.'

'What of their Majesties?' Viviane asked urgently.

'Taken to the Temple,' Madame de Tourzel replied.

'To the palace or the prison?' Viviane asked.

The older woman just lifted her shoulders and let them fall.

A few days later, the three women were taken from their dungeon and hustled upstairs to a much larger and airier cell. The Princesse de Lamballe rose to her feet as they were pushed within, holding out her hands in welcome.

'I heard that you were held here too. So I bribed the guards to let us be together. Money still holds sway in this new republic of theirs.' Her soft voice was full of disdain.

Madame de Tourzel embraced her tearfully, and Viviane and Pauline curtsied and thanked her in shaky voices.

Marie de Lamballe was dressed as exquisitely as always, in a gown of silk and delicate lace, her curls unpowdered but tied back with a ribbon. Her room was furnished with a few items of luxury – a comfortable chair, a bed with a mattress and soft counterpane, some candles, a pile of books, a sewing box.

'What news?' Madame de Tourzel asked breathlessly. 'How is Her Majesty?'

'I do not know.' The princess's eyes welled with tears. 'They tore me out of her arms so roughly Her Majesty almost fell. Oh, my poor Toinette. Why do they hate her so?'

'They are rough with her?' Madame de Tourzel clasped her shaking hands together. 'Oh, the brutes!'

'They blow smoke in her face, and call him Fat Louis.'

'*Quelle horreur!*' Madame de Tourzel sank down onto a stool. 'What is the world coming to?'

'They have created a new government,' the Princesse de Lamballe continued. 'It is those madmen Monsieur Robespierre and Monsieur Danton. They have made him Minister of Justice! His idea of justice is to break down doors all over Paris, and arrest anyone who they think supports the king.'

'What will happen to us?' Pauline asked, her voice cracking.

'Do not worry, my pet,' her mother said, trying to summon up some courage. 'The queen's brother will not let anything happen to her. He will march upon Paris and rescue us all.'

A few days later, it seemed as if she was right. Viviane heard a newsboy shouting the news outside the prison walls. The Austrians had won a great victory, and were now pressing on towards Paris. Viviane never would have thought she would celebrate a foreign victory on French soil, but the four women revelled in the news, laughing and weeping and hoping they would soon be delivered.

Their guards were surly and resentful that night, and the younger one spat in the princess's jug of water. Two days later, he came in boisterous and laughing. 'They have a new killing machine,' he told the princess. 'It chops off heads as fast as a stroke of lightning. We saw it used last night. Took off the head of an old friend of yours. Collenot d'Angremont, his name was. The great royalist enlister. What do you have to say to that?'

'God rest his soul,' the princess whispered, all colour draining from her face.

'They call it the guillotine,' he said. 'After the good doctor who designed it. Three of you treasonous royalists killed last night, as fast as you could please.'

'They will be proud to have lost their lives in service to His Majesty the King,' Madame de Tourzel said quietly.

The guard came up close and thrust his unshaven face into the old woman's. 'What about you, old bag? Would you be proud to have your head sliced from your body too?'

She tried not to flinch. 'Indeed I would,' she replied staunchly.

When the guard came the next day, he took great pleasure in addressing the women with the title *Citoyenne*, instead of Madame or Mademoiselle.

'No more monsieurs or mesdames,' he jeered. 'We are all equal citizens now. Even that fat old pig, Louis Capet.'

The older guard, a lean man with a badly pockmarked face, looked pained but did not speak. Viviane was puzzled. She did not know who the guard meant.

Madame de Tourzel exclaimed in outrage, 'How dare you name His Majesty so.'

Only then did Viviane remember the House of Bourbon was descended from a man named Hugh Capet, who had been the King of the Franks in the tenth century. It was not, however, a name that was ever used. The kings of France had no surname. They had no need of one.

'Eight hundred years our kings have ruled,' Madame de Tourzel cried, so distressed she could scarcely speak. 'The most ancient rulers in the world . . . may God strike you all down dead!'

The younger guard raised his hand as if to hit her, and she cowered away. Pauline rushed to embrace her.

'Have you no shame?' Viviane said quietly. 'She is old and sick and filled with sorrow. Leave her be.'

The gaoler bowed mockingly to her. 'As you wish, madame la duchesse . . . I mean, *citoyenne*.'

And with one hand he struck Viviane full across the face, knocking her to the ground.

Then, laughing, he swaggered away.

The older guard looked troubled. He bent and lifted Viviane up, and put her on the bed, then brought her a cloth soaked in water to press against her swollen cheek.

'I'm sorry,' he mumbled. 'Not right to hit young ladies . . . I mean, young *citoyennes*.'

He glanced at Pauline and her mother, weeping in each other's arms, and the Princesse de Lamballe, who had sunk to her knees beside Viviane, her delicate face ashen.

'Not right,' he said again, and went away, locking the door behind him.

*

On the 2nd of September, the French troops surrendered to the Austrians without a fight.

The women huddled together on the bed, listening to the rage of the Parisian mob. It sounded like a menagerie of wild beasts had been set loose. All night, bells rang the alarm, and faint screams filled the air.

Guards ran along the corridors, their sabots setting up a terrible clatter. The woman in the next cell begged for news.

'They're killing all the prisoners,' the bearded guard said shortly. 'You'll be next if you don't shut up.'

As the news spread around the gaol, the prisoners began to weep and cry out for mercy. The noise was almost unbearable.

'We must pray,' Madame de Tourzel said.

And so the four women knelt on the filthy floor, crossed themselves, and prayed.

An hour or so after midnight, Viviane was woken from an uneasy sleep by the scrape of the key in the lock. She sat up, pushing the tumbled hair away from her hot forehead.

It was the older guard, with the pockmarked skin. 'There's evil work afoot tonight,' he whispered hoarsely. 'The most evil I've ever seen. I can smuggle one of you out. Only one, I'm afraid.'

The women all looked at each other.

'Pauline,' Viviane whispered through stiff lips. 'She is still only a child. She should go.'

'Yes, please, take my daughter,' Madame de Tourzel gasped in relief. 'She is only sixteen. Please save her.'

'No, no, *maman*!' Pauline protested.

'Yes,' the princess said. She stood up, took out her purse, and pressed all the money she had into the guard's hands. 'You are a good man. I thank you. Please keep her safe.'

Pauline wept and grasped at her mother's hands. 'No, I do not wish to leave you, please, Maman.'

Her mother seized her hands and kissed them passionately. 'Go, my darling! All will be well. God shall look after me. I shall see you soon.'

Still Pauline protested. The guard looked out the door uneasily. 'We must go.'

And so, wrapped in the guard's cloak, Pauline was smuggled out.

The women left behind could do nothing but sit down, and weep, and pray, and wait.

Late the next day, they were pushed out into the courtyard. The sky was darkened with smoke, the damp ground littered with fallen leaves. A table had been set up, with men in rough coats and long trousers smoking pipes and scrawling notes on long scrolls of paper. Throngs of thin, shabby people pressed close on all sides.

Marie de Lamballe was interrogated first. The questions came as hard and fast as bullets.

'Who are you?'

'I am the Princesse de Lamballe.'

A hiss from the crowd.

'Indeed? And what is your employment, princess?' The question was asked in a mocking, sneering tone.

The princess was pale as skimmed milk, but she answered steadily, 'I am superintendent of the Household to the Queen.'

'To the woman Capet!' someone called from the crowd.

'The Austrian whore,' someone else yelled.

'Have you knowledge of the plots of the court of the 10th August?' the interrogator rapped out.

'I know nothing of any plots,' the princess replied.

'Swear to Liberty and Equality, and hatred of all kings and queens!'

'I will swear readily to the former, but I cannot to the latter. It is not in my heart.'

'Madame,' Viviane whispered in agony. 'Please, take care.'

The princess glanced at her, and gave a crooked little smile. 'I have nothing more to say. I will never swear to something I do not mean. I love and honour their Majesties, and pray for the day that they will be returned to their rightful thrones.'

There was a short pause, then the judge said in a tone of indifference, 'Let Madame be set at liberty.'

The princess staggered a little in her surprise and relief. She looked at Viviane and smiled. Then she was led through the gateway and into the street.

A great howl rose up from beyond the thick stone walls. Then a high unearthly scream. For a moment it lingered in the smoky air, and then a great thud cut it short.

Viviane's knees weakened. She put out one hand blindly, and found a chair-back to cling to. Madame de Tourzel moaned and staggered. Viviane put her arm around her. The older woman was all bones. They held each other up, unable to help the tears coursing down their cheeks. From behind the high wall came grunts, groans, thumps, thwacks.

'Who is next?' the interrogator asked.

Madame de Tourzel stumbled through her answers, shaking and weeping so hard her words could hardly be heard. The man behind the bench looked exasperated. He was about to give his verdict when the guard who had saved Pauline cried out, 'She's nothing but an old woman. Does our great nation kill old women now?'

The interrogator looked displeased and stared around, trying to see who had spoken. After a moment, he frowned and said, 'Oh very well. *Vive la Nation!*'

'*Vive la Nation!*' the crowd cried. Madame de Tourzel was led back into the prison.

It was Viviane's turn.

'Who are you?' the man rapped out.

'I am *Citoyenne* Viviane de Ravoisier,' she answered faintly.

'Is that so? And what do you do, *citoyenne?*'

Viviane thought of the Château de Belisima-sur-le-lac, floating amongst fields of deliate blue flax flowers in the spring.

'I grow flax, *citoyen*,' she replied in an unsteady voice. 'I weave linen to make babies' beds soft, and warm smocks for our workers, and handkerchiefs for the widows of our brave soldiers, and bandages for the hurt and wounded, and shrouds for the dead.'

She hardly knew where the words came from. They rang with truth, however, and the crowd shifted and murmured in appreciation.

The judge stared at her intently, then said sharply, 'And what do you think of our principles of liberty, equality and fraternity then, *citoyenne?*'

'I believe all men and women are born free and equal in rights,' she answered at once, 'and that liberty consists in the freedom to do as I wish as long as my actions injure no-one else.'

She met his gaze squarely.

One side of his mouth compressed in what may have been a smile.

'*Vive la Nation!*' he cried.

'*Vive la Nation!*' Viviane echoed.

She was led into the prison, her legs shaking so much she could only stumble along.

As they passed a window slit, she pulled against her captors' grip and peered out into the street.

The frenzied mob, dancing with glee.

Marie de Lamballe's naked body, blackened with blood.

Her head, hoisted high on a pike.

Part III

Blue Devils
September 1792 – December 1793

Blue Devils: *A fit of the blues*. A fit of spleen, low spirits . . .
Paracelsus . . . asserts that blue is injurious to the health
and spirits. There may, therefore, be more science in calling
melancholy blue than is generally allowed.
The Reverend Ebenezer Cobham Brewer
Dictionary of Phrase and Fable (1870)

19

Going to China
26 September – 9 October 1792

'Away! Aloft!'

As the order was shouted through the lieutenant's brass speaking-trumpet, sailors swarmed up the rigging like monkeys. The great canvas sails tumbled down, and were caught and tied. As they billowed out in the wind, the HMS *Lion* began to move forward and a cheer rang out from the crowd of men gathered on the main deck.

'I can't believe we're going to China!' young Tom Staunton cried.

David smiled. He felt the same fizz of excitement in the pit of his stomach. For as long as he could remember, he had been fascinated by that mysterious distant land, hidden behind its misty mountains and great stone wall, populated by mandarins with long curving finger-nails and exotically beautiful women with onyx eyes and tiny feet. In China were rare flowers with names like an incantation to beauty. *Magnolia liliiflora, chrysanthemum sinense, prunus mume, ginkgo biloba, sophora japonica.*

And, of course, the ever-blowing rose of legend, which bloomed from the sweet rush of spring to the slow chill of frost.

It was impossible not to think of Viviane when he thought of roses.

David's jaw clenched.

He had read the news of her marriage to the Duc de Savageaux in *La Gazette*. At first he could not believe it. Then his incredulity turned to hurt and anger. She had not even waited a month. The banns must have been read the very day after he had fled.

It was a bitter memory.

Hunted like a beast through the night.

The baying of the hounds. The rhythmic pound of galloping hooves. The eerie long-drawn-out blowing away of the horn.

David ran till he was winded. The frozen stream a slash of black through the white. He crouched in the shadows, strapping his skates to his boots. He had seized them from their hook in the stable as he had raced past. His only chance to escape.

His maimed hand throbbed with pain. Dark rivulets of blood dripped into the snow. He bound the wound tightly with his cravat. It hurt like hell. Then, using his teeth, he hauled on his gloves. The dogs hurtled closer, barking and yelping with excitement. Lanterns glinted through the darkness like hungry eyes.

'This way!' the marquis shouted. 'I see his footsteps.'

'He's left a trail of bloodstains for us,' the duke called back. 'How very kind.'

The thunder and steam of horses ridden hard. The tumult of the dogs. Whips cracking.

Then David was up and racing away down the frozen stream, each stroke of his skate cutting into the ice and sending a spray of frost behind him. The hunters spurred on their horses, careering through the snow-bound forest. They could not catch him. He was too swift.

On and on he skated, till the wood was silent and dark. The only sound the scrape and swish of his skates. The clouds drifted away. Stars blazed out of a huge sky, edged with the black lace filigree of the winter forest.

David felt as if he was the only living thing in an alien world.

All else was dead.

The darkness began to lift. Pallid streaks of colour smeared the sky. The stream spread out into swamp, veiled with thin translucent ice that cracked beneath his blades. White snow and black trees as far as he could see.

Go west, David thought. So he unbuckled his skates with one stiff hand, and hung them over his shoulder, and trudged into the ashen day, the sun behind him all morning and before him all afternoon.

Somehow, he made it to Roscoff, to a hotel called The Grey Cat, owned by a man named Yves. Days and days of stumbling along, hiding in hedges whenever he heard horses' hooves, sleeping in ditches, begging for bread in return for a few small coins. It was all a blur.

At first David's only thought was of Viviane, of returning to the château and rescuing her. But he was feverish and exhausted. Yves's wife put him to bed with a hot stone wrapped in fur. He had nightmares of being chased. Sometimes he was a man, sometimes a stag. His missing finger burned with fire.

It took him a long time to recover. He slept for hours, and then woke up exhausted, racked with chills.

Yves's wife refused to bring him his clothes so he could get up. She brought him a pack of cards and a stack of newspapers instead. That was when he read about Viviane's marriage to the Duc de Savageaux.

At first David had not been able to believe it. Surely it was a mistake, a printing error, a lie. He had read the few cold formal lines again and again, until they were acid-etched into his brain.

Then he was filled with horror and a sense of raging helplessness. What had they done to her? Images of Viviane being hurt and terrorised tormented him.

Yet a small doubt or fear within him unfurled a delicate root, and found purchase.

Could she not have found the strength to withstand her father? Was she so soft, so weak, that she would consent to a loveless marriage so fast? She had promised to wait for him, yet the banns must have been read the very Sunday after he had fled.

Perhaps she had never loved him. Or, if she had, her love for him had been a low, feeble thing, easily ground to dust. Not like his love for her. David had been rocked to the foundations of his being.

He felt a bitter shame, that he had been so unmanned.

David remembered how she would not flee with him, how she had hesitated and prevaricated. Perhaps she had only been toying with him for her own amusement.

No, no, his tortured mind insisted. Viviane had loved him. It had been real, it had been true.

So real that she had married another within weeks.

David could not break the repetitive circling of his thoughts, like some poor dumb creature that paces around and around a bolt at the utmost limit of its chain.

By the time he was strong enough to leave his bed, and sail home again, his hurt had hardened into rage. Obviously becoming a duchess meant more to Viviane than waiting for a penniless gardener.

A broad hand clapped him hard on the shoulder.

'Why so glum? We're finally setting sail on the adventure of our lives!'

David came back to himself to find a burly young man grinning at him. John Haxton had the rosy cheeks and rough hands of a man who worked with the soil, and exuberantly curling brown hair. He was a fellow gardener in the employ of the East India Company.

'I was just thinking that there'll be little for us to do, these next few months, there being no garden on board a ship,' David replied.

John grinned. 'We can play at being idle gentlemen, and smoke our pipes and play cards and gamble.'

'My grandfather would be horrified at the very thought. To waste our time in such a way.'

'Ah, yes, he's a parson, isn't he? Lucky he does not travel with us. What he does not know will not hurt him.'

David thought of his grandfather, more white and frail than ever. He looked as if a winter wind would snap him in two. His grandmother looked worn too, and his sisters were talking a little too cheerfully of how much fun it would be to try their hand at being governesses. David had to make a success of this expedition to China.

'I say! This is something, isn't it?' John waved his hand around at the vast expanse of gleaming deck, the thick upright masts with their fretwork of ropes, the immense fat-bellied sails.

'I've never been on such a big ship before,' David replied, amazed at the courage and agility of the sailors swinging through the ropes.

'Nor have I. I've never even left England before,' John confided. 'And now I'm going to China!'

Dozens of small boats bobbed about the HMS *Lion*, with spectators waving hats and handkerchiefs enthusiastically. Two other ships sailed on either side, the *Jackall* and the *Hindostan*.

The small fleet was sailing on behalf of King George III and the Honourable East India Company, in the hope of opening up trade between Great Britain and China. Many countries had tried in the years since Marco Polo had first travelled to the court of the Great Khan in the thirteenth century, but the Celestial Empire guarded its borders jealously. Foreign merchants were only permitted to trade on one small peninsula of land, on the southern bank of the Pearl River in the port of Canton, and then only during the time of the monsoon winds.

As the summer winds began to blow from the south in June, ships would sail in from Portugal, Spain, France, Holland, Great Britain and all the other great Western kingdoms. When the monsoon changed direction in the winter, those ships would sail away again, laden with precious Chinese silks, porcelain and tea.

Over time, Europeans had learned some of China's secrets of making silk and porcelain, but no-one had ever discovered how to grow, harvest and process *camellia sinensis*, the Chinese tea shrub. David knew the drink had been introduced to the English by the Portuguese princess Catherine de Braganza, who brought a chest of tea with her as a gift to her husband-to-be, King Charles II. It did not take long before a cup of tea was the most popular drink in the country, ousting a tankard of beer. The Honourable East India Company imported hundreds of thousands of crates of tea from China every year. The problem was the Chinese did not purchase any British goods in return. This created a serious imbalance of payments, exacerbated by the heavy taxes the Chinese merchants imposed on all foreign traders.

The Honourable East India Company – which David had learned to call by its nickname 'John Company' – resented these exorbitant costs and had sought help from the British government. So the king had appointed Lord Macartney as ambassador to the Celestial Empire. He and his second-in-command, Sir George Staunton, were to attempt to meet with the Chinese emperor, Kien Long, and request that he open up more ports to trade, allow a permanent British embassy in Peking, reduce the exorbitant taxes and duties, and, most importantly, increase imports from Britain to China.

It was also hoped the British might be able to discover the secrets of growing tea, so that they could break the Chinese monopoly. David had been given strict instructions by Sir Joseph Banks, his patron at the Kew Botanical Garden, to surreptitiously gather as many tea seedlings as he could, so they could be transplanted into British-owned land in India.

It was a dangerous mission, for the penalty for smuggling tea plants out of China was death by beheading.

The British embassy was hoping to reach China in time for the emperor's eighty-second birthday, so the three ships carried a treasury of priceless gifts. There were two coaches in imperial yellow, a diving-bell, a hot-air balloon, telescopes and other astronomical instruments, replicas of British warships, good sturdy woollen cloth, clocks, locks, firearms, a printing press, a huge gilded planetarium decorated with pineapples, and a wide assortment of 'sing-songs', the pidgin term for mechanical toys and automatons, such as a snuffbox that contained a jewelled bird that sang when the lid was opened.

Everyone had high hopes of this mission to China. It was confidently believed Lord Macartney would return with an agreement that would open China's tightly locked gates to trade with Great Britain.

The morning tide was running out swiftly, and the three ships were soon well away from Portsmouth. David and John spent the day exploring the ship, as well as they could for the tightly crowded quarters. They were sharing a tiny berth with two bunks, but soon realised they were better accommodated than most of the sailors, who slept in hammocks slung one above the other.

By dusk, the favourable east wind had shifted and ominous clouds were massing on the horizon. David and John were piped to supper at eight bells, and found themselves sharing a table with a most unusual set of characters.

There was twelve-year-old Tom Staunton, the son of Sir George, a delicate-looking boy with floppy mouse-coloured hair and deep-set grey eyes that shone with curiosity and intelligence. He was accompanied by his German tutor, Herr Hüttner, a large red-faced man with a shining bald dome of a head and ferocious eyebrows.

Opposite them sat two slender young Chinese men, dressed in long soutanes tied at the waist with cords. Small crosses hung about their necks.

A stout Scottish inventor sat beside them, wearing an old-fashioned bag-wig and a snuff-brown velvet jacket that was rather worn at the elbows and cuffs. His name was Dr James Dinwiddie, and he was delighted with everything he saw.

'I'm in charge of the curiosities, you know,' he confided to David, in a soft Scottish burr. 'I swear the emperor in Peking will never have seen the like!'

On the far side of the table were the two doctors serving the expedition, Dr Hugh Gillan and Dr William Scott. Both doctors were dressed conservatively in dark woollen breeches, sober frock coats and grey powdered hair clubbed at the back of the neck with a narrow black ribbon, but there the resemblance ended. Dr Gillan was stern-faced and learned, with a pair of eyeglasses perched on the end of his thin nose. Dr Scott was much younger, and looked strong and lean and brown, as if he spent his spare time playing cricket and tramping in the woods.

Opposite them, in a comic mirror image, sat the two artists employed by the expedition. Thomas Hickey was middle-aged, ruddy-cheeked and cheerful, and wore a long Indian dressing-gown in red embroidered silk over loose trousers and soft leather slippers with curling toes. William Alexander was young and slight, and wore a soft-collared shirt with a flowing scarf, and a sky-blue waistcoat embroidered lavishly with flowers under a vividly striped coat. His unpowdered hair was long and loose and artfully tousled.

He reminded David of Pierrick.

At the far end of the table sat Lord Macartney, stout and florid, with his grey powdered hair set in stiff rolls over his ears, and his friend and second-in-command, Sir George Staunton, a tall, lean man with grey eyes and a prominent nose. They sat with the captain of the ship, Sir Erasmus Gower, a square-faced man with wind-reddened cheeks and big capable hands. They spoke amongst themselves and paid little attention to the other men, or to the music being played by the quintet crowded in one corner of the oak-panelled room.

The food and wine was good and plentiful, though Mr Hickey assured them that they should enjoy it now, as it would not last. He had sailed, he told them, to India and Portugal and Italy, and the worst of it was always the food.

'Maggots,' he informed them ebulliently.

As the meal went on, the ship began to lurch up and down in a highly unpleasant manner. The lantern above swung violently, sending shadows skittering round the cabin. David felt his stomach drop, and wished he had not partaken of the steak and kidney pie with such enthusiasm.

'Storm coming up,' Mr Hickey said.

Plates and cups hurtled across the table, but were prevented from crashing to the floor by the table's raised edging. David caught his wine-glass in his left hand as it slid past. He saw the ugly scar, the puckered hole where his smallest finger used to be, and immediately dropped his hand out of sight. Every day it reminded him of what a fool he had been.

Tom Staunton had seen the scar too. 'What did you do to your hand, sir?'

'An accident,' David answered shortly.

'Did you lose it in a duel?' the boy asked eagerly. 'With swords?' He picked up his bread knife and pretended to feint and parry with it. 'Were you fighting for a fair lady's hand?'

'No, not at all.' David clenched his hands together under the table.

'Did you blow it off lighting fireworks?' Tom went on. 'My mother is always telling me not to play with fireworks in case I blow off all my fingers.'

David shook his head again, trying to smile.

'Then how?'

'He's a gardener,' Dr Gillan said in a bored tone. 'He probably chopped it off while trimming a hedge.'

'Oh, no, really?' Tom was crestfallen. 'Is that how you did it, sir?'

'Something like that,' David agreed.

'Couldn't the doctor sew it back on for you?' Tom asked.

'I'm afraid not,' David replied.

'Such a thing is impossible,' Dr Gillan said.

'Well, I am not so sure,' Dr Scott said. 'Perhaps, with the help of a microscope, the blood vessels could be reconnected . . .'

The two doctors began to argue, and attention shifted away from David and his maimed hand, much to his relief.

As soon as he could politely excuse himself, he went up on deck to smoke his pipe and watch the storm. The ship was pitching wildly in high seas, the crew fighting to furl the sails. Spray lashed their faces and dampened their coats. It was impossible to light his pipe. Each spark was blown out instantly. David had to grip onto the railing to avoid being thrown off his feet. All he could see was black roiling water splattered with foam. The masts creaked alarmingly.

Dr Scott, the younger of the two surgeons, climbed up the ladder to join him, his pipe in his hand. He took one look at the heaving horizon, and tucked his pipe away.

'Wouldn't it be comical if we all drowned on our very first night out of an English port?' he asked.

'Hilarious,' David replied dryly.

Dr Scott grinned at him. 'We would be immortalised forever as the finest example of a ship of fools in history.'

'That is not how I wish to be remembered.'

'Nor I, most emphatically.'

'How do you wish to be remembered?' David looked at the other man in some amusement.

'Discovering a cure for some dreadful disease,' Dr Scott replied promptly. 'And you?'

'Discovering some unknown plant that will be of invaluable service to mankind,' David responded as swiftly.

'Perhaps you will discover the plant that will enable me to discover the cure.'

'Perhaps.'

'And we shall retire rich and famous men.'

'We have to survive the storm first.' David looked back at the sea which seemed about to engulf the whole ship.

'Perhaps the *Lion* will break in two like Candide's ship did, and we shall have to try to float to shore on a plank,' a boyish voice said. Turning, David saw Tom had climbed up to watch the storm too, accompanied as always by his tutor.

'Let us pray to our Vater to spare us,' Herr Hüttner said in his guttural German accent.

'If we are to be shipwrecked, I do think it's a shame that it should happen off the coast of Dorset,' Tom went on. 'It'd be so much more exciting to be marooned on a desert island somewhere.'

'You speak like a *dummkopf*,' his tutor replied austerely. 'It is not exciting to be shipwrecked, it would be most wearisome. Come away below deck now, Master Staunton, I am getting my feet wet.'

'I don't mind getting a little damp,' the boy answered, but his tutor frowned ferociously and said, in uncompromising tones, 'I, however, do.'

The big man towed away his reluctant charge.

David and the doctor lingered a little longer on the deck, watching the sailors work in unison to curb the ship. The lash of the salty wind, the high-flung spume of the sea, the roll and roar of the ocean, all filled him with a kind of mad exhilaration, and he saw by the glow on the doctor's face that he felt the same.

'If this is what the English Channel can throw our way, imagine what it will be like rounding the Cape of Good Hope.' Dr Scott cast David a sparkling look, and he grinned back in shared excitement.

'Not to mention the typhoons of the South China Sea,' he answered.

Dr Scott shook his head in disbelief. 'I can scarcely believe that it's true, and that we are travelling so far. To China!'

'To China,' David repeated under his breath. A chill crept over his skin, like a premonition.

A few days later, the *Lion* sailed along the west coast of Bretagne.

David stood on the deck, gazing at the sea-lashed rocks and wide scoops of pale sand, thinking, despite himself, of Viviane. He imagined her at Belisima-sur-le-lac, walking in the gardens he had designed for her, smiling up at her doting husband. She would be dressed in velvet, jewels in her hair instead of wild flowers.

Perhaps one hand would rest on the swell of a slowly growing baby within her. Perhaps the linden trees would already be a blaze of gold along the lake shore, their heart-shaped leaves falling unnoticed at her feet. Perhaps she would stand at the windows of the banqueting hall, the glow of candles haloing her dark head. She would look down at the maze, and smile a little and shrug, thinking with amusement of the poor besotted gardener who had planted it.

David felt the hurt of it in his throat, like a wedged bone.

He could not dig deep, or ride hard, or tramp across a mountain, all the things he did when trying to master his emotions. So, barefoot, he climbed the rigging to the very top of the mast, and clung there, swaying from side to side, looking out across the crawling indigo sea to the horizon, which the Greeks had called the separating circle.

I have to forget her, he told himself.

*

213

Every day, Tom Staunton sat with the Chinese priests. Father Li and Father Cho did not speak English and Tom did not speak Mandarin, but they managed to communicate quite well together in their shared language of Latin. David began to join them, fascinated by the intricate symbols the young Chinese men drew so deftly with their brushes and ink.

'Look, Mr Stronach,' Tom cried one day, holding up the pictograph that he had so carefully copied. 'This means "life". It is inspired by the shape of a plant sprouting from the soil. Can you see?' With his finger he traced the black strokes. 'It means to be born, to give life, to grow. Is that not beautiful?'

'You're a quick study,' David said. 'I can't make head or tail of their script yet.'

'Do not compliment the boy, he will get a fat head,' Herr Hüttner said. 'As I tell him often, hares are caught with hounds, fools with praise, and women with gold.'

David set his jaw and turned away.

He had thought Viviane different.

On 9 October, the *Lion* and the *Hindostan* reached Madeira, where they stopped for supplies, and then – four days later – David saw the peak of Tenerife rise up out of the sea. It heralded the approach of the Canary Islands, an archipelago off the coast of Morocco conquered by the Spanish in the fifteenth century.

'The Spanish used to call this place *Isla del Infierno*,' Mr Hickey told David, as they stood side by side gazing at the sharp peak of the volcano. 'It means "Island of Hell".'

'Is the volcano still active?' David asked.

Mr Hickey nodded his head. He was wearing a red fez with a long black tassel which blew about wildly in the wind. 'Last time it erupted, it buried the whole town with lava.'

'I wonder if it's possible to climb it.'

Mr Hickey looked at him in surprise. 'They say El Teide is one of the tallest mountains in the world.'

'That's why I'd like to climb it.'

'It'll be cold. There's snow on the peak.'

David looked at him with exaggerated pity. 'I'm Welsh,' he reminded him.

Mr Hickey laughed and conceded him the point.

As the *Lion* sailed into the harbour of Santa Cruz that evening, David saw a great warship with three tall masts and a battery of guns along its upper deck resting at anchor. A flag in three broad stripes of blue, white and red fluttered from its topmast.

Suddenly the warship fired at the *Lion*. Heavy cannonballs crashed into the water all around. Smoke billowed into the sky. Shouts of alarm and anger rang out. Sir Erasmus strode to the top deck and lifted his telescope to his eye.

'What flag is that? Who is that firing at us?' Lord Macartney demanded.

'It is a provocation, no more,' Sir Erasmus said. 'If they had wanted to hit us, they could have. Perhaps it is just a welcome salute.'

David asked the harbourmaster about the mysterious ship when he came onboard to welcome the British to Tenerife.

The harbourmaster frowned. 'No salute allowed,' he answered, in heavily accented English. 'No, it was a rudeness. That ship, it is French. It has been detained by the governor, awaiting instructions from His Majesty in Spain. In case we should join the allied powers, you see, in fighting the French. As you English will, no doubt.'

'But the flag . . .' David was puzzled. The French flag was a grandiose affair of golden fleur-de-lis against a royal blue background.

'New flag now,' the harbour man said briefly. 'For the new republic.'

David stared at him, his pulse quickening. 'Pardon?'

'France republic now. New flag for new government.'

'But . . .' David could not manage to process the news. 'When?'

'We heard not long now. One or two weeks, maybe.'

'But . . . what of the king? The old government?'

The harbourmaster shrugged.

20

Slimy Pollywogs
14 October – 18 November 1792

The snow-streaked peak of Mount Teide rose above fleecy clouds, like a child's drawing of a mountain.

The party of men from the *Lion* set out from the town of La Orotava at noon, riding mules and led by two guides. David was impatient with their slowness. If he had had his way, they would have left at first light.

After David's parents had died, nothing could keep him in the house. He would slip out at dawn and roam the hills till dusk, exploring as far as his feet could carry him. He had been twelve when he had first climbed Pen y Fan, the highest peak in South Wales, and nineteen when he conquered Snowdon. Some nights he did not come home at all, but slept under the stars, rolled in his old coat. He drank clear water from the peat pools, and cut away squares of turf with his knife to kindle a fire and cook a moorhen he had caught with a net of old string. In the morning, the fire would have sunk to ashes and he could drop back the square of turf and leave no sign that he had ever been there at all.

His grandmother had worried about him, but his grandfather had only smiled and said in his gentle way, 'Leave the lad be, Manon. He's grieving in his own way. On the mountain peaks, he is as close to God as he can get.'

In his sorrow and rage, the boy listening at the door had rejected his grandfather's words violently. It was not God he was climbing to meet. David did not know how to express what it was he wanted, but it had something to do with being quick and strong and alive. To feel his hot blood thumping in his pulse, his fast breath pumping in his lungs. It was only much later that David wondered if his grandfather's idea of God and his own longing for rapture were not, perhaps, the same thing.

The guides led them slowly along a narrow path that wound up through vineyards and orchards. Gradually the cultivated land gave way to dry barren fields, an occasional stunted tree stretching out its thin twisted branches as if shrieking for help. Steep slopes of dry black lava were rent with narrow chasms, their depths hidden in shadows. Shaggy wild goats leaped nimbly over the rocks, sending pumice stones scattering in tiny avalanches. The mules picked their way forward, heads down, ears back. David had to quell his impatience, and plod along with the rest of the party.

By late afternoon, the barometer told them they had risen six thousand feet above the town, which could be seen below them like a child's game with sticks and stones. As the sun set behind the mountain, its shadow fell upon the wavering line of mules and men, and then stretched out to swallow the town. Conversation stalled. The men turned up the collars of their coats. Slowly the shadow stretched out across the sea, blotting out its dazzling brightness in a perfect vast triangle. David felt an uneasy vertigo, as if the mountain was teetering.

Clouds boiled up from the ravines. The path was hidden by mist. The temperature had dropped so low, David's breath plumed white before him.

'Better we stop now,' said the head guide, a tall spare man in his sixties. 'No go any further.'

'Oh, we can't stop,' David said. 'That would be most cowardly, to come so far and go no further.'

'Dangerous,' the man said.

'That's the point,' David replied. He looked around at the others. 'You can go back if you like, but I want to reach the top.'

'Perhaps we should go back,' Sir George said, with a worried eye on his son.

Tom straightened his back at once, and said, 'I'm all right, Father. Let's go on. Adventurers never say die!'

'That's the spirit!'

On they rode, peering ahead through the dusk and the rain. The mules began to baulk. Sir George was thrown from the back of his mount, and fell only inches away from a steep tumble down the cliff-face. He remounted without a word, but his face was white and strained.

The rain became sleet, and then snow. The sky was so dark it was impossible to see more than a few paces ahead. They came to a small flat shelf, protected a little from the worst of the storm by a bulge of mountain above.

'We must stop here,' the guide said.

'But if we stop here, we will never be able to reach the summit tomorrow,' David protested. 'We must push on as far as we can.'

'No going on.' The guide shook his head firmly. 'All die if go on.'

The stiff weary men began to dismount, and shake out their wet clothes, and look for somewhere dry to sit.

'I'll just go on a little.' David kicked his mule forward, but he could see nothing but mist-swirled darkness. Stones dislodged by the mule's hooves clattered down the precipitous slope.

At last, angrily, he turned back.

A rough camp had been made, with branches of Spanish broom lopped and spread to make beds and a tent made from a sail draped over a branch. A fitful fire spat.

'It is good to have an indomitable will,' Sir George said, as they ate a meagre supper from tin plates. 'But it is not a sign of weakness to know when one must give in.'

David set his jaw. He could not give in. He could not bear another failure. All those months wasted, building a garden he would never see blossom, for a debauched marquis and his weak-willed daughter. David had not even earned a glowing letter of recommendation, to help him find another position. If he had not written to Sir Joseph Banks at Kew

Gardens himself, and impressed the legendary botanist with his bravado, he and his family might have come close to beggary.

'If we do not climb the peak, we cannot establish how high it is or at what temperature water will boil,' David replied, trying to speak lightly. 'And then we shall not have our names published in the journal of the Royal Society.'

He knew how seriously Sir George took the scientific responsibilities of the expedition.

'I don't think that's worth losing our lives for,' Sir George answered shortly, rubbing his bruised hip.

It was a most uncomfortable night. David could not stop shivering in his damp clothes, and he could not stop worrying about Viviane.

The governor of Tenerife had told them that the new French government had massacred thousands of imprisoned clergymen and aristocrats, and the royal family were prisoners in the dank medieval tower of the Temple in Paris.

She's safe in Bretagne, David told himself. *Enjoying her new life as a duchess.*

But he could not convince himself.

He laid one arm over his eyes, and tried to steady his breathing. But fear clamped his chest tight.

A few hours before dawn, the clouds rolled back and David could see the peak shining above him in the moonlight. It rose out of a frozen sea of fog, pure and cold and unassailable.

David lay still, his blanket glittering with a faint rime of frost. All around him, men slept or lay in silence, breathing softly, but he felt as if he was all alone.

He had thought Viviane was the other half of his soul, the missing part for which he had always longed. Her absence was a constant ache, like the space where his finger had once been.

The night seemed very long.

*

In the morning, most of the men decided to turn back, Sir George dragging an unwilling Tom with him.

David was determined to press on, however. Dr Gillan, Dr Scott and Mr Barrow, the ambassador's financial comptroller, decided to accompany him. One of the guides grudgingly agreed to accompany them, the other returning to the *Lion* with the rest of the party.

Beyond their makeshift camp was a dreary waste of lava and ash. The wind was so strong it almost dragged them from the back of their mules, who were sullen and intractable and had to be kicked or lashed for every slow reluctant step. It was piercingly cold.

They had climbed another two thousand feet, the barometer told them. Then Dr Gillan's mule slipped into a chasm, and the poor doctor was only saved from a murderous fall by catching desperately at a thin bent tree. Shaken and bruised, he decided to turn back, and Mr Barrow thought it best to accompany him.

At that point, the guide refused to go on any further.

'But we are so close,' David cried. He could see the mouth of the crater a steep scramble above them. He looked challengingly at Dr Scott.

The doctor grinned back at him, and cried, 'Race you!'

But it was impossible. The ground was so thick with ash it was like struggling up drifts of powdery grey snow. Treacherous lumps of lava rock lay hidden beneath, bruising their hands and knees. An evil sulphurous smell rose around them, making David's head swim. For every step he and Dr Scott managed to gain, they slid back another two.

David made a convulsive effort to grab hold of a ledge above him, missed his mark and came tumbling down, knocking Dr Scott off his feet. They rolled down wildly, and ended up in a tangle at the foot of the slope they had begun to climb almost two hours earlier.

David rolled away and lay on his back with a groan.

'I suppose we must admit defeat,' Dr Scott said at last, staring up at the stormy-dark sky.

'I hate to give up,' David said.

'Me too, most emphatically.'

David grunted a laugh.

Dr Scott sat up, and flexed his long limbs experimentally. 'Nothing broken, by some miracle.'

David did the same. 'Just a whole lot of bruises,' he reported. 'I must admit I'm not looking forward to riding those damned mules all the way back.'

'They have the boniest spine of any animal I've ever encountered,' Dr Scott responded. They hauled themselves to their feet, dusted themselves off, and glanced up at the mountain peak towering above them.

'Ah well,' David said. 'We shall just have to return here again one day, Dr Scott.'

'You may as well call me Scotty. I think a man who has fallen down a mountain on top of me can be admitted into terms of familiarity.' With a grin, the doctor held out his hand.

David shook his hand heartily. 'Yes, indeed. I'm David.'

'And Welsh by the sound of it.'

David smiled. 'Yes, indeed.'

'Some grand mountains in Wales.'

'The grandest. Climbed any?'

'A few.'

As Scotty began to describe the hills and mountains he had climbed, they limped together back down the hill to where the guide sullenly waited with the mules.

And those blessed animals – who had plodded so begrudgingly up the mountain, impervious to kicks or slaps of the hand – took the bits between their teeth and galloped the whole way back.

David was woken out of sleep by a loud banging on the door.

'Get up, you lazy dogs!' a voice shouted. 'You're under arrest.'

The door burst open, and two burly seamen seized him by the arms, dragging him out of his bunk. Dressed only in a loose linen shirt and breeches, he was hustled down the narrow corridor.

It was late, and the only light was a swinging lantern carried by a man wearing a ferocious horned mask. His hair was covered with a wig made of seaweed.

Doors crashed open. Sleepy passengers were dragged out in various stages of undress, some laughing, others protesting angrily.

'What is the meaning of this outrage?' Dr Gillan was puce with anger.

'You're under arrest, you slimy pollywog!'

'What? On whose orders?'

'On the orders of the Old Sea Dog!'

'It's the crossing of the line.' Thomas Hickey stood in his doorway, his red silk dressing-gown on over his clothes. 'The sailors perform an initiation ceremony for all those who have never sailed over the equator before.'

'Silence!' the masked man roared.

Laughing, David allowed himself to be rushed down to the lower deck, where he and the rest of the expedition were pushed into the dark stinking hold.

The man wearing the mask began to read from a scroll.

'I am Davy Jones, and I am come out of the depths of the sea tonight to summons all you landlubbers who have not yet been initiated into the Supreme Order of the Old Sea Dogs. We of the court of His Oceanic Majesty, King Neptune of the Seven Seas, bring serious indictments against all you that still have the dust of the land on their feet. You shall answer for your crimes! And remember! Sorrow and woe await any who resist or mock His Majesty, the Great Neptune, Ruler of the Seven Seas. So beware!'

With one last dramatic shake of his fist, Davy Jones retreated and the hatches were slammed shut and battened down.

There was a loud hum of conversation. The two Chinese priests looked dismayed, while Tom was excited and a little apprehensive. His father – resplendent in a paisley silk dressing-gown over his nightshirt – spoke to him calmly. Herr Hüttner, however, stormed up and down, spitting out German phrases that were all too easily translated.

Eventually the doors banged open, and buckets of sea water were flung inside, soaking all who were unfortunate enough to be standing near.

'The court of King Neptune is in session! All those accused of crimes against His Majesty, quick march!'

A mock courtroom had been set up on the main deck, with a jury of seamen dressed in makeshift costumes – fishing nets as skirts and seaweed as hair, or blackened faces and striped turbans and scimitars made of tin. There was even a man dressed in a bearskin cloak.

King Neptune sat on a throne, a crown of golden paper askew on his tangled seaweed hair, a trident in one hand. Beside him was a huge tattooed sailor, dressed in a woman's dress with pumpkins stuffed in his bodice and a face gaudy with rouge and a multitude of patches. He minced about on ludicrously high heels, blowing kisses to the laughing crowd of seamen. There was also a man dressed in medieval costume, with a giant razor and an apron luridly stained with red.

David saw this only in glimpses, as he and the other men were forced to run the gauntlet through two rows of sailors throwing buckets of slop from the kitchen. Fish guts, potato peelings, tea leaves, onion skins, apple cores, eggshells and vegetable scraps had all been mixed in dirty dishwater, and rained on them from all sides. The smell was awful.

At last, dripping and adorned with garbage, they were pushed to their knees before King Neptune.

Sir Erasmus stood to one side, his tricorne hat held against his heart. 'We welcome you on board the *Lion*, Your Majesty. It is a great pleasure to have you on board.'

'The displeasure is all mine,' Neptune growled in answer.

'I beg your pardon most humbly. What may I do to please Your Majesty?'

'Your ship is sorely infested with slimy pollywogs, a situation which my loyal sea dogs plan to correct. We shall turn them into trusty shellbacks, fit for my service!'

'Then I turn over the command of my ship to you for as long as you wish.' Sir Erasmus bowed, then went to sit down and watch the show.

One by one the men were brought forward, ordered to kneel before Neptune, and accused of various crimes. Dr Gillan was accused of being a witchdoctor, and forced to swallow something out of a large black bottle.

From the look on his face, it tasted very nasty. Lord Macartney was accused of eating too well, and was forced to munch on some ship biscuits. He did so with great good humour, pretending to pull maggots out first.

Sir George was accused of being too serious, and was ordered to dance the hornpipe, which he did with surprising vigour and enthusiasm. His son Tom laughed and clapped loudly. Then it was his turn. The boy was accused of spending far too much time studying, and was ordered to drink some rum and gamble on the throw of some dice. He did both eagerly, though the rum made him choke.

The young artist William Alexander was accused of spending too much time combing his hair, and the Barber shaved it all off. William did his best to pretend to take it in good part, but it was clear he was mortified.

Lord Macartney's valet, Aeneas Anderson, was ordered to bark and wag his tail and lick his master's hand before being declared a proper sea dog. He refused to do so, with great dignity, and so was forced to run the gauntlet as he was pelted with raw eggs and flour and sugar syrup, while the Barber cut open pillows with his razor and tossed feathers all over him. He did not look pleased.

David and John – being gardeners – were dunked overboard 'to wash the land lubber dust off their feet'.

It was terrifying dropping down the great length of the hull and into the vast green ocean. David clung tightly to the rope, afraid that his missing finger might weaken his hold.

'I hope there are no sea monsters lurking below!' he shouted to John.

'Or sharks!' he bellowed back.

David plunged deep into the water but was hauled back on deck again straightaway, dripping and exhilarated.

'We declare you a landlubber no longer!' Davy Jones yelled.

Then the two Chinese priests were pushed forward. Both looked pale and frightened, not understanding the raucous horseplay. The Barber flourished a harsh-bristled scrubbing brush and cried, 'You two are accused of being dirty heathens so we'll scrub you white.'

The priests were grabbed and thrust headfirst into barrels of soapy water, then the Barber and Davy Jones and the other men began to scour them roughly. Flailing and gasping, they tried to resist but were shoved back and forth to the shouts and jeers of the crowd.

Father Li slipped in the soap and fell to his knees, raising his arms above his head imploringly. His cheek was red raw.

Tom Staunton ran forward and grabbed the Barber's arm. 'No! Stop! It's not fair. He cannot help the colour of his skin . . . Please! Father, you must make them stop.'

Sir George hesitated, looking about him. The huge tattooed sailor in the woman's gown bellowed, 'Anyone who speaks up against the court of His Oceanic Majesty, King Neptune of the Seven Seas, shall be flung into the hold to fester forever!'

David could not bear the look of terror on the young priest's face. It reminded him vividly of Viviane's fear, the day her father came back. He stepped forward, putting down a hand to help Father Li to his feet. 'If my grandfather was here,' he said to the grinning sailors, 'he would bid you remember that you will be judged in the same way that you judge others, and with the measure you use, it will be measured to you.'

The men's eyes fell. The Barber lowered his scrubbing-brush.

'Amen,' Father Li said, and bowed to David in thanks.

21

On Trial
11–25 December 1792

The king was playing ninepins with his son when they came for him.

Rain lashed against the barred window, and the room was so cold that the officers' breath frosted the air when they spoke.

Viviane could not hear what they said. She was on her hands and knees, scrubbing the stairwell. She could only catch a glimpse through the narrow chink where the door had been left ajar.

She saw that the two officers made no motion to remove their hats and that this discourtesy pained the king. Louis-Charles clung to his father's leg, and one of the officers jerked him away roughly. The toy spaniel leapt up, barking. The officer kicked the puppy, who yelped and ran away, tail tucked between her legs. Louis-Charles wept and struggled to be free.

Viviane rose to her feet, clutching the dripping scrubbing brush close. She wanted to rush in and comfort the little boy, but dared not.

One of the officers opened the door. '*Citoyenne*, take this boy to his mother!'

'Yes, *citoyen*,' she murmured and dropped the brush back in her bucket, wiping her cold damp hands on her apron. Louis-Charles struggled against the officer's hold, calling, 'Papa-Roi, Papa-Roi.'

The officer cuffed him across the ear. 'There is no king anymore. We are all equal citizens of the republic of France.'

'Please do not hurt him,' the king said unhappily. 'He is only a little boy.'

'I don't want to go! I want to stay with you!' Louis-Charles held out his arms imploringly to his father.

The king looked at the officers. 'May he not stay with me for just a little longer? He does not understand . . .'

'If he stays with you, he shall not see his mother again,' the officer said brutally.

The king's shoulders slumped. 'I am sorry, *mon petit*, but your mother could not bear to be separated from you. You must go to her and reassure her that all will be well.'

The officer passed the weeping child to Viviane, kicked the dog out, then shut the door in her face.

She sat for a moment on one of the steps, rocking Louis-Charles back and forth. The spaniel whimpered and put its paws up on her leg, and she lifted the puppy in the little boy's arms so that he could bury his face in her silky coat.

The only light came in through a narrow slit of a window, and the air smelt of damp and mould. The Temple, where the royal family had been confined, was a forbidding medieval tower that had once been the fortress of the Templar knights. It was surrounded by a putrid-smelling moat, and its walls were nine feet thick.

At least, Viviane thought, she was free to leave every day and go out into the streets for a while.

Unlike the king and his family.

When Viviane had been released from La Force prison, she had not known where to go or what to do. She had nothing but the filthy clothes she stood up in. She had limped back to the Tuileries, which lay in bloody shambles still. Everything of value had been broken or stolen. Rummaging through her rooms, she found some old clothes. Hiding behind a door, she hastily stripped off her ruined muslin, and pulled a grey wool dress over her head. It hung loosely on her, for she was thin from the weeks of prison rations. She washed her face and hands, and tidied her hair as best she could with a broken comb.

Looking for anything else that might be useful, she discovered the miniature of her mother kicked under a chair. The glass was cracked, but the painting undamaged. Hot tears rushed to her eyes. She kissed it, then hid it in her pocket.

As Viviane crept down the grand marble staircase, she caught a glimpse of herself in a tall silver mirror that hung high on the wall. She scarcely recognised herself. So thin and pale, with haunted dark eyes and a sombre mouth, and plain clothes like a peasant might wear.

I am no longer the Duchesse de Savageaux, she realised. *And I am not Mademoiselle de Ravoisier anymore either.*

She could be anyone she wanted.

Viviane stood still for a while, thinking about this, feeling a strange mad rush of excitement and liberation.

I can do anything, go anywhere, be anyone I want!

But then came a wave of desolation.

Viviane had not a single sou in her pocket, nor any means of earning any. And Paris was in a state of siege. Even if she could afford it, Viviane could not hire a carriage to take her back to Belisima, or pay for a berth on a ship to the New World. The new National Convention had closed all the gates of Paris and posted guards on the bridges and quays to prevent the escape of any aristocrats.

She had no friends or family in Paris to help her. Her father had abandoned her without a second's hesitation. Pierrick had taken Luna and melted away into the night, and she did not know where to find them.

The queen will help me, Viviane thought, and then remembered that she was queen no longer. Citoyenne Capet, everyone was calling her jeeringly. And Marie-Antoinette and her husband and children were in prison themselves.

Viviane began to walk slowly once more. The thought came to her: *Perhaps I can work for the queen once more. Perhaps I can help.*

She remembered Marie-Thérèse's pale face, and how she had said so bitterly, 'I thought you said no harm can come to the innocent.' She thought of Louis-Charles, hugging his puppy, his thumb in his mouth, his blue eyes blank with horror.

Her footsteps quickened.

The Temple rose high above the crowded rooftops of Paris, making it easy to find. It had a thick central tower, with four small turrets on each corner. Each tower was topped with a spire shaped like a dunce's cap. A garden at its base was protected by high walls, with a large courtyard in front surrounded on all sides with buildings. The only way was through a gatehouse, secured at all times.

As soon as Viviane arrived, she knew she had made a mistake. It was guarded by half-a-dozen men, all slovenly and uncouth, drinking from dusty bottles and smoking foul-smelling pipes, their feet up on stools, red revolutionary caps crammed on their heads. They were, nonetheless, well equipped with bayonets affixed to their muskets, and pistols slung from their belts. Her resolve faltered, and her step with it.

One guard had spied her, though, and called out to her.

'Hello there, *citoyenne*, what are you doing here?'

She did not know how to answer.

They got to their feet, circling her, plucking at her sleeves and her bodice. 'So clean and nice you are,' they jeered. 'Are you an aristo in disguise?'

Viviane was so frightened, she could scarcely breathe.

For some reason she thought of Pierrick. Last time she had seen him, he had been dressed in baggy striped trousers and a red cap, just like these men. He had put aside his white powdered wig and livery without a moment's thought.

She pulled her arm free. 'Mind my fine feathers, *citoyens*,' she said, mimicking Pierrick's accent. 'I'm in search of work, and can't afford turning up dirty.'

They made a few lewd jokes about making her dirtier. Viviane turned red, and wished she had expressed herself in different words. She tried to step away, but they pressed closer, their hands rough on her arm and waist. 'Let me go!' she cried.

A young man dressed in a big white apron, a white cap on his head, and a belt stuck with knives had been passing by, a string of fish in one hand. He turned his head at the sound of her accent.

'Are you from Bretagne?' he asked.

Her stomach flipped, but she nodded.

He said in the Breton patois, 'Are you all right? Are they bothering you?'

'*Ya*,' she answered rapidly, the Breton term for 'yes'. 'Please help me.'

'You looking for work? Can you scrub?' His quick glance took in her fine, white fingers.

She nodded. 'Yes, I can scrub, I can scrub anything,' she babbled.

He smiled suddenly. 'Good.' He turned to the guards, and switched effortlessly into French once more. 'Unhand my new scullery maid, *citoyens*, else you'll be scrubbing the floors and emptying the chamberpots yourself!'

The guards all laughed, and relinquished their hold on Viviane's arm. He jerked his head at her to follow.

'We Bretons must stick together,' he said. 'Where are you from?'

Improvising, Viviane told him she had worked in the kitchen and still-room of a château in Bretagne, but had handed in her notice and come to Paris so she could be part of the revolution. He nodded, but a faint frown creased his face.

The kitchen – along with pantries, butteries and sculleries – took up most of the ground floor of the old fortress. It was a dark, gloomy room, paved with huge uneven flagstones, and lit only by the glare of fires at either end, and tallow candles on the tables and mantelpiece. Men were busy stirring sauces and soups, kneading bread, or stripping herbs from their stems. A huge leg of mutton was being turned on a spit in one cavernous fireplace by a boy with a grubby face.

'What's your name then?' the Breton chef asked, as he showed her around.

Viviane thought fast. 'Rozenn Cazotte,' she answered, taking Pierrick's surname as her own and using her middle name, which was a good Breton name.

She could not say she was the daughter of the Marquis de Valaine.

'I'm Ivo Sezvec, from Saint-Malon-sur-Mel.'

'Why, that's not far from me!' Viviane cried, before she thought.

At once Ivo wanted to know where she had lived, and she was too tired and hungry to think fast enough. 'Near Paimpont Forest,' she said.

'So you must have worked at Belisima-sur-le-lac? That is the only château near there.'

'Yes,' she admitted.

'Was it not burned down?'

'Yes. That is why I came to Paris. There was no work there anymore.'

'So you were there when it burned down?'

'Yes,' she lied, finding herself drawn deeper and deeper into falsehood with every word.

'Was it true it was burned down by a madman who danced as he lit the fires?'

She nodded, and hoped he would be satisfied, but Ivo perched on a stool and questioned her eagerly. Viviane had no choice but to weave him a tale from all that Pierrick had told her. It upset her, talking about the fire, and she had to stop and try to steady herself.

'You lost someone in the fire?' he asked sympathetically.

Viviane nodded, but then found herself in trouble again. She could not say her wet-nurse. So she blurted out, 'My *maman*. She was the château cook. She knew the madman and ran into the fire to try and save him, but died herself.'

Tears burned her eyes, and she stopped and searched for a handkerchief. Not having one, she used her sleeve to mop her eyes.

'Ah, I'm sorry,' Ivo said. 'I've lost my mother too, so I know how it hurts.'

She nodded, and asked him about his mother and so turned the conversation away from herself.

'I will tell the *chef de cuisine* that you are my cousin, come up from Bretagne,' he said abruptly. 'We are short-staffed, and so I think he will be glad to give you the work.'

Viviane nodded, even though it was yet another lie. Each falsehood made her feel more afraid.

The *chef de cuisine* looked her over with a frown, and commented on how skinny she was.

'She might be skinny, but she's strong,' Ivo said.

'Her hands look too fine for a scullery-maid.'

'She worked mainly in the kitchen and stillroom,' Ivo explained. 'Her mother was the cook.'

The *chef de cuisine* snorted contemptuously, clearly not approving of female cooks.

'Where are your papers?' he asked.

Viviane did not know how to answer. 'They were all burned . . . in the château fire,' she managed. Another lie.

'So how did you get into Paris?' he asked.

'I . . . I told them about the fire. They said I must apply for new papers.'

'Very well. Ivo can take you to the Committee of General Security, and vouch for you, and get your papers in order. In the meantime, Rozenn, I expect you up early to get the fires lit and the bouillon on. Ivo will show you where you'll sleep, and get you an apron and cap.'

She nodded and thanked him, but thought to herself that she would never get used to being called Rozenn.

As the weeks passed, it became easier.

Although the former king and queen and their family were kept closely guarded, and allowed only one servant – the king's faithful valet, Jean-Baptiste Cléry – there was still a full team of chefs employed to feed them, just as if they were at Versailles. The *chef de cuisine* oversaw the work of the *hâteur de la bouche* who roasted the king's meat, Ivo, the *poissonnier* who prepared the fish dishes, the *garde manger* who made salads and pâtés, the *maîtres-queux* who prepared the sauces, the *gobelet* who carried drinks to the king, the *paneterie*, who cooked the bread and pies, the *fruiterie* who prepared fresh and preserved fruits for the family, the *potager* who made the soups, and the *patissier* who made all the cakes and pastries. There were also a few boys who watched the fires and the spits and ran errands, making thirteen kitchen staff in total, cooking for a family of five.

Viviane was one of four serving maids. Her main duties were bringing water from the public fountain, preparing the bouillon, peeling vegetables, washing dishes, scrubbing floors, and going to the market for fresh fruit and vegetables and fish. She was able to listen to the gossip of the market-vendors and the loud cries of the newsboys, and pass the news on to Cléry, who then whispered it in His Majesty's ear as he was shaved and barbered. That was the only news the king received. The royal family were kept under close scrutiny, and were not permitted any quills or ink or paper, or to receive notes or letters.

Viviane did what she could to help the imprisoned family – laundering the women's linen, making up tisanes for their constant coughs and fevers – but she did not see them. The faithful Cléry was the only servant permitted to them, with the chambermaids cleaning their rooms while they walked in the garden once a day. The guards were rude and insolent to the king and queen, blowing pipe smoke in their faces and sitting on chairs in their presence. Often, the royal family returned to their rooms to find graffiti scrawled on the walls. *Madame Veto shall swing. The guillotine is ready for the tyrant Louis. The wolf-cubs must be strangled.* Viviane did her best to scrub the cruel words away.

Viviane and Cléry set up a complex system of secret signals to keep Louis and Marie-Antoinette aware of the news, including the passing of tiny notes concealed within balls of strings or hidden within fruit. So they heard of the defeat of the Prussian army at Valmy and the victories of the French republican soldiers, and they knew that the new National Convention was divided between the moderate Brissotins and the radical Jacobins, who had begun to be nicknamed 'the Mountain' because they occupied the highest benches in the hall in which the deputies met.

The Mountain wanted the execution of the king.

Gradually the dauphin's sobs died away. Viviane was able to mop his face with a corner of her apron, and smooth back his ruffled curls.

'Come, let me take you to your mama,' she said, and lifted him down to the ground. With Coco scampering ahead of them, they went hand in hand up the stairs to the next floor, where Marie-Antoinette, her sister-in-law Élisabeth and her daughter Marie-Thérèse shared a few cold and gloomy rooms.

Louis-Charles had been looking up at her in puzzlement, taking in her grey gown and apron, the white cap that hid her hair. 'Are you playing dress-ups, madame?' he asked eventually.

Viviane had to smile. 'In a way, Monseigneur.' She lowered her voice. 'But in this game we are playing, you must not call me Madame and I must not call you Monseigneur. We are simply *citoyen* and *citoyenne*, understand?'

Louis-Charles nodded gravely, and she knew he must have already had such instructions from his mother.

The door to the queen's apartment stood open, and two guards sat outside, legs outstretched, puffing evil-smelling smoke from their pipes.

'I have been instructed to bring the boy to his mother,' Viviane said shortly.

'O-ho!' one cried. 'So fat Louis is to face the Convention. Won't be long and he'll be losing his head.' He made a swift, slicing motion with the edge of his hand into his palm.

Louis-Charles made a sound of distress, and Viviane drew him closer. 'Come, I'll take you to your mama,' she said in a low voice.

'No whispering! Speak up so we can hear you,' the guard ordered.

Viviane went in. She felt both anticipation and anxiety at the prospect of seeing the queen again. What if Marie-Antoinette or her daughter unwittingly betrayed her to the guards? She could only hope they would be aware of the danger.

Marie-Antoinette sat listlessly at the narrow window slit, watching the rain drench the glass. Marie-Thérèse read a battered old book. Élisabeth, the king's youngest sister, sat with her eyes closed, counting her rosary beads. All looked thin and pale, and the queen's bright hair was fading to white.

'Maman-Reine!' The dauphin ran forward and was clasped in his mother's arms, Coco leaping up and barking for attention.

'Your papa?' she faltered.

'He is with officers of the Convention, *citoyenne*,' Viviane answered.

At the sound of her voice, Marie-Antoinette looked up. Viviane instantly lifted her finger to her lips. The queen looked startled, but bit back the words she had been about to say. Marie-Thérèse's blue eyes were round with surprise, but she too managed to stifle her exclamation.

'Thank you, *citoyenne*,' Marie-Antoinette said, then stepped a little closer, saying in a low voice, 'So you are our friend in the kitchen?'

'Yes, madame.'

'We are most grateful to you,' the queen murmured.

'Speak louder!' the guard shouted.

Viviane spoke more clearly. 'I cannot stay. I will be in trouble if I do not return to my duties. Already I have been away far too long.'

Marie-Antoinette started forward, catching her hand. 'Please, bring me what news you can of the king. I am so afraid . . .' She stopped, swallowing convulsively.

Viviane answered only with a brief nod, then turned away, worried the guard would grow suspicious of her. Marie-Thérèse said, in a low voice, 'I am glad to know that you are not dead, madame.'

'So am I,' Viviane answered, with a poor attempt at humour.

The princess did not smile. 'So many people we know are dead.'

As Viviane returned to her bucket and scrubbing brush, a column of men marched up the spiral staircase. One wore a tri-colour sash across his chest.

They charged into the king's room, leaving the door wide open. Viviane decided she had best scrub away their muddy footprints before returning to the kitchen. She dropped to her knees, but moved the brush only lightly so she could still hear.

'I come with orders that Louis Capet should be brought before the bar of the Convention,' the man with the sash cried.

'I am not called Capet! That is the name of one of my far distant ancestors.'

'It is your name now,' one of the men said with a guffaw.

'I could have desired, monsieur, that the commissioners had left me my son during the time I have spent waiting for you. In any case, this treatment is in accordance with what I have experienced here the past four months.'

'You have been treated far too well, considering how badly you have treated the people of France!'

Louis's voice rose in surprise. 'I have never done anything but my best for the people of France.'

'A poor best!' the man cried angrily. 'When your people are starving in the streets and foreign troops march upon our cities!'

'That was never my intention,' Louis replied unhappily.

'Enough! You may speak in your defence before the Convention . . .'

'Much good it will do you!' one of the men jeered.

'So you must come with us now, and face your accusers.'

With great dignity, Louis replied, 'I will come with you now, not in obedience to this Convention of yours, but because my enemies are in possession of *force majeure*.'

He walked out the door, and the men all crowded after him.

Viviane scrambled to her feet and stood silently, the scrubbing brush in her hand. As the king passed her, she looked up.

He wore a simple brown coat, and looked just like any other man.

December passed.

Marie-Thérèse turned fourteen, but was not permitted to see her father.

Louis spent his days on trial. Viviane heard that he was calm and composed. Only once did his self-possession falter. When accused of being responsible for the shedding of French blood, he answered angrily and then paused, rubbing his hand across his eyes as if to dash away tears.

All day Viviane worked quietly at her tasks in the kitchen and scullery. At night she crept to her bare, icy room, so weary and aching in every limb that she could scarcely walk.

Christmas Day came. Louis spent it alone in his cell. The gossip in the kitchens said that he occupied the day by writing his will.

The staff had had their own celebration, eating leftover roast goose stuffed with chestnuts and drinking the cellar's best apple brandy. Viviane ate a little, quietly, then went to her room where she lay in her bed, curled under her thin blanket.

Christmas Day was hard for her. Five years since David had drowned under the ice. Five years since her heart had been broken.

Hearts can't break, David would have said, laughing. *It's a muscle, not a bone.*

But Viviane felt like something inside her had broken.

22

Hungry Ghosts
29 December 1792 – 20 June 1793

The albatross had followed the ship for miles, gliding effortlessly on its great dark wings just above the surge and swell of the ocean waves. Its frowning gaze, its silence, the hypnotic sway of its motionless wings, was unnerving.

It's as if it carries some secret message, David thought, *but has not got the language to tell it. Hope, perhaps . . . a promise that we will one day reach land again . . .*

'It's been flying like that for days and days,' Tom exclaimed. 'Does it never sleep?'

'Not natural,' a young lieutenant named Whitman cried. 'Why don't it flap its wings like it should?'

'The sailors say an albatross is the ghost of an old sailor who died at sea,' Mr Hickey said, puffing on his long pipe.

'A ghost?' Whitman looked at him, startled.

'Or perhaps a reincarnation,' the artist replied. 'An interesting distinction.'

Whitman looked back at the bird. 'I don't hold with ghosts,' he said.

*

On the last day of 1792, the tiny remote island of Tristan da Cunha was spotted on the horizon. The ships dropped anchors some distance away, and Whitman rowed ashore on the cutter to scout for fresh water and food, his musket slung over one shoulder. When he returned, the boat was laden with the weight of an enormous sea lion. The sailors let out a cheer, for supplies were now scarce.

The next minute, the cheers died away. With a broad grin of triumph on his face, Whitman lifted up the limp body of the albatross, wings dangling gracelessly. 'Look what I bagged!' he shouted.

'Ought not to have done that,' one sailor muttered. 'Bad luck to kill an albatross.'

'I knew His Lordship wanted some scientific specimens,' Whitman blustered. 'Besides, it weren't natural, that bird.'

The sea lion was cut up to be made into soup, while Sir George examined the dead albatross. With a wingspan of over nine feet, it weighed just three and a half pounds.

'That's half the average weight of a newborn baby,' Dr Gillan said.

'And more than the average weight of a human brain. Whitman's, anyway,' Scotty added dryly. David exchanged a quick glance with him, knowing his friend felt as angry at the slaughter of the magnificent bird as he did. Whitman was hacking off one of the dead bird's feet, declaring he would make a new tobacco pouch from it. The sailors looked at him askance, but no more was said.

Sir George was pleased at the reports of fresh water and many different species of birds and plants on the island, and decided to send an expedition onshore the following day. A feast for New Year's Eve was prepared, and extra rations of grog handed out.

But that night, a heavy gale rose up and the *Lion*'s anchor was torn loose. The ship was almost wrecked upon the rocks.

Then the deaths began. The cook of the *Hindostan* died of a fever. The ship's carpenter was killed by natives while washing his linen on a beach. A sailor fell from the mast into the ocean and was drowned. Then, two weeks later, another sailor was lost overboard. The fever spread, and could not be checked. Dysentery and scurvy worsened.

Many a glance of anger and loathing were directed at Lieutenant Whitman, who glared back as he puffed at the long pipe he had made from the wing bone of the albatross.

'Superstitious fools,' he complained. 'It was just a damned bird.'

On the evening of the 16th of January 1793, the king was to be sentenced.

Each deputy had to make his vote publicly.

Along with thousands of other Parisians, Viviane fought her way into the *Salle du Manège*, the old riding stable where the National Convention held its meetings. A roaring trade was made by selling hot chestnuts and mulled wine. Girls carried baskets of oranges around, shouting their wares hoarsely, and some even sucked on ices, despite the crippling cold.

Voting began at eight in the evening, and continued all night. The king's legal counsel was denied a seat and stood, swaying visibly, for thirteen hours as, one by one, the deputies cast their votes. Again and again, the same word was cried.

'Death.'

Viviane recognised a few faces, among them Camille Desmoulins and Maximilien Robespierre, who had been the first to vote.

The last man to cast his vote was Louis's own cousin, the Duc d'Orléans. He had changed his name to Philippe Égalité. When he pronounced the dreadful word, in a calm measured tone, the king bent his head into his hands.

Viviane sat frozen. She could not believe it.

Louis XVI was a gentle, pious man. He liked to read, and make things with his hands, and play games with his children. He had never asked to be king. He had never liked being king.

Viviane stood and made her way blindly to the door.

He was just a man, she thought. A man who made mistakes, it's true. A man who could have done more. But surely not a man who deserved to die?

*

240

The king was guillotined on the 21st of January 1793.

His wife and children were informed by the great shout of joy that rose from the throat of Paris. The moment that his head was sliced from his body, his young son became the next king of France.

The prison laundress, a fervent revolutionary named Alouette, had been in the crowd. She had come back to the prison, laughing, her face splattered with gore.

'They told us that his blood would be on our heads. And see? It is!'

The coffin was carried on a bamboo litter on the bowed shoulders of four young men, dressed in sackcloth, white rags bound about their foreheads.

The smoke of incense hazed the air with a blue tinge. Monks in saffron-coloured wraps and beads walked ahead of the coffin, shaved heads bent, chanting. Behind, men carried paper lanterns inscribed with golden dragons. One man threw handfuls of rice to the watching crowd; another scattered money which the half-naked beggars fought to catch. Tall banners inscribed with strange intricate characters fluttered on all sides. Musicians played a strange wailing music upon wooden flutes and cithers. Drums thumped. Cymbals clanged.

Behind the coffin stumbled several young men, clad all in white, weeping and crying aloud to heaven. Sedan chairs, curtained in white, were carried behind. David could hear the sound of women wailing. More women followed behind, their faces heavily painted, black tear tracks running down their cheeks, grimacing theatrically with grief.

'What is it, what's happening?' David asked.

'It looks like a funeral procession,' Tom Staunton answered.

'But why are they wearing white instead of black?' Scotty asked.

'White is the colour of death in China, I believe, sir,' Tom answered.

Herr Hüttner frowned. 'It is most messy and noisy. Do they not know Orderliness is next to Godliness?'

As if in response to his words, two young men began to throw handfuls of firecrackers down on the ground. Bangs and pops. White light snapping on the ground. Smoke billowing past. Showers of paper confetti. The reek of gunpowder.

Tom clapped his hands over his ears. 'I don't think they do, sir,' he replied, trying not to laugh.

'Fireworks at a funeral seem disrespectful,' John Haxton said, gazing around bemusedly. 'Why would they do that?'

'I don't know,' David answered, just as puzzled.

Scotty turned to Father Li, who was walking with them, his hands tucked inside his sleeves, and asked him, in careful Latin, to explain.

The Chinese priest answered, 'To scare away malevolent ghosts.'

'The Chinese believe in ghosts?' Tom asked eagerly.

'Many ghosts in China,' the priest replied. 'Hungry ghosts, trickster ghosts, venomous ghosts, pestilence ghosts, nightmare ghosts, goblin ghosts.'

David was not sure if he had understood him properly. Despite all his grandfather's careful tutoring, Latin had never been his strong suit. He had learned as much as he needed to study botany, and little more.

Tom looked at him doubtfully. 'But you don't believe in ghosts anymore, do you, Mr Plum?'

Father Li did not speak for a moment, then replied 'not yes' in Mandarin.

There did not seem to be a single word meaning 'no' in his language. Sometimes Father Li said 'not right' and sometimes 'not true' and sometimes 'not can'. Such subtleties of difference made it a very difficult language to learn. David had tried hard to master it on the long months spent sailing on the ocean, with only the company of birds and whales and flying fish to break the monotony of the never-ending ocean. It had stumped him, however. David recognised the sound of some spoken words and the pattern of some written characters, but the two did not always seem to belong together. The way the word was pronounced could change its meaning considerably. David had sent Tom into paroxysms of laughter by telling the Chinese priest that he 'wished to kiss him', when he meant to say he 'wished to ask him'.

Tom had learned the language much faster and more easily than David or any of the other adults on board the *Lion*. He delighted in the Chinese love of puns and double-entendres, and so had begun to call the Chinese priest Mr Plum, since the symbol for his surname 'Li' was also the symbol for a plum tree. Tom took great care in practising his Chinese logograms, and loved the multiplicities of meaning behind just a few simple strokes.

Four swift scratches of his quill, and he created the logogram for fire. Yet that simple character could also mean light, bright, burning, passion, anger, ammunition, rage, wrath, war, weapon, explosion, inferno and imminence, depending on how many times the figure was drawn or what other logograms it was combined with.

China itself was imminent, David thought. They had sailed that very morning, the 6th of March 1793, into the harbour at Batavia, on the north coast of the island of Java, in the East Indies. It had been their first sight of civilisation since Rio de Janeiro, ninety-five days and nine thousand, five hundred and ninety miles away. They needed only to navigate through the islands and they'd be in the South China Seas, with the peaks of the fabled Flowery Kingdom slowly rising on the horizon.

They had seen Chinese junks in the harbour as the *Lion* had sailed towards the town, with flimsy high-pooped decks and red sails fluted like a fan. Father Li and Father Cho had fallen to their knees, crying aloud and bowing their heads to the ground. It was, Father Li had later explained, the first sight of anything Chinese since he had been sent away to Italy as a boy, at only twelve years of age.

There had been fear in the priest's face as well as joy. Afterwards he had been greatly agitated, walking the decks, rattling his rosary beads, turning often to stare at the junks. Later, when they had all embarked, the two Chinese priests had found their compatriots who had sailed on the *Hindostan*, and there was much loud jabbering in their own language. It had sounded like a furious argument.

The funeral procession reached what looked like a street altar, painted lacquer-red with golden characters inscribed upon it and smouldering joss sticks stuck in ceramic jars. The grief-stricken young men in white suddenly dropped to their knees in the filth of the street, and knocked their foreheads against the ground.

'That's the *ko-tow*,' Tom said knowledgeably. 'A ritual prostration performed by the inferior to the superior. Did you know the people of China have to *ko-tow* to the emperor's throne, even if he is not sitting in it, and to any letter that carries the imperial seal? And if they are in the presence of the emperor himself, they have to do the grand *ko-tow*, which is three kneelings and nine knockings of the head. My father says Lord Macartney swears he shall not demean himself so, as he is the representative of King George.'

'No man should kneel before another, or kiss his feet, or doff his hat,' David said. 'All men are created equal.'

'But you would kneel to the king, would you not, and kiss his hand?' Tom asked, shocked.

'As it is most unlikely that I will ever be presented to the king, I have no need to worry about that,' David responded.

'I would like to meet the king,' Tom said. 'One day perhaps I shall. I am to meet the emperor, you know. I'm to act as Lord Macartney's page and carry his train. The emperor is very old and wicked, I have heard. He has two empresses and twenty-nine concubines, and orders people to be executed by the death of a thousand cuts.'

The boy spoke with a certain breathless excitement, not at all shadowed by trepidation.

But Father Li, gazing back at the young Chinese men bowing low to the altar, was tense-jawed and fist-clenched.

The crew and passengers of the British ships were very pleased to be on firm land again, and enjoyed themselves bargaining in the markets, drinking vast quantities of palm wine, and buying monkeys and parrots. David had no cash to spare, since his salary was sent straight to his grandfather, so he spent his time in Batavia at the botanical park, studying the plants and trying to secure samples and seeds.

He was most pleased to be given a fragrant young nutmeg tree, and a nut supposed to be close to germination, and arranged for them to be sent back to Sir Joseph Banks at Kew Gardens on the very first ship returning to England. Sir Joseph had given David a job, despite his lack of a letter of recommendation from the Marquis de Valaine, and had put his name forward for this journey to China. David was determined to prove himself to his patron, and took a great many notes about the care and harvesting of clove, cinnamon, pepper, and the fruit of the mangosteen tree.

He was interested to learn that pineapples were as common as turnips. In England, they were rare and precious and grown only in the glasshouses of the tremendously rich. Often they were not eaten, but displayed on the table as proof of wealth and power. A man wishing to impress could even hire one for the evening, for an exorbitant price.

Here, in Batavia, pineapples were so unexceptional people often cleaned their swords by running them through the yellow flesh, thought to be so full of acid it would dissolve any dirt or rust upon the metal.

After ten days, the *Lion* set out once more. Lord Macartney was ill, as were many of the crew, but the admiral was keen to try and catch the strong surge of the monsoon winds that were meant, at this season, to blow towards China.

But the wind died away. The fleet was becalmed.

Pacing the quarterdeck in the heat of the blazing sun, gazing out at a sea as calm as bath water, David could not help but wonder uneasily if all this bad luck had anything to do with the shooting of the albatross.

At last, the monsoon came and the fleet of ships sailed on.

But all felt the shadow of the ill omen.

'Madame Guillotine is thirsty today!' a woman said to Viviane, passing her a calf's liver wrapped in bloodied paper.

Another loud cheer echoed across the rooftops of Paris.

'May she drink deep,' said Alouette, the Temple prison's laundress. A passionate revolutionary, she wore a short, striped tricolour skirt and a red cap crammed over her dark curls, which had been chopped *à la jacobine*.

'Such a damned shame we have to work today, Rozenn, else we could go watch.'

'I'd rather not,' Viviane answered, stowing the package away in her basket. Seeing Alouette's quick frown, she added, 'You know I don't like crowds.'

'Oh, the smell, the crush!' Alouette pressed one hand against her forehead, pretending to faint. 'You are such an aristo,' she added.

'I am not,' Viviane answered sharply. 'It's not my fault crowds make me feel sick.'

It was not exactly a lie.

'All right, then, such a clodhopper.' Alouette grinned at her. 'Though you'd think the smell of pigs and cows would be worse than the smell of Paris.'

'Trust me, it's not,' Viviane replied, and moved on to look at the chicken giblets laid out on the next table.

She and Alouette were at the markets at Les Halles, crowded as always with women buying and selling and talking and arguing. The market square was only ten minutes away from the Place du Carrousel, so they could hear the roar of the crowd as another tumbril deposited its human cargo at the foot of the guillotine. Since the Revolutionary Tribunal had been set up a month earlier, the nation's razor had been busy.

It had been a tumultuous few months in France. Peasants in the provinces had rebelled against the National Convention's *Levée des 300,000 hommes*, which demanded men leave their fields and families and go and fight in the army. France was now officially at war with Britain, Austria, Prussia, Holland, Spain and Sardinia, and fighting on all fronts. Food riots in Paris had led to the formation of the Committee of Public Safety under the leadership of Georges Danton, famous for having shouted, 'The kings of Europe would dare challenge us? We throw them the head of a king!'

This in turn had led to the Revolutionary Tribunal, formed to prosecute anyone believed to be an enemy of the revolution. Meanwhile, the National Convention was bitterly divided on the best way to govern the country. The Brissotins were popular in the provinces, where people were shaken and disturbed by the execution of the king, and the Jacobins had the support of the *sans-culottes*, the angry and often violent mob of Paris.

Alouette attended the assemblies at the National Convention whenever she could, knitting as she listened for she had nine younger brothers and sisters, all hungry and cold. She cheered and clapped at the speeches she approved of, and booed and hissed at those she did not. Sometimes she hammered on the wooden benches with the hilt of the dagger she always carried, useful for cutting wool, skewering mutton in a stew, or holding off an amorous soldier. 'Besides,' she said, 'a *sans-culotte* always has their weapon well sharpened, ready to cut off the ears of opponents of the revolution!'

At the moment, her most bitter enemies were the Brissotins, who had tried to arrest Jean-Paul Marat, the journalist who had once accused Marie-Antoinette of trampling on the cockade. The Brissotins had charged him with trying to incite violence, but Marat had been acquitted of all charges. His accusers had then been arrested themselves, and the National Convention was now ruled by the Jacobins, led by Maximilien Robespierre.

The Jacobins' first task was the drafting of a new constitution. The one written in 1791 had been for a constitutional monarchy, but the monarchy was no more. So, in just two weeks, Robespierre and one of his acolytes, Louis-Antoine de Saint-Just, formulated a new system of government for the new republic. It was adopted by the Convention on the 24th of June, and then submitted to vote by popular referendum.

'It's all very well and good,' Alouette grumbled, 'but they've forgotten about us women. Why aren't we allowed to vote for the constitution too? They don't mind us throwing flowers and hanging wreaths on statues, but when it comes to being a real citizen, they give us nothing. Surely the so-called "rights of man" means our rights too? What has the National Convention done for us? There's no flour for bread, no soap for us poor washerwomen to do our job, no coal to light our stoves to heat our irons. Those bloodsuckers are hoarding it all for the rich, and letting us starve.'

The next day, a mob of washerwomen stopped two carts full of bars of soap on the Rue Saint-Lazare, and commandeered it for themselves.

They sold the soap to each other for only twenty sous. The unrest spread, and shopkeepers and merchants found themselves mobbed by angry women, forcing them to sell soap, tallow candles, sugar, salt and coal at more reasonable prices. A house on the Rue de Provence was besieged by two hundred women who believed the owner was hoarding soap for rich merchants. By the following morning, more than a thousand women were attacking the cargo boats moored at the Quai de l'École. They were dispersed by policemen, but marched on the Convention and presented a petition protesting the cost of everyday items such as flour and beer.

Alouette returned with a black eye and a torn blouse, filled with satisfaction.

Viviane told her that Jacques Hébert, Deputy Prosecutor of the Paris Commune, had said, 'Damn it! You spend your time catching flies when there are lions to be fought. Great heavens, are we to make war on sugar and soap?'

'It's fine for him,' Alouette had said. 'He's not the one that has to queue up all night for bread, and then try and wash sheets all day without any soap. He's probably eating *foie gras* and truffles, and sleeping on silk. All men like him ever do is make promises and then shrug and say sorry when the whole cost falls on the shoulders of the poor, like always. We should send him to the guillotine too!' And she had laughed.

Viviane could not understand how anyone could find the guillotine a source of glee. So, as another roar of approval resounded through the streets, she hesitantly asked, 'Why do you want to go and watch the guillotine, Alouette? It's people dying, people with mothers or lovers or children left behind to grieve.'

The young woman was silent for a moment, looking down at the filthy cobblestones. 'It's justice,' she said after a long moment. 'Justice for all the wrongs we *sans-culottes* have suffered. Thousands of years crushed under the red heel of the tyrant.' Suddenly she looked up, her dark eyes ablaze. 'And vengeance! Vengeance at last!'

*

On 20 June, David had his first sight of China. Soft blue billows of hills, rising from sea smoke. He and the other men raised a resounding cheer. Nine months they'd been at sea, and at last their objective was in sight.

As the fleet sailed closer, clusters of peaked islands, bare and windswept, rose from the water, looking like fragments broken from the continent. The rocks were dark, almost black, and honeycombed with erosion. Ahead lay the peninsula of Macao, with its high summit looking down on the bay, and behind, the great dark landmass that was China.

The bay was crowded with junks, with stiff-battened sails like red silk parasols. Smaller boats with flat bottoms were propelled along by a single oar. Father Li said they were called sampans, which meant 'three planks'. The boats were crewed by men with heavy-lidded black eyes, wearing loose trousers and tunics and pointed straw hats. Their queues hung in long thin braids down their backs.

Some of the boats carried bamboo crates filled with live chickens, all squawking loudly. Another was hung with strings of still-flapping fish. One had a hull piled with strange-looking bristled fruit. Yet another sampan trailed smoke from a small charcoal furnace. An array of razors, tweezers and brushes hung from a bamboo pole, and the man on the boat made a great noise clanging tongs against a cymbal. Someone nearby gestured to him. The barber poled over, jumped on to the other boat, and within moments was shaving the man's forehead with a glinting razor.

At the sound of the local boatmen's high-pitched jabbering, Father Li and Father Cho shrank away and hid themselves from sight.

'What is wrong?' Tom asked in Latin, laying his hand on Father Li's sleeve.

The priest looked down at him with a troubled face. 'We are in China.'

It was as if he had never expected this day to come.

23

A Great Mandarin
21 June – 3 July 1793

'**B**ut why can't we go ashore, sir?' David demanded. 'We have come so far, and we are so very close. I want to walk on Chinese soil, and see a Chinese garden, and smell the perfume of a Chinese flower.'

'I understand your frustration,' Sir George replied patiently. 'But Macao is not really China, it's a little corner of Portugal. It is walled off from China, with a single gate that no-one but the Chinese can pass through. So you would be as distant from the real China as you are now.'

'But I would get a taste of what China is like, and have solid earth beneath my feet instead of this infernally rocking boat,' David responded.

Sir George smiled. 'So the old sea dogs failed to wash the landlubber out of you after all! I'm sorry, I'm afraid Lord Macartney's instructions are clear. Until we know how the emperor has responded to our overtures, the embassy must be careful not to offend in any way. I am hopeful to receive a favourable communication from the emperor soon, but until then only myself and my servant are to go ashore.'

David sighed in disappointment.

Someone tapped on the door. Sir George's manservant opened it, showing in Father Cho and Father Li, both looking nervous and uncomfortable.

Father Cho bowed and begged pardon. He could not travel any further. It was too dangerous. If the emperor found out . . . he would be punished most cruelly. He had left China without permission . . . he had *ko-tow*ed to another god . . . he must not risk his neck anymore . . .

In vain, Sir George protested. They had an agreement. Father Cho had been already paid for his services. They needed an interpreter.

Father Cho could not be swayed.

At last, Sir George turned to Father Li with a cold contemptuous expression. 'I suppose you wish to desert us too?'

But the young priest shook his head. 'I will stay. I will rely on your protection. I must be Mr Plum.' He drew himself up, put on an expression of superciliousness and disdain. 'I will wear your clothes and hats, and they will not know me.' He gestured at Sir George's breeches and frockcoat.

It was clear Father Li thought he could disguise his Chinese origin with English dress.

But the idea made David's heart sink.

He did not think anyone would be fooled.

When the brig set forth for Macao, it carried three of the Chinese priests.

They had paid the barber to come and shave their heads, and glue on long thin plaits of black hair to hang down their backs.

'Where did the barber get the queues?' David asked. 'Surely they are not easy to come by?'

Father Li seemed to understand his words, for he turned and said sombrely, in Latin, 'Dead men.'

In Macao, Sir George met the commissioners of the East India Company, and was given a message from the emperor. He read it out to the men that night at dinner:

> His Imperial Majesty says that, as such a great Mandarin has come so far to visit him, he must be received in a distinguished manner . . .

A ripple of indignant laughter.

'The idea of his lordship being called one of those heathen mandarins!' the valet, Anderson, cried.

Sir George glanced at Lord Macartney, sitting at the high table with a crystal glass of claret at his elbow. 'My lord, the commissioners say that – despite his welcoming words – the emperor urges us to sail to Canton, to stay with the other Europeans in the enclave they call the Thirteen Factories and speak there with his representatives.'

Sir George took a moment to read the proclamation more closely. 'As your Excellency knows, European merchants are only permitted to trade within the confines of the factories. His Imperial Majesty says there is no reason to insist on travelling beyond. The emperor's mandarins will assess the rarity and value of His Excellency's tributes to his Imperial Majesty there.'

Lord Macartney's bushy eyebrows rose. 'Tributes? I do not bring tributes. Our cargo are gifts from one king to another!'

'Perhaps the word has been mistranslated,' Sir George said.

'I suppose it is possible,' Lord Macartney answered, frowning.

'The mandarins are most insistent that we do not sail any further north, my lord. Go to Canton, they say, and wait upon the emperor's indulgence.'

Lord Macartney did not speak, swirling the claret in his glass then taking a sip.

After a moment, Sir George continued reading. 'The emperor says there are no pilots available to show us the way north, through the Yellow Sea, to Peking. And, given the shocking accounts of the recent confusions in France, the emperor feels he is justified in taking strong precautions against the incursions of uninvited foreigners. Go to Canton, he says. Follow the established procedures.'

There was a long silence, then Lord Macartney looked up and smiled.

'I think not. Tell the captain we sail north. To Peking.'

*

252

Through squalls of rain, the small fleet headed north.

The coast of China was hidden by mist. David stood on the quarter-deck, gazing to the west. But no amount of looking summoned up a glimpse of the land, let alone its forests and gardens. He had to walk out his impatience by striding round and round the quarterdeck, stepping over the coils of rope, counting his steps till he had reached two thousand, which he and Scotty estimated would be a good mile. Then he began again.

How he longed for good firm ground beneath his boots, and a rolling vista of meadows and woods and hills beckoning him beyond. He remembered the last good tramp he had had, the day before he had said goodbye to his grandparents and sisters and set off for Portsmouth. He had slowly climbed above the mist and rain, and seen one bright star burning out like a beacon of hope in a miraculously clear sky. The mountains had floated in a sea of moonlit clouds. David had lit a low campfire, as red as the last smears of sunset, and then rolled himself in his coat to sleep, weary in body but exultant in spirit.

He had been so sure then that he was doing the right thing, leaving England and his family and sailing so far away. He dreamed of finding many rare and wondrous plants, and making his name and his fortune. Perhaps he would even be knighted by the king, as Sir Joseph Banks had been, or made an earl, like Lord Macartney. David imagined stalking into the great hall at Belisima-sur-le-lac, at the head of a procession of servants carrying pots of the finest blue-and-white Chinese porcelain, all planted with roses of the deepest ruby red. He would incline his head and say with cold courtesy, 'Madame, the rose that you requested. I regret that I cannot name it after you, as I once intended, but that honour must be reserved for my wife, Lady Stronach.'

Except that he would never marry. He would become a plant hunter, spending his life battling through jungles and scaling high mountains, searching for the rarest, most exotic flowers in the world. He would see such things and go to such places. And Viviane, bound to a man more than forty years her elder, would be sorry.

*

Sometimes a whole day would pass without Viviane speaking more than a word or two to anyone.

She was too afraid of betraying herself in some way. An unwise word, an involuntary quiver of her lips, a flash of expression on her face. So she kept her eyes down and her hands busy.

Ivo always stopped to speak to her when he saw her, and once or twice intervened when one of the other maids teased her for being hoity-toity, or made her do the dirtiest chores because she was the newest.

Every evening, when she could, Viviane slipped away and walked by herself in the garden. Tonight the avenue of horse-chestnut trees was blooming with pale candles of flowers. She picked some hyssop and sage and thyme for her bouillon, lifting them to her nose to smell their fresh scent, and wondered if the garden at Belisima was now just a wasteland of weeds.

Coming slowly through an archway in a hedge, she found Ivo, sitting and smoking his pipe in the dusk.

'Oh, I beg your pardon,' she said. 'I did not mean to intrude.'

She would have turned to leave but he smiled at her. 'Come and join me,' he said. 'You like the garden too?'

'It's the only good thing about this place,' she answered, then flushed. 'A thousand pardons, I did not mean to be rude.'

'Oh, no, I agree,' he answered. 'I'd gladly not work here, but there are so few jobs for chefs now, with the nobility all dead or fled.' He spoke lightly, but she thought there was a shade of bitterness in his voice.

From over the hedge came the sound of raucous laughter, and then loud singing. *Ah! ça ira, ça ira* . . .

'You don't join the others in the evenings?' Ivo asked.

She shook her head. 'I like the garden better. The beauty and the peace . . .'

'I'm the same. Maybe it's because we are both from the country. I often wish I could just go home again, but . . .' His voice trailed away. They both knew it was too dangerous to go travelling through the countryside without an urgent cause. The city gates were well guarded, and permission to travel rarely given.

'Why did you come to Paris?' she asked.

'Things were hard for us. My mother died and my father lost his job. He was a chef too. There was no work in Rennes, at least work I wished to do. And I wanted to see Paris. I wanted to see all the shops, and go to the theatre and the ballet and the opera.'

'Oh, yes, I wanted to do that too.' Viviane sighed. Her husband had not been interested in music, so she had not seen even one show.

'You haven't been? Oh, but you must.' Ivo looked at her in amazement.

'I haven't got any money.' Viviane was saving all her coins so that – when Paris at last opened its city gates – she could obtain a pass and go home to Belisima.

'But the theatres all have nights when you can buy cheap tickets, or even go for free. That's one good thing about this damned revolution at least!' Then Ivo realised what he had said, and flushed. 'I mean . . .'

'Do not concern yourself,' Viviane said. 'I know exactly what you mean.'

They smiled at each other a little sadly.

'Why don't you come with me?' Ivo said. 'No-one else here is interested in the opera. It will be nice to have the company.'

She hesitated, not knowing how wise it was to confide in him.

'You need not fear I will importune you with unwelcome advances,' he said, after a moment.

She flushed, and laughed, and shook her head. 'It's not that . . . though I thank you. It's just . . . I am afraid to go out. I do not much like crowds anymore, or places that are too noisy. Oh, it's so hard to explain.'

'You've seen too much in this past year or so?'

She nodded. 'Far too much.'

'But going to the opera is not like going to the fishmarkets,' he said. 'Beautiful music, amazing costumes, angelic singing . . .'

Still she hesitated.

'Come with me once. Then if you do not like it, you need not come again.'

So Viviane had gone to the opera with Ivo, at the Theatre de la Porte Saint-Martin. Antonio Salieri's *Les Danaïdes* was playing. It was a tragic and rather gruesome tale in which the fifty daughters of King Danaus are betrothed to marry the fifty sons of the family of Egyptus, in order to end a long feud between the families. But Danaus reveals to his daughters that the reconciliation is a trap, and orders them to kill their husbands on their wedding night. All the daughters agree to do so, except one. She is in love with the man she is to marry. After a great deal of heart searching, she tells her betrothed about the plot. He survives, but all his brothers die. In his grief and horror, he attacks the palace of Danaus, slaughtering the king and his daughters, but saving the one who loved him.

The final scene was set in the fiery underworld. Danaus is chained to a rock, his entrails pecked by a vulture, his daughters tormented by demons. Great spouts of flame and waterfalls of sparks drew gasps of surprise and alarm from the audience. Even Viviane had her hands over her mouth. Smoke billowed out into the theatre, making everyone cough.

'That was wonderful!' Viviane made her way through the crowd with Ivo. 'The music, the singing. I've never heard anything like it.'

'I wonder how they created those jets of flame! I thought the whole theatre would burn down.'

'Oh, that's easy,' Viviane said. 'That'd be flash powder. It's made from clubmoss, the little plant they call wolf's-foot. You pound it up and light a brimstone match, and then throw the flash powder over it. It ignites into a great gush of fire! Or you could mix nitrate of potash with sulfuric acid . . .'

She became aware that Ivo was staring at her in amazement, and went red.

'My brother liked to play with fire,' she stammered. 'He was always experimenting. He made us fireworks once, for the birth of the dauphin. But he burned off his eyebrows and eyelashes, and was forbidden from ever doing it again.'

'He was lucky not to have been blinded!'

'Pierrick was always doing experiments. He used to make lightning to scare my great-aunt, who was terrified of storms. It was just spirit of nitre and oil of cloves, but it made such a noise and crack of light. I was so grateful to him for it, because she'd go to bed and pull the pillow over her head, and I'd be free for a few hours.'

'So what did you and your brother do with your free hours?' Ivo asked, laughing.

Viviane smiled. 'Oh, we'd go to the kitchen and steal apples and cakes to eat in the mill, or go and visit the weavers in their cottages. Pierrick was sure he could invent a machine to spin and weave cloth with the power of the mill rush. It was one of his favourite places. When we were younger, Pierrick and I used to drop sticks from the bridge, and then run to the other side to see whose stick boat sailed through first. And he'd make all sorts of different designs to make sure his stick would win first.'

'You seem to have had the run of the château,' Ivo said.

Viviane's cheeks burned. 'Monsieur le Marquis was rarely there.'

'That was lucky.'

'Yes.'

There was a long silence. They were walking together along the Rue de Vertbois, towards the towers of the Temple. Viviane felt stiff and awkward. She had said too much, revealed too much.

'Where is your brother now?' Ivo asked. His voice was gentle, his eyes downcast.

Viviane shook her head. 'I don't know. I've lost him.'

'He probably wouldn't be too hard to find, in these days of identity papers and certificates of public spirit.'

Another silence. Viviane did not dare to make such a search. What if her own papers were scrutinised? What if they realised there was no Rozenn Cazotte?

'You're lucky to have a brother,' Ivo said at last. 'I always longed for one.'

'Any sisters?'

He shook his head.

'A sweetheart?' she asked. Anything to keep the conversation on him.

Ivo shook his head again. He glanced at her, and she saw in surprise that his face was as hot as hers.

'I'm not made for that kind of love,' he said with difficulty.

It took a moment to know what he meant, and then her whole body burned with embarrassment. 'Neither was my brother,' she managed to say at last.

'Really?' He looked at her full in the face. 'Do you mean . . .'

She nodded and laughed, all embarrassment falling away from her. 'Oh, yes! Pierrick was always much more interested in boys than girls.'

'I might have to meet your brother.' Ivo grinned. 'That's another good thing about the Revolution. Boys like me and your brother used to be burned to death. But now it's only aristocrats who need to fear.'

By 1 July, the flotilla was close to the Chu-San Islands, the most easterly point of China. Progress was slow because, as the ships began to approach the shore, hundreds of junks and sampans crowded around them, the fishermen within gesturing in astonishment.

'They have not seen ships like ours before,' Scotty said.

'I wonder what they think of us,' David replied, and was answered by loud hootings of amusement as the Chinese gestured towards the naval officers in their powdered wigs and cocked hats.

Soon the ships were immobilised by a floating city of little boats, all tethered together, while the locals clambered up to the decks. The soldiers were tense and alert, but there was so much good humour in the faces of the men who swarmed up the ropes that the admiral told the men to be at ease, and let the sightseers come.

The Chinese were amazed at everything. They fingered the embroidered facings of the men's coats and were thunderstruck by their pockets, putting their hands in and out so many times that everyone began to feel uncomfortable, and took great care to keep their snuffboxes and watches safe in their hands.

The fishermen wanted to explore the whole ship, so David found himself escorting small parties around, showing them the hammocks on the cannon deck where the sailors slept, and his own tiny hole in the wall that he shared with the other gardener, John Haxton. Then, with Lord Macartney's permission, he showed them the ambassador's great cabin.

Hanging on the wall was a long silk scroll which depicted the Emperor of China, dressed in an elaborately worked yellow robe, a red hat on his head, pearls about his neck.

The Chinese men instantly prostrated themselves, pressing their foreheads to the ground again and again.

It was hard not to laugh.

David met Lord Macartney's eyes in amusement, but they waited patiently till the men had finished their *ko-tow*, then accepted their many low bows of thanks with equanimity.

'It is a good thing that I do not need to pay homage to the emperor every time I enter my cabin, else I'd never get any work done,' Lord Macartney said, as David ushered the visitors out.

For the first time, David wondered what the consequences would be if Lord Macartney refused to prostrate himself before the emperor.

He felt a sharp twinge of unease.

The admiral was able to secure the services of one of the fishermen as a pilot, and he guided them through the hundreds of small islands, atolls, shoals, reefs and sandbars till the ships came into a bay where they could drop anchor.

Then David was able to set foot on the soil of China for the first time.

He could not help being disappointed. The island was bare, with few trees. One or two low mud-coloured houses, stands of ragged-looking bamboo, and small fields cultivated into rice-paddies.

A peasant gazed at them in open curiosity. When Father Li spoke a few words to him, he rather unwillingly allowed them to look inside his dwelling. It was flimsily constructed of timber and rice straw, with hanging mats parting it into sleeping and living quarters. The floor was beaten earth. Two small spinning wheels of uncommon design stood near the hearth, still rotating slowly, but there was no sign of the women who must have been sitting there just moments before.

Dissatisfied, David and his friends returned to the *Lion*, and the next day the flotilla set sail once more. Slowly the ships glided through the channel, steep islands rising out of the water on all sides. It felt like they were floating through a drowned valley, and that they must run aground on a submerged mountaintop at any moment.

At last Ting-hai came into view. A walled city, set on the harbour with mountain peaks behind. David saw tall pagodas over the wall, and his heart quickened in excitement.

The *Lion* dropped anchor, and an official in a long robe with a bird gorgeously embroidered on his chest came aboard to ask their business. He was dressed in a heavy silk robe, with a black hat upon his head, and a string of heavy coral beads about his neck. His beard was long and white, and the nails of his smallest fingers had been allowed to grow to extraordinary lengths. He was accompanied by a servant in a loose indigo smock who carried all his pens and seals and papers in various pouches and bags suspended from his girdle. The servant had a cringing servile manner that bothered David. He wanted to tell him sharply to stand up like a man.

It took some time to open up a dialogue with the mandarin, for he did not understand a word Father Li spoke. It seemed the young priest had been away from China too long, or spoke a different dialect. Tom had the bright idea of writing down a few characters, however. The mandarin recognised them at once, and so they were able to communicate through the written language.

As soon as the mandarin realised the flotilla was escorting the English ambassador, his haughty manner changed. He bowed, and willingly agreed to give them supplies and to organise a meeting for Lord Macartney and Sir George with the town governor.

David and the other men went to explore the town.

Ting-hai was guarded by a wall thirty feet high, set with stone towers every hundred yards. The wall was battlemented, but there was no sign of any cannons.

A wooden gate was guarded by soldiers in medieval-looking garb, wearing steel caps with a sharp metal point. While Father Li tried to communicate with them, scratching characters in the dirt with a stick, William Alexander quickly drew one of the soldiers in the sketchbook he carried with him everywhere. Eventually the gate was opened for them, and they stepped through into the walled city.

Ramshackle grey houses with upturned eaves huddled together along narrow alleys, running north to south and east to west, in neat squares. Overhead hung dozens of long banners and signs, painted in unfathomable Chinese characters. Ahead was a bazaar teeming with people, arguing and bargaining. Chickens and songbirds were crammed in small bamboo cages, and thin dogs rooted through piles of rubbish. Outside one shop were barrels of water filled with flapping fish. Another shop sold exquisite fans, with scenes of lovers in gardens painted on fluted silk. A man carrying a huge wrapped bundle on his head pushed past David, glancing at the Englishmen with suspicion.

Everywhere David looked was something strange and marvellous. A set of lacquer-red temple doors guarded by immense stone lions with stylised curls like a judge's wig. Vermilion lanterns inscribed with gold. Tiny paper kites of dragons bobbing and darting in the air, long tails writhing. An old man with a long white beard, dressed in a cerulean satin robe embroidered with peonies, fanning himself with a pink silk fan painted with cherry blossoms. A pine tree in a pot, no larger than his handspan.

And over it all loomed the monumental city walls, frowning down on the buildings below like the ramparts of a prison.

'There are no women in the streets,' William said.

David realised he was right. The people jostling on every side were all men.

They walked on through the marketplace, uneasily aware of how everyone stared at them. David in particular attracted attention, with his bronze-red hair, grey-blue eyes and unusual height. It made him most uncomfortable.

'There's a woman,' William said, pointing. 'In that shop.'

David turned and saw an old lady with sunken cheeks and sparse white hair, sitting on a stool inside one of the shops, weighing rice with a small set of scales. She was dressed, like most of the men, in a blue smock over loose trousers.

William said, in a low shocked voice, 'What's wrong with her feet?'

David looked down, and realised that the old woman's shoes were impossibly small. It looked as if half of each foot had been amputated. The remaining stumps were clad in tiny silk slippers, with a narrow pointed toe, intricately embroidered with flowers.

Just then another woman hobbled into sight from the back of the shop. She was much younger, but her feet were as unnaturally small. She moved with the awkward jerkiness of a small boy trying out new skates for the first time.

A man saw the Europeans gazing in, and with unintelligible shouts and flaps of his hands shooed them away from the door.

But not before they saw that the woman carried a little girl on her hip. The child's feet were tightly bound in bandages that were soiled with blood and pus. She was sobbing in pain.

The men walked away in silence.

'I had read that Chinese girls' feet are bound to keep them small, but I had not imagined they would be so sorely maimed,' Scotty said at last. 'Surely the foot must be broken and crushed to be so tiny?'

'It is a wonder they can walk at all,' David said, filled with a sudden rage.

Tom turned to Father Li, and said in a voice that trembled, 'Why do they do that to the girl's feet?' For once, his Latin was not perfect.

The priest looked down at the ground, his face impassive. 'The women do it,' he replied in his precise Latin.

'But why?'

'So their daughters will be number one wife.'

'It's horrible,' David said.

In his mind's eye, he saw Viviane running barefoot in a meadow, laughing and graceful and lissom, her dog leaping and playing about her like summer lightning.

That little Chinese girl would never be able to run so free.

24

The Cobbler
3 July – 2 August 1793

Viviane kicked off her sabots, reaching down to rub her aching foot. The clock on the mantelpiece said it was almost ten o'clock. Outside, the other maids sat drinking rough wine and smoking with the off-duty guards. Alouette was strumming a guitar and singing:

> If some want a master,
> In a world filled with kings,
> Let them beg for shackles.
> Unworthy to be called Frenchmen,
> Unworthy to be called Frenchmen!

Alouette had liked to sing such songs when the king and queen and their children were walking in the garden but, since Louis's death, Marie-Antoinette could not bear to pass his door. She had not walked in the garden in the months since his execution. So Alouette had to sing loudly under the queen's window, and hope she heard.

Viviane had little time for drinking and singing. The kitchen staff had been reduced to eight and she had taken on extra chores as a result. Besides, she did not have the heart for it.

She rubbed her other aching foot, then drew a leaflet of papers out of her apron pocket. They were creased and stained, Viviane having read them many times in the past few months. It was a pamphlet, entitled *The Declaration of the Rights of Woman and the Female Citizen*, written by a woman named Olympe de Gouges. It began: 'Man, are you capable of being just? It is a woman who asks you this question: who has given you the authority to oppress my sex?'

Alouette had brought the booklet back from one of her political meetings, as she had done ever since she had learned that Viviane could read. Alouette liked to pore over the tracts, following the words with one dirty finger, committing them to her memory and then repeating them triumphantly whenever she wanted to win an argument. This was one of her favourites, and had become Viviane's too.

'Woman is born free and lives equal to man in her rights,' she read. 'Liberty and justice consist of restoring all that belongs to others; thus, the only limits on the exercise of the natural rights of woman are perpetual male tyranny.'

The words always made Viviane think of her father with bitterness and pain. Viviane wondered where he was. She could not imagine him living in this new France. Perhaps he had fled to England or Austria, and was even now plotting to restore the monarchy under the name of the little boy-king kept prisoner in this cold, dank tower.

The pamphlet ended with the rousing words: 'Woman, wake up; the tocsin of reason is being heard throughout the whole universe; discover your rights!'

Viviane murmured Olympe de Gouges's words over and over to herself, trying to commit them to memory. If her father ever came back, and tried to force her to marry against her will again, or impoverish her land and her people for his vanities and gambling debts, she would shout them in his face.

Ivo came through the kitchen, drawing on his coat. 'I'm off to the theatre,' he said. 'Do you want to come?'

Viviane shook her head. 'Too tired.'

He nodded, having expected the answer, and went out, shutting the door behind him.

The truth was Viviane really did find crowds difficult to bear. The smell, the roar of many voices, the fear of being crushed. It had been nine months since the Paris mob had torn apart the Princesse de Lamballe and paraded her head on a pike through the city. The Temple prison had, strangely, become a place of refuge and protection for Viviane, and she took pride in windows that sparkled and the delicious smell of bouillon that she had made herself.

The tramp of booted feet in the hall. She looked up anxiously. Even after so long play-acting the role of Rozenn Cazotte, Viviane feared the day when she would be discovered.

She stood up, crushing the booklet in her hands. The marching boots did not come into the kitchen, but kept on going up the stairs. Viviane crept through to the front hallway and listened. Up one flight of stairs, and past the first floor where the maidservants slept. Up another flight, and past the apartment which Louis had once used. It had been locked since his execution, but had been opened up and aired by the maids that very day, and a fire laid in the main bedroom.

Viviane frowned, as the boots kept on marching up another turn of the stairs. It was late, the queen would be preparing for bed, the little king would be asleep. What could they want with poor Marie-Antoinette and her children at this late hour?

She began to hurry up the stairs, telling herself all the while not to be so foolish, to go to bed and put the pillow over her head, and pretend she had heard nothing. But the thought of the queen and her two young children, so thin and white and sorrowful, made it impossible. Viviane had to know what was happening, had to try to help if she could.

She needed some excuse. Viviane got out a chamber-pot from a cupboard, threw a cloth over it, and hurried up the steep circular steps.

Suddenly she heard Marie-Antoinette cry out, 'No! No! Don't take him. Please, I beg you!'

Then the little boy's shrill cry of terror. 'Maman!'

Viviane ran up the last flight of stairs. The only light shone through the door to the queen's apartment, standing ajar.

One of the officers was saying, 'The Committee of Public Safety orders that the son of Capet shall be separated from his mother and delivered into the hands of a governor.'

'Please, you cannot . . . be so cruel. He's been sick . . . he's only a little boy . . . he needs his mother.' Marie-Antoinette was almost incoherent with fear.

'You must release him,' one officer said, 'else we shall be forced to strike you.'

'Strike me all you like, just leave me my son.'

'If you do not let him go, we shall have to drag him away and then he may be hurt. Let him go!'

Viviane did not dare go in. She crouched in the darkness, listening, hating her fear and her impotence. A brief scuffle, then the boy screamed, 'No, no, maman, maman!'

'Where are you taking him?' Marie-Antoinette cried. 'Oh, please do not hurt him.'

'He's not going far,' one of the men said kindly. Viviane recognised his voice. His name was Jean-Baptiste Michonis, the superintendent of the prison. 'Just downstairs. Just to his father's rooms.'

'But why? Why? He will be so frightened all alone. He's only just eight years old, he needs me.'

'He will not be alone. The Commune has found a tutor for him.'

'A tutor? But who?'

Nobody answered her. Viviane heard Marie-Antoinette sobbing.

'Get him dressed,' another man said.

A low murmur, and the high-pitched voice of Marie-Thérèse, questioning her aunt. 'But why are they taking him away, Tante Élisabeth? Who will care for him? Who will hear his prayers at night?'

'Oh, please, don't be so cruel!' Marie-Antoinette cried once more. 'He needs his mother.'

'That's enough! Be silent, or we shall silence you. Come, take the boy!'

Viviane retreated swiftly, as the officers came out of the queen's room, one carrying the boy over his shoulder. Louis-Charles was crying and hammering his fists on the officer's back. His golden curls were damp and ruffled, his thin face flushed and hectic.

His spaniel Coco raced out, yapping madly and nipping at the officer's boot heels. He kicked out, and the puppy tumbled over, yelping.

Viviane could not bear it. 'Oh, let him take his dog! What harm could it do?'

The officers glared at her, but Superintendent Michonis bent and scooped up the spaniel and carried it away.

The door to the queen's room was locked securely behind them. Viviane was left standing on the steps. She kicked her feet out of her sabots and tucked them inside the chamber-pot, then went silently down the steps in her stockinged feet. Sabots made such a clatter, and she did not want the officers to know she was following them.

She stopped in the shadow of the curving steps, peering around the central pillar.

The officers had flung open the door to the lower apartment.

A tall, beefy man stood waiting, dressed in rough clothes with a red cap on his greasy, matted hair and stout leather boots on his feet. He held a leather strap in one hand, and a bottle in the other. Viviane knew him. His name was Antoine Simon, and he was a cobbler by trade. He and his wife Marie-Jeanne had been employed at the Temple for some months as servants.

'Ho, so here is my young charge!' Simon slurred. 'Well met, little Capet.'

'That is not my name,' the boy answered defiantly.

The man slapped the strap in the palm of his hand. 'Your name is what I say it is!'

The child shrank back, but was dropped roughly to the ground and shoved through the door.

'So what is your name, toad?' the man asked, stepping forward so he loomed over the child.

'Louis-Charles of France,' the little boy replied at once.

The man struck him across the face. 'No! That is wrong. You are Charles Capet. No-one is to be called Louis anymore – that name is soiled by treason and betrayal. You'll be Charles from now. Do you hear me?'

The little boy sobbed, holding his cheek.

'Do you hear me?' The man held high the leather strap.

'Yes, monsieur,' the boy whimpered, and was struck again.

'Call me *citoyen*!' the man cried.

'*Citoyen* Simon, is this really necessary?' Michonis asked in a pained voice.

'Yes, it is necessary,' Simon replied. 'Have I not been hired to teach our little Capet to be a good revolutionary? By the end of the week, I'll have him spitting on his father's portrait.'

As he spoke, the door was swung shut and Viviane heard no more. She was trembling, close to tears. She wanted to fling open the door, take the little boy in her arms, and tell those bullies to leave him alone.

But she dared not.

It would do no good. They would simply throw her back in prison and punish him more harshly. She knew what men like Antoine Simon were like. Her father had taught her well.

For the next few days, there was no sight of the little boy.

Viviane occasionally heard the sound of pitiful sobbing, or brutal yelling, but the child was not taken out for his daily walk. The Convention sent orders that Simon must make sure the boy was seen, as rumours were flying about that he had been murdered. So Louis-Charles was taken to the garden. He walked slowly, his shoulders hunched, wavering a little in his step as if dazed. He wore a red revolutionary bonnet on his head.

'Poor little mite,' Viviane whispered, sitting on the back step peeling potatoes.

Alouette looked at her askance. 'You should not pity him. Was he not suckled on the blood and sweat of the poor? Why should you pity him, and not my little brothers who spend their days rummaging through refuse looking for rags they can sell?'

'I pity them too,' Viviane said.

'Citoyenne Simon told me this morning that her husband is teaching the little Capet to call his mother "that damned whore",' said Jeanne, another maid, in a tone of frightened wonderment.

'And to spit and trample on the Bible,' Alouette said, laughing.

Viviane herself heard, a few days later, the little boy singing, in his clear piping voice, the words of *La Marseillaise*, which she had first heard the terrible night of the attack on the Tuileries.

> To arms, citizens,
> Form your battalions,
> Let's march, let's march!
> Let an impure blood
> Water our furrows!

It all brought back awful memories for her. Viviane found it hard to sleep, starting awake at the slightest sound, the faint memory of nightmares shadowing her days. She was close to tears at all times, and stupidly clumsy, cutting and bruising herself as she went around her work. She thought of her own lonely childhood, starved of love, willing to do anything her father ordered in the hope of a scrap of praise or affection. If she did not stand the second he came into a room, she was beaten. If she did not remember the right depth of curtsey for each rank of nobility, or did not deploy her spoon in the accepted manner, she was beaten. If she laughed, or cried, or spoke spontaneously, she was beaten.

And when her father was at court, her governess Madame Malfort made sure his methods were followed scrupulously.

No wonder the little Capet sang *La Marseillaise* when he was told to, and cursed God.

Viviane would have too.

*

On the eve of the fourth anniversary of the fall of the Bastille, Jean-Paul Marat was murdered in his bathtub by a young woman named Charlotte Corday.

She was only a year younger than Viviane. She had travelled up by stagecoach from Caen, a journey of four days, purchased a newspaper, a sharp kitchen knife, and a hat with green ribbons, and gone to Marat's house in the Rue des Cordeliers. Turned away several times, she at last gained admittance to his house. Marat spent much of each day in the bath, because of a painful and debilitating skin disease rumoured to be caused by hiding out in the sewers of Paris in the early years of the Revolution. Charlotte pretended to betray the Brissotins of her home town. Marat was pleased, and promised her they would be sent to the guillotine. And so she drew her knife and stabbed him.

The news spread fast. Viviane heard it that night. No-one could talk of anything else. Charlotte was arrested and interrogated. It was impossible she acted alone, most said. A young woman could not act with such force of mind, such ruthlessness. Paris was plunged into mourning. Alouette joined hundreds of other women in holding a wake over Marat's body, crowning him with everlasting flowers. They paraded the blood-stained bathtub in which he had died through the streets of Paris. Odes were read over his heart, which was embalmed and set in an urn at the Cordeliers Club.

'But why?' Viviane asked her friend. 'Marat was no friend of women.'

Alouette said sharply, 'He was the friend of the people!'

As she turned away, Viviane saw a flash of fear in her eyes. She thought she understood. Alouette and other women of the *sans-culottes* could not be associated with the monster that had murdered Marat.

Charlotte Corday was guillotined on the 17th of July. A few days later, Olympe de Gouges was arrested. She had spoken out against Marat and Robespierre and the other Jacobins, and was thought to have sympathy for the imprisoned Brissotins.

'A woman has the right to mount the scaffold, she must also have the right to mount the rostrum,' she had written. Viviane feared that her words were prophetic.

Antoine Simon was enraged at the murder of Jean-Paul Marat. His own lodgings were next door to Marat's in the Rue des Cordeliers and his well-paid job had been won as a result of the journalist's patronage. For hours, the sound of his drunken ranting echoed through the prison. Viviane could hear Louis-Charles crying out for mercy, and was once again overcome with anger.

She did what she could to help. She made rich beef broth and carried it upstairs to Louis-Charles's room, handing it through the door to Citoyenne Simon. When the boy was out in the garden for his daily walk, she stripped the bedding from his low cot and plumped his pillow, then burned some juniper to purify the air. And she took the queen a little nosegay of sweet-smelling flowers, hiding it within the clean chamberpot as she had once hidden her sabots.

Shyly she laid it next to Marie-Antoinette's hand. The queen managed a faint smile, but her eyes returned at once to the gap in the shutters, where she could see just a glimpse of the garden. Marie-Antoinette crouched there all day, in the hope of seeing her little boy.

Viviane picked up the dinner tray – hardly touched – and carried it away with an aching heart.

One evening in early August Viviane was sitting in her usual spot by the kitchen fire, reading Olympe de Gouges's latest pamphlet, released just before her arrest. The outspoken playwright fully expected to be executed, and so had written a mock will: 'I leave my heart to my country, my integrity to men (they need it). My soul to women, not an indifferent gift; my creative genius to authors, they are sure to find it useful . . . my compassion to the ruthless, my philosophy to the persecuted, my spirit to the fanatics, my religion to the atheists, my guileless gaiety to women past their prime, and all the sad debris of an honest fortune to my natural heir, my son, if he survives me.'

What a gift to be given, Viviane thought. *Olympe's indomitable soul and her guileless gaiety.* It lit a spark somewhere deep inside her. She felt suddenly restless and got to her feet, moving about the kitchen and tidying it once more.

The door to the garden opened with a bang, and Ivo came in.

'I met your brother tonight,' he said abruptly.

Viviane had a strange sensation, as if the floor rocked under her feet. 'What?'

'Your brother. I met him tonight.'

A tall white dog with three red feet came bounding through the door. On her side was a large spot, as round as the moon. 'Luna!' Viviane cried and ran forward.

Luna went mad with joy. She leapt and pranced, wagging her tail, then sprang into the air and put her only front paw on Viviane's shoulder so that she could lick her face. Viviane embraced her, caressing her soft ears, weeping with surprise and gladness. Then she saw that Pierrick had come in with the dog, and flew to him, embracing him. 'But how . . . where? Oh, Pierrick!'

All was tumult for a moment.

'I wanted you so badly,' Viviane cried. 'Where have you been?'

'Working at the opera as a stage hand. I create the fiery pits of hell where the villains end up.' Pierrick's familiar cheeky grin. How she had missed it.

'But how? I don't understand.'

'I needed work, and they needed someone happy to play with fire.'

'I didn't know where you were, or how to find you. Why didn't you come to the prison, or write to me?'

His grin faltered. 'It was too dangerous. Anyone associated with an aristo was in danger of being arrested themselves. Besides, I had to look after Luna.' He patted the dog's head, and she licked his hand, tail wagging madly.

'I didn't know where to go once I got out, or what to do . . . I was all alone.' Viviane had to mop her eyes with the corner of her apron.

'But how did you end up here?' Pierrick looked around at the dark, cavernous kitchen, with its vast medieval hearths and heavy oaken beams.

'The queen,' Viviane faltered, 'and the children of France.'

'You came to serve them?'

'To help if I could. I didn't know where else to go.'

'You told me you were a peasant girl,' Ivo said accusingly. 'You lied to me. I helped you get papers. False papers! You're an aristocrat! If anyone knew . . .'

'I'm sorry. You must know I couldn't tell anyone the truth. Besides, I didn't want . . .'

I didn't want to be a duchess anymore, she was going to say.

Ivo gave her no chance. 'I thought we were friends. But everything you've told me is a lie. You've put my neck at risk.'

'I didn't know what else to do.' Viviane's words tumbled out as she tried desperately to explain. 'Besides, it wasn't all a lie. I did grow up at Belisima, in the kitchen, with Pierrick, and he really is my brother, or my half-brother at least . . .'

'What?' Pierrick stiffened. His laughter died away. 'What did you say?'

Viviane pressed both hands against her mouth. 'Oh, I'm sorry,' she faltered. 'Your mother made me swear not to tell you.'

'What do you mean?' Pierrick demanded. 'Not . . .'

As realisation dawned on him, horror grew on his face. 'No! It's not true! My mother would never . . .'

'It was not her fault,' Viviane cried. 'She never wanted anything to do with him. But our father always took what he wanted, you know that.'

'He is not my father!' Pierrick shouted.

'That is why she was given the job as cook . . .'

'To pay her off?'

'No, no, to support . . .'

'Me, the bastard child.'

Viviane took a deep breath. 'I'm so sorry, Pierrick. I so wanted to tell you. Your mother made me promise on my mother's grave. She told me the night the mole-catcher's house was burned ... there were three children, all born so close together, you and me and the mole-catcher's daughter ...'

'You, the marquis's daughter, given everything, and me, the bastard, given nothing.'

'That's not true,' Viviane said. 'You, at least, were loved.'

For a moment, Pierrick stared at her. His face was burning. Then he shook his head dazedly. 'No. It can't be true. You're wrong. Or lying.' He turned to go.

'Oh, Pierrick, please ... I'm sorry ...' Viviane reached out her hands to him, but he jerked away from her as if she was made of poison. He gave a quick whistle, and Luna leapt to his side. In a moment, they were gone.

'I can't believe it,' Ivo said. 'You lied to me ... you risked my neck ... I don't even know your real name!'

'I am Héloïse-Rozenn-Viviane de la Faitaud de Ravoisier,' she told him. 'Or I was. Before they made me marry the Duc de Savageaux.'

He shook his head. 'A duchess,' he whispered. 'Here in my kitchen. They will kill me if they find out.'

'I'm sorry,' she tried to say, but he turned and ran out after Pierrick.

Viviane stood, silent and trembling. She heard the faint clatter of sabots outside the kitchen door, and looked that way. Had someone been listening? She went slowly, as if struck down with an ague. But when she opened the door, no-one was there.

At two o'clock in the morning, Viviane and the other maids were woken by the tramp of marching feet on the stairs.

Ten minutes later, shawls flung over their nightgowns, they watched silently as Marie-Antoinette walked down the steps, between heavily armed guards. Dressed in black, she looked thin and hunched. She carried a small bundle in one hand.

'Where are you taking her?' Viviane asked one of the guards, who glanced at her.

'To the Conciergerie,' he answered.

Viviane bit her lip. The Conciergerie was known as the most pestilent of the prisons.

As Marie-Antoinette came down the steep spiral staircase, a guard insolently blew his pipe smoke into her face. She stumbled and knocked her head sharply against the stone beam.

'Are you hurt?' Micholet asked, putting out his hand to help her.

Marie-Antoinette shook her head. 'Nothing can hurt me now.'

25

The Forbidden City
6 August – 5 September 1793

'For all their fine words, you've got to admit we're little better than prisoners,' David grumbled. 'It is ridiculous! We've been in China for seven weeks now, and still we have not been permitted to visit any gardens.'

'I haven't seen a single peony,' John said wistfully.

And I've not seen a single rose, let alone one as red as blood, David thought.

'They promise us everything we desire, but do not have the slightest intention of delivering,' Scotty said. 'It does not bode well for our embassy.'

'It is most humiliating that they continue to call our gifts to the emperor "tribute",' said Anderson, the valet. 'And his lordship "the bearer of tribute"!'

'And they expect us to eat our dinner with nothing more than a couple of sticks!' Dr Gillan exclaimed.

The men were seated cross-legged on the floor, trying to convey morsels of food to their mouths with chopsticks. There was no table or chairs or cloth or knife or fork or spoon, only a few low tables on which the men could rest their bowls of food.

Their dining parlour was the main chamber of a wooden junk, one of a small fleet moored along the banks of the River Pei Ho. Lanterns of coloured paper bobbed from the masts of the junks, their light reflecting in ripples of vermilion on the water. The embassy's Chinese entourage were camped on the banks of the river, in round tents with high pointed roofs. It was nearly as noisy at night as it was during the day, with shouted orders, arguments, strange high-pitched music, the beating of drums and the striking of gongs.

The last few weeks had passed slowly, with many small misunderstandings. It had taken several days to transfer all the cargo from the British ships to the junks, which were dragged up the river by teams of half-naked Chinese men, harnessed like mules with heavy wooden collars and leather straps.

Meanwhile, Lord Macartney and Sir George had endless meetings with mandarins, some of whom were eager to please, while others were pompous and suspicious. The ambassador had been angered by the banners fluttering from the junks, which read 'Tribute-Bearer to Great Emperor'. He had protested, only to be met by shrugs. Gifts to the emperor were always described as tribute, and those who carried them as tribute-bearers, they said, not seeming to understand the insult to the ambassador and King George.

Lord Macartney was also perturbed by the attitude of the Imperial Legate deputised to attend them. His name was Zhengrui, and he found it necessary to constantly instruct the ambassador on the rigid etiquette of the Celestial Court.

According to Zhengrui, there were eight salutations of respect in China. The lowest was the *kung-show*, in which hands were clasped together and raised high. The next degree of respect was the *tsa-yih*, which meant to bow from the waist with hands clasped. Third was *ta-tseen*, the bending of the knee. Then came the act of kneeling, called the *kwei*. The fifth act of respect was the *ko-tow*, which meant to kneel and knock one's forehead against the ground. The *san-kow* meant to strike one's head three times. To give the seventh degree of respect, *luh-kow*, one must kneel and knock one's head three times, rise to one's feet, then kneel once more and knock the head three times again.

The highest act of respect was the *san-kewi-kew-kow*, in which the supplicant knelt three times, each time knocking his head thrice against the earth for a grand total of nine. That was reserved only for Heaven and his son, the emperor. Marco Polo had called this ritual abasement 'the adoration'.

Lord Macartney was amenable to being taught the first four obeisances, but he refused to lower his forehead to the floor. He made some joke about being too stout. Zhengrui, who was far stouter, was most displeased. He shouted something in Mandarin, which David took to mean, 'You must!' Then Zhengrui dropped to his knees, bent forward till his silk-clad bottom was lifted high in the air, and banged his forehead to the ground again and again. Every now and again he looked up, shouting. Ripples of stifled laughter ran through the watching men and even Lord Macartney had trouble maintaining his composure.

When Zhengrui heaved himself to his feet once more, his face was suffused with rage. He said something in rapid-fire Mandarin, then swept out of the room without waiting to be dismissed. His servant had to race to pick up his fan and cinnabar snuff bottle, left discarded on the table. He then hurried from the room, bowing so low and so often it was as if he sought to demonstrate to the British how it should be done.

'What did the Legate say?' Lord Macartney asked Father Li, who inclined his own head and said briefly, 'The emperor must not be insulted.'

'It is hard to imagine an act of more profound submission,' Lord Macartney said to Sir George, frowning. 'And there is no evidence that such subordination leads to the loosening of trade restrictions in any way. The Dutch have been *ko-tow*ing for years and haven't won a single concession. Indeed, I heard the Dutch ambassador returned home to Holland in utter ignominy after *ko-tow*ing to the sound of the emperor's name, his letters, his empty throne, abasing himself in every possible way for no gain whatsoever.'

'It is a vexed question,' Sir George replied. 'We do not want to cause offence and so jeopardise our mission.'

Lord Macartney thrust out his jaw. 'I will not do it unless a Chinese official equivalent to my own rank stands before a portrait of His Majesty the King and prostrates himself in the same way!'

'That they will not do,' Sir George answered.

'Then they cannot expect me to do so. I shall write to the emperor and say so!'

Lord Macartney and Sir George had gone that very evening to meet with Zhengrui and another high-ranking mandarin, Liang Kentang, the viceroy of Zhili. They had been carried away from the junks in gilded palanquins.

David could not help wishing that he had been able to accompany them. The junks, picturesque as they were, moved at only five miles an hour on a river that meandered back and forth through plains planted with millet. Any attempt to disembark was met with vigorous denials from the soldiers who guarded the fleet. If David insisted, he was watched with such a degree of suspicion and mistrust, he felt uncomfortable. Besides, there was little point. Sir Joseph Banks was interested in tea plantations and rare flowers, not millet.

The ambassador and his secretary returned soon after sunset, and Sir George came with his son Tom to tell the men the outcome of the meeting.

'We are to see more of China than we expected,' he said with a rather forced smile. 'It seems the emperor Kien Long is not in Peking anymore. He has retired to his summer palace, up in the mountains at Zhe-hol in Tartary.'

'Does that mean we do not get to see Peking after all?' David asked.

'Zhengrui did his best to make sure we did not have a chance to see the capital,' Sir George said. 'We think it was the emperor's intention to keep us away from Peking. But His Excellency insisted that some of the gifts were too delicate to be transported through the mountains and asked for a residence in Peking to keep the more precious items.'

'Zhengrui was not pleased about that!' Tom said, grinning.

'His Excellency would not be bullied, however.'

'The new official interpreter from Canton was no use at all,' Tom cried. 'The Legate would say, "After touching the ground with your forehead before the Great Emperor, you may lay your tributes to his greatness at his feet." And His Excellency would reply, "We have travelled many miles to bring gifts from one great sovereign to another," and the new interpreter would translate it to, "We have come from afar to pay homage by knocking our forehead to the ground." I think he didn't realise that Mr Plum and I could understand him.'

'He will be sent back to Canton,' his father said. 'We cannot have an interpreter so in awe of the mandarins that he misrepresents our words.'

'I'll translate for you, Father,' Tom said.

Sir George ruffled his fine brown hair. 'And a far better job of it you would do too, my boy. I am afraid, however, that the Legate would find it too demeaning, having a boy of thirteen as his mouthpiece. We will just need to rely on Mr Plum, and the Jesuit missionaries.'

'I was hoping we'd get to see inside the Forbidden City,' John said wistfully. 'I'd like to catch a glimpse of the emperor's concubines!'

'No-one sees the concubines,' Dr Gillan said. 'The only men allowed inside the Forbidden City are eunuchs, you fool.'

'At least we'll get to see the Great Wall of China,' David said. 'And, if we are lucky, the emperor's gardens!'

The embassy reached Peking on the 21st of August.

Lord Macartney and Sir George and his son were carried in red lacquer palanquins, gaudily painted with golden dragons, but the rest of the entourage were crammed into common hired carts, with a roof of coarse straw matting. The horses were raw-boned and harnessed with rope, and no attempt had been made to match one to the other. It took seventy carts to carry them all, with four hundred porters trudging ahead, carrying the baggage.

'This is not how the British embassy should be received!' Anderson cried. 'Where is the pomp and spectacle of one great nation welcoming another? Are we not the first nation in the west and China the first nation in the east?'

David and Scotty and a few of the other young men preferred to ride, and – after a great deal of argy-bargy complicated by the language divide – were at last given some short rough-coated ponies to ride. It was a relief to be free of the carts, though, which had no springs of any kind, and David relished the chance to see more of the countryside.

Thousands of people had gathered to watch the procession. Some were struck with wonder and fear, hiding their children behind their gowns. Many others pointed and made unpleasant scoffing sounds. Some even spat.

'Why do they stare so?' David asked uncomfortably.

'They think you devils,' Father Li explained, in his oddly accented Latin. 'In Chinese theatre, only devils wear such tight clothes, or have red hair. And your eyes are wild beast eyes, devil eyes.'

'Maybe I should wear tinted spectacles,' David muttered, and fixed his gaze on the dusty road.

At last the city walls of Peking reared above them, nearly fifty feet tall and immensely thick. One could have galloped a horse along the wall's broad top. As the ambassador approached, he was welcomed by the ritual firing of guns which cast a pall of smoke over the scene. The mandarins led the way into the city, their servants shading them with silk parasols, soldiers keeping back the crowds with whips.

The road was lined with shops decorated with tall gilded pillars and intricately carved woodwork. Long banners hung with Chinese characters swayed in the breeze. Riding on his pony, David was able to see over the heads of the teeming crowds and down the alleyways, lined with rows of dilapidated grey houses with grey tiles. They were so low and uniform, and so lacking in windows, it looked like an encampment of army tents.

Men with long bamboo poles resting on their shoulders carried straw baskets filled with persimmons and dragon fruit. An old pedlar with a weathered face and no teeth sat behind a table piled high with desiccated bats, dried snakes in stiff coils, animal horns, ginseng and severed tiger paws. In flimsy street-stalls, blind fortune-tellers read horoscopes, singers warbled to the accompaniment of strangely shaped stringed instruments, and storytellers beguiled their audiences with tales of love, betrayal and reunion.

For the first time, David saw women walking freely in the streets. Their faces were painted white, and the middle part of their lips delineated with a narrow vermilion strip. Their black hair was drawn high into elaborate hairstyles decorated with jewelled pins and flowers. To his relief, their feet were not mere stumps, though they wore ugly wooden platform shoes, shaped like horses' hooves, that raised them a good two inches above the ground. He rode up to the palanquin where Father Li sat, and asked him – in his best Latin – why these women had not been crippled by their feet being bound.

'Tartars,' Father Li replied. He flashed David a proud look. 'I am Tartar. We do not bind our women's feet.'

'You are to be applauded for your wisdom,' David said, and the priest bowed to him.

Ahead, David saw a glimpse of a high grey wall, and above it a roof of varnished yellow tiles with gently upturned ends, adorned with an array of fanciful figures, shining like gold under the brilliant sun. His heart thumped hard.

'Look,' he said to Scotty. 'The Forbidden City.'

They passed a set of immense double doors, painted lacquer red and decorated with rows of gilded studs.

'Nine rows of nine,' Father Li said. 'It is the emperor's number for it sounds like "jiu" which means everlasting. He wears nine dragons on his robes, and there are, I have heard, nine-thousand-nine-hundred-and-ninety-nine rooms in the Forbidden City. Only one gate does not have the nine rows of nine studs. That is the Flowery Gate, which has nine rows of eight studs. That is the gate through which the dead pass.'

'May we go in?' Tom asked ebulliently. 'I'd so love to see inside.'

'No,' Father Li replied.

Then the Forbidden City was lost behind them, and soon the city of Peking too.

The Englishmen slept that night in cramped and crowded conditions in a small ramshackle house, much to Lord Macartney's displeasure and his valet's horror. Anderson did his best to make his master comfortable, but his feelings could be discerned by the stiffness of his back and the force with which he thumped down the chamber-pot.

The next day they were conducted to the Garden of Perfect Brightness, the emperor's country residence outside Peking. David felt an almost painful eagerness. At last – eleven months after leaving Great Britain – he was to see a Chinese garden for the first time.

The palace was composed of many small pavilions with sweeping curved eaves. Small courtyards centred around a single fantastically shaped rock, or one ancient magnolia tree, pruned so hard it was half its natural size. A circular gateway led to another courtyard, containing an oblong pond and a stand of bamboo arranged to cast delicate shadows against a white wall. A tiny wooden pavilion on a bare rock overlooked the pond, like a pagoda in miniature.

It was not what David had expected. He had imagined something like the Jardin du Roi in Paris, vast gardens laid out in formal patterns, with lawns and gracious old trees and mixed herbaceous borders overflowing with the gorgeously coloured, and as yet unseen, flowers of China. These small, spare, secret gardens, each centred around a single tree or rock or pool, unsettled him. He did not understand the design principle.

Beyond the walled gardens off the pavilions was a vast lake that stretched towards blue undulations of mountains beyond. An extraordinary marble bridge of seventeen arches vaulted across the water to an island with a temple. In the distance, a tall pagoda lifted tiers of tilted roofs to the sky. A long, covered walkway painted in emerald, scarlet and gold zigzagged though the park. Father Li said it had been built so that the dowager empress could walk in rain, snow or blistering heat.

'But why did they not make it in a straight line?' David asked.

'Evil spirits can only fly in straight lines and so the zigzag confounds them,' the priest answered.

All was mysterious and strange, with poetic names like the Hall of Dispelling Clouds or the Garden of Virtue and Harmony. It took hours to walk round. David saw a pond laden with lotus leaves and flowers, but otherwise all was woods, lakes, rocks and temples.

David asked Father Li where he could find roses growing, and the priest frowned at him. 'Roses are unfortunate,' he said, in his precise Latin. 'We Chinese consider they bring ill fortune. Because of the thorns. They bring hurt and suffering, and so are planted on graves, not in gardens.'

David felt such a pang of bitter disappointment he had to remind himself that Viviane was married to someone else. She was not pining in her château tower, waiting for him to return to her with a fabled blood-red rose. She had long forgotten him.

Viviane was arrested on the 5th of September.

The officers named her Héloïse-Rozenn-Viviane de Gagnon, daughter of the Marquis de Valaine, widow of the Duc de Savageaux. As she was led away, a small bundle of belongings in her hand, Alouette spat in her face.

Viviane was taken to the Conciergerie, on the Île de la Cité in the middle of the River Seine. It was a beautiful palace of pale stone, with steeply pointed spires. The Seine rippled past, smooth as green silk. Behind, the towers and spires and flying buttresses of the Notre-Dame Cathedral were silhouetted against the sky.

The beauty of the day was lost as soon as she stepped through the doors. Beyond was a maze of dark cramped rooms and corridors that smelt of sweat and tobacco smoke and sewage. Viviane could hear moans and cries, and the barking of ferocious dogs.

She was interrogated in a small, bare cell.

'Are you Citoyenne Gagnon, the former Duchesse de Savageaux?'

'I do not use that name. I was married against my will and hated my husband.'

'But you were married to the Duc de Savageaux?'

'Yes. For a short time only. He died some years ago.'

'And you were in service to the widow Capet?'

'For a short time only.' Viviane shivered with cold and rubbed her arms.

'But you went to serve her again at the Temple?'

'Yes. I needed to find work. I had nowhere else to go.'

Viviane wondered who it was who had betrayed her. Was it Alouette, eavesdropping the night Viviane admitted who she really was? Or Ivo, perhaps? He had not returned to the tower; she had not seen him again. Was he so angry at her deception that he would betray her? Or perhaps he was just trying to save his own neck.

She could not believe that it was Pierrick. He would never do such a thing.

The questions continued a long time. Viviane answered honestly. It was a relief, really, not to have to guard her every word and inflection. And it seemed this official knew it all anyway.

But then the tenor of the questions changed.

'Are you acquainted with Citizen Michonis?'

Viviane was surprised. 'I know him by sight – he was superintendent of the prison. But I have never spoken to him.'

'Did you not suggest that he let the young Capet keep his dog?'

Her surprise grew. 'Well, yes, but . . .'

'So you have spoken to him.'

'I did not speak to him in particular. I spoke to all the men there.'

'Because you felt pity for the Capet.'

'Yes. I would feel pity for any little boy wrested from the arms of his mother.'

As the questions continued, Viviane became more and more puzzled. They asked her about the flowers she had brought the queen.

'Were they carnations?' the man demanded.

Viviane shook her head. 'No, just a few violets I gathered from the garden.'

They asked her how she knew the Chevalier de Rougeville. Viviane shook her head and said she did not know him. They asked if she had ever passed notes to the queen, or plotted to help her escape. Viviane admitted she had passed news to the king's valet, but said that it was only ever information she had heard from the town criers.

'I never tried to help the queen escape,' Viviane said. 'How could I? I barely ever saw her.'

The official seemed to get frustrated. His questions grew terser. But eventually he threw down his pen. 'You say you know nothing about the recent attempt to rescue the widow Capet?'

He spoke with bitter irony.

'No!' Viviane cried. 'Someone tried to rescue her? From here?' She gestured at the thick walls, the heavy oaken door barred with iron. 'But who would do such a thing?'

Then she remembered how closely he had questioned her about Superintendent Michonis.

'Did they succeed?' she asked quietly.

He smiled. 'Prisoner 280 is safe in her cell. No-one escapes from the Conciergerie.'

When Viviane was taken to her cell, she could understand why. Each corridor was blocked off by a huge iron door, with another door – only three feet high – set within it. The iron gate was manned by a turnkey. As she was hustled along the corridor, there was another iron door every ten paces or so, each being unlocked and relocked as she passed through. Guards were accompanied by huge mastiffs, their ribs showing through their mangy skin. They barked like the hounds of hell.

'Do you have any money?' the guard asked her.

'A little.'

'A bed will cost you eighteen sous a day.'

Viviane blanched. 'What happens if I can't afford it?'

'Then you sleep on the floor in the dungeons.'

She hesitated. He said, with a certain rough kindness, 'It is damp and filthy and infested with rats and lice down there. Best pay for a bed if you have any money at all. Besides, it won't be for long.'

'No?' she asked with a certain faint hope.

'No. The Revolutionary Tribunal is very efficient.' He hesitated, then said in a lower voice, 'There is a reason why they call the Conciergerie the antechamber to the guillotine.'

Numbly Viviane agreed to pay for a bed, and was shown to a long dark cell. There were rows of cots, each furnished with a stained mattress stuffed with straw and a thin woollen blanket that smelt vile. Crude wooden stools and a bucket in the corner were the only other furnishings.

Her cell looked out on the Seine. Viviane pressed her face to the window, desperate for the sight of the sky, for a glimpse of a green tree. A boy was standing on the Pont au Change below, waving a sheaf of newspapers in his hand. His shrill voice piped out, 'Convention votes to make terror the order of the day! The people of Paris want blood? We shall give them blood!'

26

The Shining River
5 September – 1 October 1793

'Look!' David stood up in his stirrups and pointed. 'There it is.'

Above them a long serpent of stone twisted along the mountain ramparts, writhing down precipitous cliffs and climbing up to great square guard towers and smaller watchtowers. Beyond, sharp mountains like jagged teeth.

A chill ran over David's body, raising the hairs on his skin.

'The Great Wall,' he whispered.

'What a stupendous piece of work,' Lord Macartney exclaimed, moved to awe for the first time since arriving in China. The mandarins were surprised, considering the dilapidated old barricade to be of little interest.

'But it is two thousand years old,' David exclaimed. 'And more than five thousand miles long.'

Sir George set his surveyors to measuring the ramparts and parapets, and testing the geology of the stones. The Chinese guards were wary and suspicious, with some reason. David had to admit the British officers had surreptitiously been taking notes of the country's defences and armaments at every step of their journey.

David and Scotty and a few of the other men set out to climb to the top, accompanied as always by Father Li and a bevy of disgruntled mandarins.

The steps were so steep, the back of David's legs were soon aching. Panting and laughing, they scrambled at last to the highest watchtower. It had the most extraordinary view across steep mountains and valleys, the stone wall scaling the peaks as far as the eye could see.

It was no wonder the wall was called the Stone Dragon, he thought. One could almost imagine it had once flown the skies and now only slept, waiting to be awoken again.

David stood as long as he was permitted, watching the shadow of the Great Wall stretch long. At last, his arms tugged on by three or four different mandarins, he allowed himself to be hustled back down the rough, uneven steps. As he left the wall, he bent and picked up a fragment of broken stone and put it in his pocket.

That night, the sky was so clear David could see the crenelated shape of the watchtowers silhouetted against a sky luminous with stars. The dazzling curve of the Milky Way arched above the long twisting spine of the stone dragon below.

'What do the Chinese call the Milky Way?' he asked Father Li, in careful Latin.

The priest looked up, a faint smile on his face. 'The Silvery River.'

'That's beautiful.'

'There is an old story,' Father Li said. 'A young man fell in love with the goddess of heaven's seventh daughter and married her secretly. The two lovers were very happy, and had two children. When the goddess discovered her daughter had married a mere mortal, however, she was angry. She dragged her daughter back to heaven.

'The young man's ox spoke to him. "Kill me," it said, "and disguise yourself in my skin, and then you will be able to climb up to heaven and find your beloved." The young man did as he was told and, carrying his two children, ascended into the starry vault of the sky. But the goddess saw him and was angry. Pulling out her hairpin, she scratched a long slit across the sky to keep the two lovers apart forever.'

With one hand, he mimicked slicing the sky apart.

'Once a year, though, on the seventh night of the seventh moon, all the magpies in the world take pity on the lovers' sorrow and fly up to form a bridge so they may be together again, just for one night.'

David's eyes were unaccountably hot, his throat thick. He rose to his feet and went to stand at the edge of the clearing, looking out into the darkness. He found he was rubbing the pit of the scar on his left hand.

'You feel story is just like yours?' Father Li asked softly. 'You too have been parted from your beloved?'

David could not answer.

At last, on 7 September, the embassy reached Zhe-hol. Crowds of Tartars came to stare. They did not laugh, like the people of Peking had done. They were suspicious, hostile. Hundreds of monks with shaved heads and burnt-orange robes pressed close to the entourage, carrying smoking joss sticks, ringing bells and chanting. The sound was deep, guttural, outlandish. David was fascinated but also afraid. They were only a few hundred men, a very long way from home, surrounded by thousands of unwelcoming strangers. If the emperor chose, he could have them slaughtered where they stood and news of their death would not reach Britain for another year.

There was no grand procession, no formal reception. The British embassy was shown to a cold, bleak pavilion and left alone. Lord Macartney was told to make his own way to meet with the emperor's chief minister, a handsome young man rumoured to be his lover. Offended, Macartney refused.

The next day, their rations were reduced practically to bare bones. Lord Macartney ordered all the men to refuse to taste a morsel, and sent a formal complaint. Within twenty minutes, trays of steaming delicacies were sent, as if the kitchen had been prepared and waiting but forbidden to serve. Everyone was angry and affronted.

Every day the mandarins tried to convince the ambassador to perform the adoration at the emperor's feet. Proudly Lord Macartney told them he fell to his knees only before God.

'The emperor is the son of Heaven,' Father Li told them. 'He is God incarnate.'

Lord Macartney gazed at him in astonishment.

'Or so it is believed,' Father Li said with his usual composure.

On the tenth day of the eighth lunar month in the fifty-eighth year of his rule, the Great Emperor and Son of Heaven, Kien Long, at last permitted the English ambassador and his entourage to appear before the celestial court.

They were roused at three o'clock in the morning and hurried through pitch darkness, only the occasional paper lantern showing the way. For an hour they stumbled through the mist-wreathed night, in wild confusion, like children playing blindman's bluff. Then they were left to wait in the cold and dark for hours, stamping their feet and blowing into their hands, muttering testily to each other.

At dawn, a long procession of minor nobles and court officials rode in upon horses, their rank expressed in the embroidered panels upon their robes and the tiers of the jewelled finials upon their hats. They were accompanied by standard-bearers holding aloft long silken banners.

Then the emperor was carried into view, seated in a gilded chair borne by sixteen men. He was thin, a little hunched, with smooth skin and dark eyes. He wore a loose robe of yellow silk embroidered with five-clawed dragons and stylised clouds, mountains and waves. On his head was a black velvet cap decorated with pearls and peacock feathers. A servant held a long-handled parasol above his head, while musicians playing their strange instruments followed behind. As he came into view, every single man in the crowd dropped to his knees and banged his head to the ground again and again.

With great dignity, Lord Macartney dropped to one knee, removed his hat and bowed his head. David and the other men did the same. The emperor ignored them.

The Son of Heaven was carried within a vast vaulted tent of yellow silk, and Lord Macartney, Sir George, Father Li and Tom were ushered inside. The other Englishmen had to remain outside. There was a great feast, and performances by wrestlers, acrobats and tightrope walkers. David, however, was only interested in what was happening within. He and Scotty lurked by the tent entrance, sneaking glances inside. He saw Lord Macartney led up the stairs, where he bent his knee and handed, in a casket set with diamonds, the formal letter written by King George. The emperor passed it to a mandarin with a polite smile, then offered Macartney a ceremonial sceptre in return. Speeches were made, translated awkwardly between the ambassador, Father Li and one of the court officials who seemed to add a great many unnecessary genuflexions and prostrations.

When the emperor heard Sir George's son had learned to speak Mandarin, he beckoned Tom forward and bade him speak. His back very straight, his hands behind his back, Tom said a few words without a single stammer or stumble. The emperor gave his first genuine smile, and unfastened from his belt a golden purse with the figure of the five-clawed dragon embroidered upon it. Tom went red, and took it with shy thanks.

No formal meeting was granted to the ambassador.

That banquet, shared with many hundreds of other vassals and tribute bearers, was the closest Lord Macartney came to the emperor. He continued to try for a private audience but was politely but firmly rebuffed.

David and the other men, meanwhile, amused themselves by riding around the vast imperial park, which was named the Garden of Innumerable Trees.

'It should be called the Garden of Innumerable Temples,' Scotty muttered, after they were shown to yet another little pavilion set on the edge of a pool filled with lotus flowers. 'Why does the emperor need so many temples?'

'Many gods, many temples,' Father Li replied rather curtly, when asked.

David spied a most unusually shaped mountain peak on the horizon. It looked like a monumental obelisk, balanced precariously on the edge of a huge boulder. At once he wanted to explore it, but the mandarins shook their heads in a most emphatic manner.

'It is called the Thumb of God,' Father Li translated. 'It is sacred. Not for white devils to climb.'

'Is that what they call us?' David said.

'Of course,' the priest responded.

Some of the pavilions held the imperial collection of curiosities. Lord Macartney was mortified to realise that the emperor had all kinds of toys and clocks and music boxes, so that the gifts of Great Britain must seem rather unexceptional.

Each evening was spent attending stiff formal banquets and watching theatrical performances. The actors wore masks on both the front and backs of their heads so that they may never be seen to turn their backs on the emperor. Afterwards there were fireworks, which filled the air with clouds of smoke.

During all this time, the emperor did not speak more than polite formalities to the British ambassador or any of his entourage. All of Lord Macartney's requests for further meetings were denied. At last he wrote the emperor a letter, and asked Father Li to deliver it. Dressed in Western-style clothes, Father Li did his best but was seized and roughed up by the guards. In the end, Lord Macartney's letter was delivered and polite responses made, but no further meeting with the emperor was allowed. Discomfited, the embassy quit Zhe-hol and returned to Peking, where they were greeted with inexpressible joy by those who had been left behind. They had been kept as prisoners, Dr Dinwiddie reported, not permitted to even look over the wall of their residency.

On the first day of October, almost exactly one year after they had sailed from Portsmouth with such high hopes, the British embassy was told it was time for them to return to England. Everyone was startled and upset.

Lord Macartney protested. 'What about all our gifts?' he said rather petulantly at one point.

The next day word came that the emperor would inspect the tribute, since it meant so much to the ambassador. Kien Long looked the gifts over with an unsmiling face. 'Such things,' he said, 'are fit only for a child's amusement.'

On the third of October, Lord Macartney received a long letter from the emperor. Father Li read the scroll aloud, translating the Chinese characters into his precise Latin. Slowly, and with many hesitations, Tom then translated his words into English.

'We, by the Grace of Heaven, Emperor, instruct the king of England to take note of our charge. Although your country, O King, lies in the far oceans, yet inclining your heart towards civilisation, you have specially sent . . .'

'Wait just one moment,' Lord Macartney said, his face darkening. 'Did the emperor just say that *China* is civilisation? Implying Europe is not?'

'In Mandarin, the word for China and civilisation is the same,' Tom explained.

'Go on,' the ambassador said.

'You have specially sent an envoy to our Court to *ko-tow* and present congratulations for the imperial birthday,' Tom translated. Macartney's frown deepened, but he did not interrupt again. A long passage of formal courtesies followed, listing all the gifts and kindnesses lavished on the Englishmen.

One by one, all of the ambassador's requests were denied. 'How can we go so far as to change the regulations of the Celestial Empire because of the request of one man – of you, O King?'

Finally, the emperor's letter concluded, 'The Celestial Empire, ruling all within the four seas, concentrates on carrying out the affairs of government and does not value rare and precious things.'

'Now you, O King, have sent us gifts of tribute from a long distance and offered them with profound sincerity. Therefore, I ordered my officials to accept them. The virtue and power of the Celestial Dynasty is known, however, throughout the world, to many other kingdoms who have also come to render homage to us. All kinds of precious things are sent to us over mountain and sea. We have never valued such things, nor do we have the slightest need of your country's produce.'

'Therefore, O King, as regards your request to send someone to remain at the capital, it is neither in harmony with the regulations of the Celestial Empire nor of any advantage to you. Hence we have commanded your tribute envoys to return safely home. You, O King, should act in conformity with our wishes by strengthening your loyalty to us and swearing perpetual obedience so as to ensure your country continues to share the blessings of peace.'

There was a long silence. Then Lord Macartney said, in a shaking voice, 'We cannot take such a missive back to His Majesty. It must be moderated in tone, softened somehow. It is an offence!'

He looked around at the small group of Englishmen gathered in the pavilion, with its red-lacquered doors and latticework, its rafters carved with writhing dragons and demons. 'No word of this must leak out, else we shall be at war!'

27

Practising Dying
8 October – 17 December 1793

Viviane's twenty-fifth birthday was a sad and lonely affair.

She spent the day the same as every other day. A scanty break-fast – black bread and a little bitter coffee – and then she walked around and around the small courtyard set aside for the women's exercise yard, listening to the gossip and rumours.

'A law has been passed to make it illegal for any woman not to wear the tricolour cockade. I'm almost glad I'm in here, so no-one will see me dressing like a barmaid!'

'Did you know the queen's little spaniel followed her here from the Temple, and is now sitting outside the prison gates? The guards keep driving it away with kicks and threats, but it keeps coming back, poor little mite. You think they'd let it in to comfort her.'

'I heard they've been to the Temple and cross-questioned His Majesty the King for hours upon end. How could they be so cruel? He's only eight years old.'

Viviane listened, but did not speak. She feared some of the women were spies who reported conversations back to the gaolers.

The day ended with another sparse meal, and the clunk of iron bars being bolted.

Viviane had been permitted a few personal belongings. She kept the miniature of her mother, the rose-enamelled ring David had given her, and his signet ring hidden on her in case of theft. She did not know why she guarded these things so carefully. Her mother was dead, David was dead – what did any of it matter?

Yet somehow it did.

Sometimes Viviane saw the queen's thin white face peering out of the window of her cell. She was never permitted outside with the other women. Her trial would begin soon, it was rumoured.

On the morning of the 14th of October, the queen was taken from her cell and accompanied through the dark echoing corridors to the Revolutionary Tribunal. The news flew fast through the prison exercise yard. Many women wept.

That afternoon, the guards were mobbed for news.

'What happened, what did she say?'

'There were a great many accusations,' one of the guards said hesitantly. 'She denied them all.'

'She was accused of molesting her son,' another said, brutally frank. 'The little Capet swore to it.'

Cries of horror and alarm. 'Such a thing is impossible,' one grey-haired lady said.

'What could they have done to His Majesty to make him say such a thing?'

'What did Her Majesty say?'

'The woman Capet did not answer. When she was pressed, she said she had not replied because Nature itself refuses to answer such a charge laid against a mother,' the guard said. 'She turned to the crowd and appealed to any mothers most piteously. Quite a few called out it was a damned shame, and the proceedings should be stopped. They were made to sit down and be quiet.'

A loud buzz of conversation.

'What would make him say such a thing?' one woman said.

'He's just a little boy,' Viviane cried. 'He'd say anything they told him to!'

She found she was so choked up she could not say another a word. She went back to her cell, lay on her damp stinking mattress, and tried to stop shivering.

The queen was condemned to death, and taken from the Conciergerie in an old wooden cart. Viviane watched with her face pressed against the bars, wiping away tears with her sleeve. Marie-Antoinette was dressed in a shabby white gown, and her hair had been roughly cropped. Her hands were tightly bound behind her back. Huge crowds lined the bridge and the street. They shouted and shook their fists and spat at her. She sat calmly, her head a little bent.

The cart turned the corner and was gone from Viviane's sight. Once again, she knew the moment the blade of the guillotine fell by the great shout of exultation that echoed over the city.

Later that night, one of the guards told her the queen's little dog Mignon had followed the tumbril the whole way to the guillotine and had begun to howl when the queen's head had fallen. A soldier had run the spaniel through with his bayonet, shouting, 'So perish all that mourn an aristocrat.'

Viviane did not know if it was true, but it had made her cry all the harder.

After the execution of the queen, the pace of prisoners taken to the guillotine accelerated.

The former deputies of the National Convention were executed on the 31st of October. It took only thirty-six minutes to chop off all twenty-two heads.

Olympe de Gouges followed a few days later, doing her best to be gallant.

Women were taken to the blade still breastfeeding, their child wrested from their arms moments before they knelt to lay their heads upon the block. Sometimes the scaffold was so slippery with blood, people fell as they stepped forward. Some people died in the overcrowded tumbrils on their way through the screaming crowds. Their corpses were decapitated anyway. The Duc d'Orléans – the man who had financed the revolution – died in the same way as his cousin, the king. The former mayor of Paris was guillotined, and a former mistress of King Louis XV, and a man who had taught his dog to howl at the word 'republican', and his dog too.

In the midst of all this madness, a solemn procession of young girls clad in white, laurel wreaths on their hair, burning torches in their hands, crossed the Pont Notre-Dame and marched, singing, to the cathedral. It had been renamed the Temple of Reason. An actress, dressed provocatively, played the role of Goddess of Reason, carrying a flaming Torch of Truth. The smoke stained the sky black. The air reeked of sulphur. It made Viviane's eyes sting, her throat catch. The sun setting through the fumes made the Seine shine like a river of fire.

Everything was hellish.

Winter came, and Viviane's breath hung like smoke above her mouth. She felt as if her heart had frozen. Carts came every day, bringing the accused to face the tribunal and taking the condemned to the scaffold. Death haunted her dreams.

One day Viviane saw a familiar face in the crowd of women clustered in the prison yard, stamping their feet and blowing into their hands.

'Clothilde?' she asked incredulously.

Her stepmother turned a woebegone face toward her and said her name in a tone of weary surprise. 'We thought you were dead,' Clothilde said. 'You disappeared after the September massacres – we could find no trace of you.'

'You abandoned me!' Viviane cried. 'You left me there to face the mob alone.'

'Your father wanted to make sure I was safe,' Clothilde said. 'I thought . . . we thought . . . I was with babe. He planned to return for you later. But he could not find you. He was most displeased to find you gone.'

'I was in prison,' Viviane said flatly. 'As I am sure he could have ascertained if he had truly wished to find me.'

'Well, it was a great bore,' Clothilde said crossly. 'Everything is!'

Suddenly her pretty face screwed up, and she began to sob. Viviane patted her shoulder, and gave her a crumpled handkerchief to blow her nose.

'What of my father?' she asked.

'He is here too, somewhere.' Clothilde waved her hand vaguely. 'It is all his fault. If only we had fled to Austria when we could! Madame de Ravoisier tells me the émigrés are all the rage in Vienna. Balls every night, and the opera and the ballet. But, no, he had to stay and make stupid plots and spend all my money on schemes to save the king.'

'My father is here?' Viviane looked around in sudden and unreasonable dread.

Clothilde nodded. 'But not for long. I expect they'll chop his head off any day now.' She began to weep again, and Viviane thought for a moment her stepmother was overwhelmed with grief at the thought of losing her husband. But then Clothilde said, 'They'll chop mine off too, and I've done nothing wrong. Oh, I don't want to die!'

'Neither do any of us,' Viviane said dryly. She did her best to comfort her stepmother and arranged for Clothilde to share her cell, for the young heiress was now a pauper, unable to afford even the eighteen sous a day needed to pay for a bed.

That night, as she lay with her arms about her weeping stepmother, Viviane remembered how – long ago – she had wondered if she might befriend and comfort her father's young wife. It had never occurred to her they might share a cell one day.

Every morning, at ten o'clock, the gaolers came in and read out a list of names. As each name was pronounced there were groans and gasps, prayers and pleas. Some fainted and had to be carried away. Others stood, white-lipped and silent, and went stoically to face the tribunal. Most were executed the same day.

After the condemned women were taken away, a feverish gaiety broke out amongst those left behind. Some danced and sang, some gambled with desperation for more food or blankets, some crept to the guards and begged to be taken to see their husbands, promising them whatever they wanted for just a few moments with their beloveds.

Many began to practise their last moments. They all wanted to die like the queen, with grace and composure. As snow began to drift down from a leaden sky, they took turns in playing the roles of prosecutor, executioner, victim.

One night, after Viviane had helped her stepmother eat and wash and tucked her up under the blanket as if she was a child, Clothilde whispered to her in the darkness. 'He did not die, you know.'

'Who?'

'Your lover. He did not die.'

It took a while for Viviane to understand her meaning. 'David?' she said at last, stupidly.

'The English gardener. He escaped. I'm not quite sure how. Your father was furious.'

'David's alive?'

Clothilde nodded.

Viviane bent her face down into her hands. An agony of regret, a glorious joy. *He's alive!*

She did not sleep that night. She lay on her lice-infested straw mattress, shivering under the rank blanket, the shadow of bars striping her face, and spoke to David in her mind. *I am so sorry, I thought you were dead. My father lied to me. I should have known. Please forgive me and know that I love you.*

She sent her thoughts outwards towards David with all her strength, then lost herself in daydreams of searching for him, finding him, holding him in her arms. Her lips curved. For the first time in a long while, Viviane felt happy.

'Citoyenne de Ravoisier!' the prison warden read out.

Viviane stood as if struck to stone. *It has come*, she thought faintly. *Today I will die.*

It was only when the gaolers clamped their hands on Clothilde's arms and she had begun to shriek that Viviane realised it was her stepmother who was to go to the guillotine. She almost swooned with relief. The pang of guilt and self-reproach which followed was almost as overwhelming. Viviane sank to her knees. She watched as Clothilde was dragged away.

Clothilde had been determined to go to her death with her head held proudly high, her face pale but composed, her golden tresses rippling down her back, so the screaming mob at the foot of the guillotine would be struck with pity and admiration for her beauty.

Instead her chemise was torn, her hair hacked off, her face swollen and smeared with dirt and tears.

'Please! I am too young. I will do anything . . .' Clothilde clung with all her strength to whatever she could grasp. An iron bar. A gaoler's leg. A doorjamb. Her grip was broken ruthlessly. She was thrown into the tumbril. When she tried to scramble up, the gaoler knocked her down.

Viviane clung to the bars of the gate with all her strength. Her stepmother was only twenty-one years old. It seemed so cruel, so futile, a death.

The men were brought out. A weeping boy who looked no older than sixteen. A few old men, their bare legs spindly beneath their grimy shirts. One raised his hand to her. It took Viviane a long moment to realise it was her father. She did not recognise him without his white wig and maquillage. He looked old and haggard, his eyes deep sunken.

Her father had never once spoken a word of love to her. He had beaten her and mocked her and lied to her. Yet still she wept for him as if her heart was breaking.

That evening, Viviane crouched in the shadows while the women around her rehearsed their coming deaths. She tore a scrap from the hem of her chemise, pierced her finger with a pin, and painstakingly wrote a few words with her own blood. She tied the rag about one of her last coins and flung it out the window with all her strength. She could only hope in the goodness of heart of whoever found it.

'Viviane!' another of the women called. 'Will you not come and join us? We are practising dying.'

Viviane shook her head. 'No. I am done with playing at death. I plan to practise living.'

Part IV

Blue Wonder

A 'blue wonder': an improbable tale, something to
make one stare. The French, contes bleus.
The Reverend Ebenezer Cobham Brewer
Dictionary of Phrase and Fable (1898)

28

The Deep Story
19–20 December 1793

I t was cold.

David's breath misted white. *Dragon smoke*, he had once called it.

He stood on the deck of a barge, gaily decorated with banners, gazing out at the Pearl River. It was crowded with vessels of all shapes, sizes and purposes. Ferries laden with people in conical straw hats were rowed from shore to shore. Small junks piled high with sacks and boxes sailed past. An old man stood on a narrow boat made of five bamboo poles lashed together. He had one big straw basket, a long fishnet, and half-a-dozen huge black cormorants perched around him.

'Look!' David pointed. 'I'd heard Chinese fishermen trained cormorants to fish for them. I thought it was a myth.'

'They have some kind of ring fastened about their necks,' Scotty observed. 'To stop them swallowing the fish, perhaps.'

A junk headed towards the sea, its high prow painted with a crane with wings outstretched. Along the river banks, thousands of houseboats were tied in rows, creating a floating city. Women crouched on their haunches, cooking over small braziers.

'Look at the pretty lady.' Tom gestured towards a languid woman in emerald silk being rowed towards an elegant yacht. Her black hair was fastened on top of her head with ornate gold and turquoise pins, hung with tassels. Her face was white, her mouth crimson, her eyes obsidian. One servant held a pink parasol over her head, while another entertained her by plucking the strings of a Chinese lute. Yet another held a long ornately carved pipe to her lips. She breathed out a long plume of blue smoke and relaxed back into her cushions, as the servant began to pack the pipe for her once more.

'Opium?' David said in a low voice.

'I hope not,' Scotty said. 'It will destroy her beauty in the end.' He sighed. 'It is strange how something that has so many uses for good can also cause so much harm.'

'Dr Hickey tells me the British merchant ships are smuggling opium into China from India, and then sailing home full of tea.'

'I have heard the same thing,' Scotty said. 'To address the trade imbalance. China doesn't wish to import any of England's commodities, wanting the British to pay for their tea in silver. So they bring in opium, sell it at auction and use the proceeds to pay for the tea.'

'I was hoping to acquire a few *camellia sinesis* seedlings for Sir Joseph, but they were too closely guarded. I have many other rare plants, though, that I hope will please him.'

David could not help smiling. For months, the Chinese mandarins had controlled their every step, preventing them from seeing anything of interest or use. But after their summary dismissal from the emperor, their guardians had relaxed their vigilance. Travelling from Peking to Canton down a network of rivers and canals, the Englishmen had often been allowed to step off the junks and walk along the shore.

David had seen mulberry groves and taken cuttings of *morus alba*, the white mulberry used to feed the silkworm. The West had known the secret of silk for centuries, ever since two Christian monks had smuggled silkworms out of China concealed within hollow bamboo canes. The Honourable East India Company, however, wanted to know how the Chinese managed to keep their silk snowy-white, when British silk yellowed with age. So David had also taken samples and asked questions of the mulberry farmers about propagation and pruning and the composition of the water in which the silkworms were boiled.

He also collected the little yellow sunbursts of *chrysanthemum indicum*, and was shown how to make an infusion from its petals said to relieve chest pain and dizziness. Another useful plant he found was *panax*, which meant 'all-healing' in Greek and was named gin-seng by the Chinese, or 'man-root', for the roots of the plant were forked like a man's legs.

John Haxton had found a sweet-scented pink double rose, still flowering despite the wintry weather, and had been permitted to dig up a small bush and wrap its roots in damp hessian. It was the only rose they had seen in all their travels, and David was acutely jealous of his discovery. If only he had not stopped and turned to see how Tom was faring, following so faithfully along behind. David could only console himself with the knowledge the rose was blush-pink, not ruby-red.

By mid-afternoon, the embassy fleet had reached a palace built on an island in the Pearl River, where Lord Macartney and his entourage had been invited to stay. The palace belonged to one of the great Hong merchants, a man named Shy Kin Qua, said to have made a fortune from tea. The palace was built as usual in a series of elegant wooden pavilions with high flying eaves and scarlet latticework, connected by covered walkways. The main pavilion was two storeys high, and was guarded by two lion statues made of bronze, one resting its paw on a patterned ball, the other on a sleeping lion cub.

The embassy was met with great ceremony, a mark of favour that did much to smooth the ambassador's ruffled feathers. Scores of mandarins in silk gowns bowed low, again and again, and the Englishmen were led to an open pavilion overlooking a large pond, where they were served tea with milk from cows that had been brought over especially on flat barges, lowing mournfully all the way.

Willow trees trailed their golden tresses in the water, and lotus flowers spread their wide green leaves. A moon bridge led to an island where a tiny lacquer-red temple was situated under flowering plum trees. David was enchanted.

A stage had been set up in the courtyard, where clowns and acrobats and musicians performed, and a magnificent feast was spread out on high tables, with white tablecloths and napkins and proper chairs.

Afterwards, the men were showed to their quarters. The pavilions had all been fitted out with glass windows and fireplaces in the European way, with soft beds piled high with warm quilts and pillows instead of straw mats and hard ceramic headrests. These small signs of comfort and civilisation were met with much appreciation and a general thawing of the mood, though Dr Gillan loudly regretted the continued absence of water closets.

David was sharing a pavilion with Scotty, John Haxton and John Barrow. A moon gate led into a small sequestered courtyard centred around a tiny juniper tree in a pot. David had been curious about these miniature trees since he had first seen them in Ting-hai, but he had never been permitted to examine them closely. Now he and John pored over it, marvelling at the perfection of the form.

'A *juniperus chinensis* would normally grow up to sixty-five feet tall,' David said. 'This is only twenty-five inches.'

'I wonder how they do it,' John said. 'Imagine, if we could learn the secret we'd make our fortune. Every English lady would want one for her drawing-room.'

'It must take years,' David said, noting how the roots of the tiny tree had been trained to grow over rocks, and how its trunk had been encouraged to develop twists and knots just like a juniper tree in the wild.

It was cold that night, and David woke to find a faint frost glittering on the ground. It was only just dawn. Well wrapped up, he went out to explore more of the gardens.

Everything looked magical in the low-hanging mist. David walked down towards the pond, and saw an old man dancing alone beneath the willow trees. It looked as if he was waltzing with a ghost. David stopped in his tracks, wanting to watch but not wishing to intrude. The old man did not acknowledge him, but kept slowly dancing. Each movement was as graceful and flowing as water, his hands lifting and gesturing as if offering an invisible flower. He was dressed in simple robes of indigo blue, padded for warmth, and his long beard was wispy and white, his face heavily lined. Black slippered feet lifted and were set down with controlled precision. His long white plait swayed from side to side.

David did not like to stare so he moved away through the gardens, looking back often. When he returned ten minutes later, the old man was gone.

He walked back to the main pavilion to see a theatrical production was being staged on the front porch. Actors with garishly painted faces and long robes with flowing white sleeves were moving through a sequence of stylised gestures that were almost like a clown's mime. Musicians plucked moon-shaped lutes with their fingernails and blew into flutes made of bamboo, while the actors sang a high wailing tune.

A group of Englishmen watched, laughing and commenting rudely, secure in the knowledge no-one could understand them.

'What an infernal noise!' Dr Gillan said. 'How can they call that music?'

'It's barely dawn,' yawned Dr Dinwiddie. 'Must we be woken by such a racket?'

'I have a good mind to tell them to pipe down,' said Anderson. 'His lordship is worn out and needs a good rest.'

'I wonder what the emperor would think if he visited London and the king sent a flock of Covent Garden opera singers to serenade him at dawn each day?' John Barrow said.

David saw the old Chinese man standing at the edge of the crowd, his hand folded into his wide sleeves, his face inscrutable. Although he knew the old man could not understand him, he felt uncomfortable and so said, 'I think it is very kind of them to provide for our entertainment.'

'You call this entertainment?' Dr Gillan said incredulously.

The singers came to the end of their song, bowed low and retreated off the porch, replaced by boys who spun through the air as if they were made of hollow bone and feathers.

'You must admit their acrobats are incredible,' David said.

Dr Gillan snorted loudly. 'If you admire such circus tricks.'

David suddenly felt as if he could bear no more.

'I do,' he said, then turned and walked away. He found John still sleeping and shook him awake, saying, 'Let's go and see what we can do about getting our plants settled safely.'

Within the hour, David and John were being rowed across the river to the Thirteen Factories, as the principal warehouses of the foreigners were known, on a flat barge crammed with all the plants they had collected on their journey south from Peking.

The Thirteen Factories were built in a narrow strip along the Pearl River, and guarded on all sides by high walls. Inside were their warehouses and residencies, while their ships were moored outside on the river. Traditionally the Western merchants came with the monsoon winds between June and September, then departed once the wind changed direction in the winter months. Now that December was here, many of the merchant ships were returning to Europe, laden with tea, silk and porcelain. David hoped to find an East India Company vessel with room for his botanical specimens.

The British factory was a white palatial building, crowded with merchants and sailors. A Scottish gardener named James Main was deputised to advise them. He was in service to one of the East India Company's top men, Gilbert Slater, now retired and spending his wealth on rare and beautiful plants. James had been sent privately to hunt down magnolias, peonies, camellias, begonias, black lilies and roses.

'You are so lucky to have been allowed to travel within China,' James said enviously, as he inspected their haul. 'The Chinese are so jealous of their secrets they'll not permit us to visit any of their gardens or nurseries. I've managed to see only a few since I've been here. The nurserymen come here to the Factory, with little paper envelopes full of seeds which they try to sell us, and half the time the seeds are for common weeds, or are mislabelled.'

'We've not seen many gardens either,' David said. 'Only the imperial parks and a few courtyards hidden inside pavilions.'

'Chinese gardening is peculiar,' James said. 'There is a littleness in all their designs. They build tiny lakes where a mackerel would be puzzled to turn, surrounded by rocks which a man could carry away under his arm, and ancient trees that are only fifteen inches high. I swear, if a Chinese had ten acres to beautify, he would cover it with the same kind of childish, fanciful freaks repeated a thousand times over.'

'There's something fabulous and magical about it all, though, don't you think?' David said. 'Nothing has been left to chance, everything wrought with such care and harmony. It is as if they seek to paint a picture with the landscape.'

'Perhaps in the palace gardens,' James said sourly. 'I've not been permitted to visit them. The only gardens I've seen are tiny courtyards at the back of merchants' houses, and it is all rocks and raggedy bamboo and those vegetable cripples they like to make.'

'Do you not like the little trees?' David asked with interest.

'I'd rather see a tree growing wild on a mountain than bound within that tiny pot,' James replied.

'But what if you cannot go to the mountains?' David said. 'It's a way to bring the wild hills and forests into your home. And such skill, such patience, in the way the trees are wrought.'

'I suppose so,' James said with a shrug. 'You are lucky if you've been given a chance to examine one closely. I have not.'

He gave them advice about dealing with the Cantonese nurserymen, and suggested they visit the famous Fa Ti nursery about three miles from Canton, on the southern bank of the river. 'Go to the picture shops first and purchase drawings of the plants that you want,' he suggested. 'Then you can show them to Samay, the old gardener there, and he will find them for you. Ask him "how much-ee dollar" and never give him what he asks for.'

They made arrangements to go to the nurseries the following day, and then returned to the merchant's palace just as the sun was setting. Men stood about in groups, looking worried and agitated. Most had open letters in their hands.

'Mail from home!' Scotty called to David. 'We're at war with France.'

313

The words a blow to his solar plexus. 'But why? What has happened?'

'They've murdered their king,' Tom called, sounding most indignant. 'Months ago, and we had no idea of it. The scoundrels!'

'It is an action most execrable,' Herr Hüttner said.

'They invented a new killing machine that is really most efficient,' Dr Gillan said, in a tone of scientific curiosity. 'It's a beheading device with a sharp blade that falls like lightning and lops off the head. They are calling it the guillotine after the doctor who designed it. Apparently, the executioner can cut off a dozen heads in just thirteen minutes. Quite remarkable.'

David's first thought was of Viviane. Was her husband not one of the king's courtiers? What would the king's execution mean for her?

Oh, please, God, let her be safe, he prayed.

He hurried to find Sir George, wanting his own letters. The secretary was in his room, a great pile of correspondence at his elbow. He looked tired.

'You've come for your mail, Stronach?' he asked, scattering sand over the letter he had just finished writing. 'Give me just a moment.'

'I've heard we are at war with France, sir!'

'Yes, I'm afraid so. The situation there is rather awful, I believe. I have a letter here from Sir Joseph Banks. Take a look while I find your package.'

He tossed David an open letter. It was dated February. A whole ten months earlier!

> We are tolerably well here, though situation is somewhat tremendous. The French nation are certainly in a state of canine madness, very desirous of biting all mankind, and by that means infecting them of the disease they themselves are vexed with. I conceive them like a pack of mad foxhounds who cannot be confined to their kennel and feel sometimes a kind of horror lest they should infect too many of the quiet animals who are feeding around them . . .

'Have they really executed the king? What of his court? Is there news of them?'

Sir George looked up at him shrewdly. 'You were in France a few years ago, weren't you, Stronach? Working at the Jardin du Roi? I suppose you must have made friends there. I'm afraid that is all I know.'

He passed David a slim package, and dismissed him with a weary smile.

David instinctively sought the peace and silence of one of the hidden courtyards. He sat on a stone bench, his letters unopened in his lap, and tried not to be afraid for Viviane.

There was a plum tree in the centre of the courtyard, buds bursting into life on its bare twigs. Bamboo cast delicate shadows against the white wall. The water in the pond shivered under a catspaw of wind. David shivered too, and the papers in his hand rustled. He used his penknife to cut the cord.

The first letter was from his grandmother, full of news from home, enclosed with lighthearted notes from his sisters. His grandfather had appended just a shaky postscript, saying simply, *Bless you, my boy*. David's heart smote him. He opened the next letter.

Your grandfather is not well, his grandmother wrote. *We hope his health will improve with the warmer weather. He sends you his love. Angharad has started teaching music to the Morgan girls, and says they sing as sweet as songbirds. We are glad indeed of the extra coin, for the doctor's bills mount up. But don't you worry your head over it, Ceridwen and I have been taking in sewing and we live in hope the church will relent and give your grandfather his living back.*

More letters, all determinedly cheerful, all hiding the hardships they were clearly suffering. David set his jaw, and wished that he had some way of helping them. But his salary was already their main support. He would need to find a way to earn extra.

He came to the last letter, written in his grandfather's tremulous hand.

My dear boy

I do hope all is well with you and God is watching over you. I was sorry to find you so blue-devilled when last we saw you. It was clear to me that you had suffered some great blow to your spirit during your sojourn in France. I hope you will forgive me, but I asked

Mr Morgan to make some enquiries on my behalf, for he has business acquaintances in Paris. He was able to ascertain that the Duc de Savageaux was murdered in July 1789. His young widow was then arrested in August 1792, and incarcerated within La Force prison. It seems that as many as three thousand persons, chiefly of the nobility and wealthier classes, were arrested at that time. At least two thousand of those imprisoned were put most cruelly to death, among them many priests, women and children. It is not known what happened to the Dowager Duchesse de Savageaux. I am sorry that I cannot give you any better news. It was clear to me that you had developed an affection for the marquis's daughter and had been downhearted at her marriage. I pray that she was spared, and is safe. If any further news of her is discovered, I will advise you at once.

Wishing your business a profitable end and you a safe and speedy return to us.

Warm regards

your loving Grandpère

Darkness was falling, and David was cold to the bone.

He should never have left her. He had been afraid, and had run for his life, leaving Viviane at the mercy of her father. He should have stayed and fought, preferring to die than to leave her. His cowardice meant Viviane had been forced into a loveless marriage with a cruel man, and had suffered through all the turmoil of revolution and war, her brief sweet life ending at the hands of an enraged mob.

He was to blame for her death.

Light kindled behind him. David dashed his hand across his eyes and shoved his letters into his pocket. Rising and turning, he saw the old white-bearded man carrying a red Chinese lantern into the courtyard.

'Is all well? Are you not cold?' the old man said in heavily accented English.

David gazed at him in surprise. Although he had heard some of the mandarins and merchants in Canton speak in a strange English-Chinese compound they called pidgin, this was the first Chinese person he had met who spoke a single word of his own language. He remembered the rudeness of his compatriots, thinking no-one could understand them, and was embarrassed and ashamed.

'I'm so sorry, sir, I did not realise you could speak our language,' he said clumsily.

The old man smiled, his skin creasing into hundreds of fine lines. 'I merchant in Canton long time. It good to speak some words of customers, no?'

David nodded in agreement.

The old man laid his hand on his arm. 'But you sad. Bad news, yes?'

'Yes,' David agreed. Suddenly his throat closed over. He could not speak or breathe. His eyes and chest burned, his legs felt weak, his vision swam with black dots.

'Sit,' the old man said. 'Put head down. Breathe deep.'

David obeyed. The old man knelt by the pool and scooped up some water in his hands. He brought the water to David and told him to drink. 'Rain water, not dirty.'

David drank from his cupped palms, and the water was icy cold and refreshing.

'Breathe deep,' the old man told him again. 'In through your nose and down into your belly. Let all the bad air out. Now breathe again, as deep as you can.'

Gradually David's breath steadied and his vision cleared. He went to stand up but the old man pressed a gentle hand on his shoulder. 'No get up too soon.'

The lantern cast warm light across the courtyard, creating intricate plum blossom shadows on the wall and gilding the rippling water.

'It is very beautiful here,' David said.

The old man smiled, showing broken yellowed teeth. 'Most white devils not think so. Most think Chinese garden ugly.'

'Gardens here are very different to what we are used to,' David admitted.

'Chinese garden a poem.' The old man waved one gnarled brown hand. 'Chinese garden a deep story.'

'I do not understand,' David said. 'Please explain it to me.'

'Made by hand of man, it must look as if made by hand of God. Yet we are only men. We can only make small.'

'So the little trees, the rocks arranged in piles, the ponds, all mimic forests and mountains and lakes?' David said.

'Yes but no,' the old man said. 'Not mimic. Not playacting. It is big made more powerful by being small.' He made a gesture of frustration at the limits of his English. 'Like flower boiled down to medicine.'

'Like a distillation . . . it concentrates the essence of the thing.'

'Yes. The essence. The world's vital spirit. All concentrated and made more potent. You white devils, you plant a garden for the eye, with flowers you think lovely. But we yellow devils, we build a garden not for how it looks, but for what it means.'

The old man gestured around the garden. 'Bamboo is deep rooted and so means strength. Its stem is strong and straight and so means honour. It has one root and many stems, and so it means all things are connected together. Plum tree blossoms in winter. It tells us winter shall go and spring come. So it means hope.'

He pointed to the pond of water. 'Water is cool, dark, mysterious, like woman. It is mirror that reflects the moon.' He indicated the rock set at the far end of the pool. 'Rock is water's opposite. Warm, strong, forceful. Like man. Together, water and rock make a whole. Together, water and rock and tree and bamboo make a poem.'

The old man gave a heavy sigh, and sat down beside David. 'Too hard to explain.'

'I think I understand,' David said. 'A Chinese garden is like a poem because it shows the hidden meaning of things, in a secret language of symbols and metaphor. Its meaning needs to be pondered, wondered at, thought deeply about if one is to understand.'

The old man smiled at him. 'You are a poet.'

David remembered how Viviane's father had called him a gardener with the tongue of a poet, and was pierced once more with grief and remorse.

The old man saw the change in his face and said simply, 'You sad. Stay here a while. Garden good place for grief. But remember the plum blossom's deep story. Its flower tells us that sorrow will pass and joy come again.'

'I don't see how,' David said. 'It can't ever. Not for me.'

The old man pressed his hand and went silently away, leaving the lantern to shine its rosy light into the wintry garden.

29

The Blue Rose
21–25 December 1793

Numb with grief, David felt like one of Dr Dinwiddie's sing-songs, a brass automaton that walked and talked at the turn of a brass key.

On Christmas Eve, Lord Macartney and Sir George were engaged once more in a formal banquet, and the younger men were restless and bored. One of the more agreeable of the mandarins offered, in a low voice and with many sidelong glances, to take them to the Garden of Perfumed Lotus Flowers. It was difficult to understand his pidgin English and he was most insistent that they did not call for Father Li to translate. It was this reluctance that helped make his intention clear. He proposed to take the men to a courtesan house.

Such a thing was strictly forbidden, of course, but a combination of curiosity and long-frustrated desire tempted them to go.

'After all, we leave China soon and have hardly clapped eyes on a girl,' John Haxton said. 'What shall I tell all the fellows back home?'

'And it is most likely they will have bound feet,' Scotty said. 'I would very much like to see one, and ascertain what damage such binding does to the skeletal structure of the foot.'

'I've heard that a fairy foot is a powerful provocation for many men,' John Barrow said. 'I must admit I would like to know why.'

'I am sure the girls at the courtesan house must be very beautiful,' William Alexander said. 'Do you think they will let me draw them?'

'I won't be wasting my time *drawing* them,' John Barrow said with a laugh.

David just shrugged, and said, 'I'll come. Nothing better to do.'

Christmas Eve was difficult. He thought constantly of the night five years earlier, when he had given Viviane the ring with its secret message hidden behind enamelled roses. *Nothing is impossible for a valiant heart*, it had read. The fool that he was, he had believed it.

Home in Wales, his grandfather would be playing his harp, and his sisters would be singing, and his grandmother cooking taffy over the fire. Evergreen branches would decorate the mantelpiece, scenting the air with pine, and a fresh-made wreath would hang on the door. Neighbours would come by, stamping snow from their boots, and his grandmother would pass around slices of hot plum cake and cups of spiced wassail punch. At three o'clock in the morning, they'd wrap themselves up warm and light their lanterns, and go through the frosty, star-hung night to the church, and sing till dawn.

The bees would hum in their hives, and the cows would bend their knees in adoration.

Thinking of home, thinking of Viviane, David was as blue-devilled as he had ever been.

The Garden of Perfumed Lotus Flowers was not a house, as they had expected, but a gaudily painted junk with red furled sails moored in the middle of the river. Chinese music floated over the water. They descended a short ladder into a cabin and found their mandarin friends reclining on fat silken cushions, while a bevy of onyx-eyed young women played instruments and sang, or carried trays of food and drink around, or sat, drawing deeply on long opium pipes.

The women were all gorgeously dressed in slim-cut embroidered silk dresses with high collars, their black hair pinned up with jewels, their mouths painted into a red bud. They spoke no English, but between their funny coquettish pidgin and the Englishmen's few stumbling words of Mandarin, some communication was established.

Each of them had doll-sized feet, clad in red silk slippers. At first, Scotty's request to see their feet bare caused much consternation. They shook their heads and refused. When he asked them why their feet had been bound, one answered, 'Only servants have big feet.'

Another said, 'A beautiful face is given by heaven but beautiful feet must be earned.'

'Big feet are a sign of weakness,' another explained.

'But why? Surely you've been weakened greatly by such a thing being done to you. You can hardly walk, let alone run or dance.'

Some of the girls began to demonstrate how well they could dance, unfurling silk fans and swaying their slim bodies. Their hobbled feet moved in small, precise steps; all the motion was in their upper bodies and graceful arms.

It made David sad. 'Why? Why do they do it to you?'

The young women exchanged glances. One shrugged. 'Love,' she answered in English, and crossed her hands over her heart.

David could not bear it. He got up and went outside.

Canton spread out before his eyes, hung with red lanterns, ringing with gongs and strange music. Even the air smelt wrong. It smelt of sewage and incense, spices and vinegar, firework smoke and brackish water.

The ferryman was startled to see him so soon, but agreed to take him back to the palace. David clambered down and the boat was just casting off when Scotty came racing out. 'Wait!' he cried. 'I'll come with you.'

He jumped down into the boat and sat down beside David. 'It is a cruel practice,' he said after a long moment.

David grunted.

'She let me take a peek,' Scotty said. 'As far as I can tell, the metatarsal bones have been bent down and the calcancus – the heel bone – pushed forward to form a deep cleft. The smaller toes are all folded and atrophied under the sole of the foot. It must hurt like hell, and done when they are still little more than babies!'

322

Worse than the binding of their feet was the binding of their souls, David thought. It was impossible not to think of Viviane, and the narrow furrow of her life. He had thought her weak-willed. *Why would she not run away with me?* he had thought. *Does she not love me enough to leave behind her château and her fine silks?*

He had not thought of how a songbird, confined all its life in a tiny cage, its wings clipped, might hesitate at a latch suddenly swinging open.

'Davy, boy, what is it?' Scotty asked hesitantly. 'Bad news from home?'

David nodded. It was hard to speak. 'There was a girl . . . we were in love . . . but it was impossible . . . and now . . . I am afraid she may be dead.'

'I'm sorry,' Scotty said with the same difficulty. 'Hard luck.'

They got drunk on gin, and David told him how beautiful, how gallant, how bewitching Viviane had been.

That night, David dreamed he ran through a midnight forest. Hounds bayed behind him. Horses' hooves pounded. Horns blew. Snow like whirling stars. He strapped on his skates and skimmed away across the frozen river. Each stroke of his blade was a score into the ice. A scratch, a slit. Black water seeped up. The ice cracked. Faster and faster he skated, but it was no use. His skates cut the ice open. The gleaming river broke and splintered and struck him down. Deep he plunged, into black freezing water. Air fizzed from his lungs like globules of light.

Then slim arms reached for him, strong hands caught him. Dragged upwards. Gasping. Shivering. Water pouring away. He was in her arms, her mouth on his.

'Viviane,' he cried. He saw her dark tumbling hair, her black eyes, her smiling mouth. Joy springing.

And then he woke.

It was cold and bright. Light pierced through the glass, all fogged with frost flowers.

David brought his arm over his eyes. Head pounding. Mouth parched.

His grandfather had always called gin 'blue ruin'. David now understood why.

At last he got up and dressed, and went out in search of water. He found the courtyard with the plum tree and the pool of fresh rainwater. It tasted wonderful, and he gulped down handfuls of it and splashed it over his face. The shock of it was invigorating. He thought of the old man he had met here, and how kind he had been, and how wise. He thought of his dream. Viviane alive and laughing. It had seemed so real.

David wanted to speak to the old man again.

He ruffled his hair dry, pulled his cocked hat low over his eyes to shield them from the sun, and went out to the courtyard that lay before the main pavilion with its great bronze lions. He looked down to the pond with its willows and hump-backed bridge, but the old man was not there, dancing alone in the dawn.

He heard music and singing, and then the faint sound of one person clapping. He looked towards the main pavilion, and saw that a small theatrical group was performing on the front porch again. A row of low stools had been set up before the steps, but only one person sat there.

The old man in his plain indigo-blue suit, a round black cap on his head, his thin white plait hanging down to his waist.

David went to greet him, but he put his gnarled finger against his mouth in a shushing gesture. 'Play just begun.'

So David sat beside him and watched the show.

A man, dressed in imperial yellow embroidered with a dragon, was speaking. At his feet knelt a beautiful young woman, her black hair piled high and pinned with jade dragonflies. She had her hands clasped together imploringly.

'The emperor wishes daughter to marry,' the old man whispered. 'But she begs him not to force her against her will.'

The emperor raised one finger. His daughter drooped her head sadly, but nodded.

'He says she may choose one condition her husband must meet.'

The emperor left the stage, and the girl rose from her knees and sang a sad-sounding song. Another voice rose to meet her. It was a young handsome man, barefoot, dressed in rough peasant clothes. He carried a straw basket on his back and a rake in one hand. David sat up a little. He was clearly meant to be a gardener. The emperor's daughter and the gardener spoke together, and then he put both hands on his heart.

'What are they saying?' David asked.

'She is sad. She does not know what to do. If she says her husband must be handsome, perhaps he cold and cruel. If she says her husband must be kind, perhaps he old. If she says he must be rich, perhaps he mean. Her old friend, the gardener, says she must find what is hidden in their hearts.'

On the stage, the two actors were singing another song. When the princess was looking away, the gardener clasped his hands towards her. When he had turned away, she did the same to him. It was clear they loved each other, but neither knew the other's feelings.

'They sing now of the blue rose,' the old man told him. 'She will send her suitors to find one.'

'There is no such thing as a blue rose,' David said.

The old man twinkled at him. 'That is the point.'

'Oh, I see. It's a quest for the impossible.'

The old man nodded. 'Exactly.'

One by one, the princess's suitors went in search of the impossible blue rose.

The first was a warrior, mounted on a ferocious-looking horse made of papier-mâché and silk. He carried a sword, and made great play with it. He attacked a lord, whose bodyguards were armed only with painted parasols and silk fans, and stole from him a giant sapphire carved into the shape of a rose. But when the warrior showed the flower-jewel to the princess, she shook her head and put out her hand in a negative gesture.

'That is not the blue rose I am waiting for,' the old man translated.

The second suitor was a fat merchant, carried about on a palanquin by eight slaves. He went to the flower market and ordered the rose-grower grow him a blue rose. The rose-grower protested and was threatened.

At last he and his wife dipped a white rose into a vat of dye, till it was dripping blue. But when the merchant showed the dyed flower to the princess, she once again shook her head.

'That is not the blue rose I am waiting for,' the old man translated once more.

The third suitor was an aged minister who read many scrolls and consulted many wise men, then called to him the best spinners and weavers in the land. He ordered them to make the most beautiful gown in the world, embroidered with blue roses. But once again the princess rejected the offering.

'That is not the blue rose I am waiting for,' the old man translated for the third time.

The princess went out into the garden. The sun – cut from golden paper – sank, and the pale blue moon rose. The gardener sang to her most beautifully, and then he plucked a white rose from the garden and gave it to her. In the light of the full moon, it was the softest, most mysterious blue. Smiling, she took the rose and kissed him, their shapes silhouetted against the shining moon.

'That is the blue rose I have been waiting for,' the old man said, and mopped his eyes with his handkerchief.

David had to swallow a lump in his throat as hard as a plum stone. Simple and strange as the story was, it had got under his skin.

'It is as if they know,' he whispered.

The old man turned to him. 'Know? Know what?'

'My own story.'

The old man looked puzzled.

'I am like that gardener. I too fell in love with a princess – well, with a marquis's daughter anyway – and wanted to marry her. But we were parted . . . I ran away and left her . . . and I'd promised her I'd find her a blood-red rose . . . and so I came here to China as if I was on some ridiculous quest . . . as if I could find a red rose and bring it back for her and that would somehow save her . . . but it's no use, it's all no use.'

To his dismay, David found that he was close to tears.

The old man passed him his handkerchief, and ashamedly he scrubbed at his eyes.

The actors up on the makeshift stage were bowing, and the old man clapped enthusiastically. The actors pressed their hands together in thanks, then moved away. The emperor's daughter pulled off her elaborate bejewelled wig, and David saw that she had been played by a young delicate-featured man. He remembered that women were not permitted to perform in public in China, so female roles were always taken by boys whose voices had not yet broken, just like in Shakespeare's day.

'Blue Rose my wife's favourite story,' the old man said. 'She like emperor's daughter and me like gardener. We too in love, not permitted to marry. But I made fortune selling tea and so in the end permitted.'

David tried to smile. 'That's good. I'm glad.' He could manage no more, his throat thickened with grief.

'She dead now,' the old man said abruptly. 'My fault.'

David stared at him. He felt dazed and off-kilter. 'How? How did she die?'

The old man got up from his stool. 'Come. I show you her grave. I tell you.'

He led David through the garden, away from the pavilions. It was still very early. The rising sun's rays struck down through the willow trees, making their golden leaves glow. The grass was white with frost that glittered like tiny diamonds. A faint mist rose from the water, wreathing about the red temple.

'I born poor,' the old man said, 'but got rich. I built all this and I went to Ying Yui's father and I said, "Let me marry her, I will care for her always." So we married. We lucky and had sons.'

David was surprised by the old man's words. Because he was dressed so simply, David had assumed he was some kind of servant, perhaps a gardener like himself. But it was clear now that he was the rich Hong merchant who owned this palace. David tried to remember his name. Shy Kin Qua, he thought it was.

'But then, some years ago, fire destroyed tea warehouse,' Shy Kin Qua said. 'All lost. I rich no more. So I worked hard. Must make riches again.

327

One day Ying Yui said to me, "I hot. I sick. Stay look after me." But I wanted make-ee much-ee dollar.' His voice was bitter with sarcasm. 'So I go. When I come back, Ying Yui dead.'

'What did she die from?'

'Smallpox.'

'I'm sorry.' David's words seemed so lame, so inadequate, but what else could he say? There was no way to comfort the bereaved.

They had come to another wall, set with another moon-shaped gate. This one had red-painted doors, and an inscription in Chinese above.

'I bury her here, in her garden that she loved.' Shy Kin Qua paused and turned to David. 'Blue Rose always her favourite story. But I cannot plant blue roses for her. No such thing. And white roses mean unhappiness and death. Anything that grows on a thorn is a reminder of life's sorrow and pain, you see?'

'Yes,' David said, understanding the old man was telling him the rose's deep story.

'But here in China, red means blood, means life, means brides and joy. So a red rose is both sorrow and joy, pain and pleasure, death and life, ashes and fire. So I plant it for my wife, on her grave.'

A sudden quickening of his pulse. 'You have red roses here?' David asked, hardly believing it.

The old man nodded. 'Come see.'

He unlocked the red moon doors, and stepped forward into a small enclosed garden. A pathway led to a horseshoe-shaped tomb made of stone and inscribed with gilt characters. Two lions guarded the tomb, one with its paw on a ball, the other on a lion cub. Before the tomb was a pool of still water, dappled with lotus leaves. Behind it were rocks, piled together to make a miniature mountain.

Growing over the tomb, and all through the garden, were rose briars in their hundreds. Bejewelled with rosehips, festooned with flowers as red as blood, the roses grew from ground still silvered with frost, for the morning sun had not yet struck over the grave.

'You want to pluck?' the old man said. 'Take home to your love?'

David's throat muscles worked. At last he said, unsteadily, 'I think she is dead.'

'You think? You do not know?'

He shook his head.

'Better go find out, yes?'

'Maybe she won't want to see me. I left her, I ran away like a whipped cur.'

The old man scratched at his thin white beard. 'Sit,' he instructed. 'Tell me.'

So David told him about how he had met Viviane, and loved her, and abandoned her.

'But you in danger? Her father want kill you?'

David nodded his head. 'Yes. He slashed at me with his sword. Cut off my finger.' He pulled off his glove and showed the old man his scarred hand. 'Viviane pushed me away, and held her father back, and I ran. I barely managed to escape.'

'So she save you.'

'Yes.' David dropped his head, not wanting Shy Kin Qua to see the shame on his face. Viviane had saved him, and all he had done was blame her for betraying him.

'So she want you to live. She save you. Why she not want to see you?'

David lifted his shoulders and let them fall. 'She was married to another, against her will. And there has been much death and bloodshed in her country. The king was murdered, and many of his nobles. Perhaps she was too.'

'But you don't know?'

David shook his head, rubbing the scar of his missing finger.

'So she may not be dead.' The old man's eyes were bright and intent.

'Last night I dreamt she was still alive. I dreamt she saved me from drowning. But there's no sense in that. It's just what I wish was true.'

'The soul can travel far when sleeping,' the old man said.

David did not answer. The hope blossoming within him was too hurtful.

Shy Kin Qua pulled scissors from his girdle and passed them to David. 'Cut the rosehips, take the seeds, take whatever you need. Then go and find her.'

'But it's been so long. Five years today.'

The old Chinese man twinkled at him. 'Better late than never.'

30

Wolf's Foot
25 December 1793 – 22 June 1794

On Christmas Eve, her brother came to her.

Viviane could hardly believe it. 'You got my note?'

'Miraculously. A boy brought it to me. It was a wonder he could read the address, it was so faint and spidery. What on earth did you write it with?'

'Blood.'

Come, I need you, she had scrawled that day with a bloodied pin.

There was a long pause. Pierrick put out both his hands. They were warm and strong.

'I should've come earlier. But times are hard and I was scared of risking my neck.'

Viviane nodded. 'And you were angry with me.'

'Yes. I'm sorry. I don't know why – none of it is your fault.' He gave an apologetic shrug. She squeezed his hands.

'I have something for you.' Pierrick looked about cautiously, but the guard was smoking his pipe and reading a newspaper, and the other women were all talking and weeping with their own visitors. He drew a small leather purse from under his coat and passed it to her. Viviane hid it under her shawl, and then swiftly passed him the velvet pouch with her few treasures within. She did not need to tell him to keep them safe.

Viviane leant forward and whispered, 'Pierrick, I think I know a way to escape. But I cannot do it without you.'

He drew his hands away, frowning at her.

'I promise you it can work,' she said.

The guard noticed them whispering, and shouted at them to sit back. Viviane obeyed, her eyes fixed imploringly on Pierrick's face.

He sighed. 'What madcap scheme have you up your sleeve now?'

'I can only hope it will work. You will need to keep an eye on the execution listings. When you see my name, you will know it's time. Then you must get some clubmoss – you remember, the little plant they call the wolf's foot.'

'A-ha!' he said. 'I see the light.'

She smiled at him. 'You'll know what to do.'

Pierrick grinned, his eyes dancing devilishly. 'Well, at least if I'm to die, I might as well have some fun doing it.'

The guard glared at them again, and told him it was time to go. She begged the guard for just one more minute, and Pierrick grinned and slipped him a coin.

'Ivo is sorry,' he said. 'He swears he did not denounce you.'

'I'm glad. Give my love to him and to Luna.'

'Hopefully you'll be seeing them soon.'

Viviane bent her head, blinking away tears. It was almost unbearable, the pain of hope. She rubbed at her eyes with her kerchief, then looked steadily at her brother.

'He's dead, you know.'

'Our father?'

'Yes.'

'May he burn in hell!'

'It feels so strange,' Viviane said. 'I thought I'd be dancing on his grave, but I just feel so sad. I can't help wishing things had been different.'

'I wouldn't waste your energy mourning him,' Pierrick said. 'Just think, you are free of him now!'

'If only I was free of this prison too,' she said.

'If all goes to plan, you will be.'

'You will not fail me?'

'Never again.' He pressed her hand warmly, then stood up and went swiftly away.

Back in her cell, Viviane opened the leather purse Pierrick had given her and smiled in relief at the sight of the coins within. Her own savings were almost all gone, and Viviane had dreaded the thought of sleeping down in the dungeons with the rats.

She wondered if Pierrick understood what she wanted him to do. But all their life they had communicated with little more than gestures and facial expressions, and she had to trust him.

All she needed now was to be condemned to die.

That night, Viviane lay and thought of David, as she always did. She imagined she was back at Belisima-sur-le-lac, and it was summer and the roses were glowing as red as rubies. The château was reflected in the smooth waters of the lake, and the flax fields stretched away, golden and ripe. She was running though a meadow, barefoot, wild flowers on her hair. David chased after her, laughing and calling her name. Luna bounded before them.

She slipped into sleep, smiling.

But it was cold. Outside the thick prison walls, snow fell. The Seine was grey as lead. Icicles hung from the iron bars. Viviane shivered under her thin blanket.

In her dream, she saw the château muffled in fog. The mill wheel did not turn, the stream was a cascade of crystal. All was dark.

David ran like a hare. The hunt galloped behind him, hounds baying. The terrible long drawn-out cry of the horn. David fell. Ice cracked beneath him. Into the black waters he sank.

Viviane picked up her skirts and ran. Her breath sharp in her side. She raced on to the ice and flung herself down at the gaping fissure. Nothing to see. She plunged her arm deep into the icy water. For a moment, nothing.

Then her fingers touched soft, undulating hair. She reached deeper, grasped him by the neck and shoulder, dragged him out with all her strength.

She saw the steam of his living breath and, in her joy, drew him close and kissed him.

When Viviane woke, she was trembling violently. The water in her tin cup was frozen solid. The window was starred with frost.

She pressed two icy fingers to her mouth.

Her lips were warm.

On the 8th of January, the British fleet left Canton at last.

David said farewell to Father Li, who stayed behind to spread his missionary zeal throughout China. They had become good friends, despite not sharing a language, religion or culture, and David hoped that the priest stayed safe and found happiness.

In the hold of the *Lion* were three large blue-and-white ceramic pots with tight-fitting lids that Shy Kin Qua had called ginger jars. The old man had given them to him, each decorated with designs of blue roses. Inside, buried in rice, were handfuls of rosehips, red as pomegranate seeds.

It made David smile to think of them.

The HMS *Lion* reached Macao on the 15th, and was warmly welcomed by the Portuguese. David was glad to have earth under his feet again, and to visit the botanic gardens. It was strange to hear church bells ring on Sunday.

The Chinese celebrated the beginning of the new year with the coming of the first new moon. Red and gilt lanterns were strung across the streets in their thousands, and every house was decorated with banners. Fire crackers filled the air with loud bangs and sputters, while acrid-smelling smoke billowed through the air. Long writhing dragons made from silk and bamboo undulated through the streets, held aloft by poles. Girls danced ahead of the fearsome painted heads, holding aloft round baubles. For fifteen days, the festivities continued, till the moon was full again.

It was an extraordinary way to bid farewell to China.

*

It was impossible to know the date anymore.

The National Convention had introduced a new calendar, with names devised by a poet. Each month was divided into three weeks, and each week was ten days long. The guillotine worked every day of the week except the tenth, when the executioners were allowed to rest.

On that day, Paris was eerily silent.

Viviane could only tell what season it was by the narrow view afforded by her cell window. She watched the snow melt, the leaves bud, the sun arc across the rooftops.

The days were marked by deaths. Georges Danton and Camille Desmoulins died on the same day as the poet who had named the months. They said Desmoulins went mad when he heard his wife had been arrested too. He fought and struggled the whole way, ripping his shirt, but they manhandled him to the guillotine all the same.

Six weeks later, the king's sister Élisabeth was killed. She had been a sweet, devout woman who should not have had an enemy in the world. Viviane cried for her, and worried about the young king and his sister, now in the Temple alone. She hoped their gaolers let them be together, but knew it was in vain.

Pity is treason, Robespierre said.

The small fleet of ships rounded the Cape of Good Hope on the 2nd of June.

It had been a swift journey, with the winds blowing fair. A French squadron was known to be cruising the Straits of Sunda, so a sharp lookout was kept. A few ships had been encountered, but all flew the British flag.

On the 18th, the fleet reached the shelter of St Helena, a tiny island in the Southern Atlantic Ocean. It was a bare, windswept rock, used by John Company as a rest stop and rendezvous point on ships returning to Europe from the East. Many on board were ill, and were glad of the chance to rest and recover. They were able to bury their dead, take on fresh water and food, and hear the news. All anyone could talk about was the situation in France.

'Not everyone wants this new republic of theirs,' one man told David. 'There's fighting all through the countryside, I've heard.'

'And on the high seas,' David replied. 'The French royalists have their own fleet of ships, and whenever they see a boat carrying the new republican flag they give chase. One will shout "Long live the king!" and the other will shout back "Long live the nation!", and then they fire on each other.'

'It's as if they've all run mad,' the man said.

Summer came, and the stink of the buckets was unbearable.

The Conciergerie was crammed, people sleeping on straw flung on the ground, over-laden carts rattling away over the cobblestones every day. Hair cropped to bare their neck for the blade, they were taken out through the iron teeth of the gate and into the seething streets, for the long parade of humiliation and shame before the final swift blow.

Soon the ground at the Place de la Révolution was so saturated with gore the horses dragging the tumbrils could no longer be induced to go near it, no matter how ferociously they were whipped. The people who lived nearby complained that dogs came each night to lap up the puddles of blood. So the guillotine was moved. First to the Place Saint-Antoine, where it stood for only five days. The shopkeepers there complained of the stench and the sound and the horror of it all, ninety-six people having died in just those few days. So then it was moved further south-east, to the Barrière du Trône, at the very limits of the city. A special sanguiduct was built for the blood to pour away.

Viviane did not know why she was still alive. Every day she waited to hear her name read out, and every day she was passed over.

Perhaps it was simply because there were so many others to kill.

Cécile Renault, for example, a young seamstress who went to Robespierre's house because – she said – she wanted to see what a tyrant was like. When she was searched, two small knives were found in her basket. Cécile and her family and friends – sixty in all – were sent to the guillotine wearing the red shirts reserved for parricides, for Robespierre was considered the father of the Republic. Jean-Baptiste Michonis, the man who had tried to save the queen, died the same day.

On the twenty-second day of the Prairial month of the Year II, a law was passed to enable the guillotine to hack faster. The Revolutionary Tribunal, it said, was created to punish the enemies of the people. Anyone who opposed the Republic was an enemy, and the penalty for all was death.

The rate of executions quickened. From five or six deaths a day, the tempo quickened to sixteen or seventeen, and then to two dozen. Every single day.

Viviane walked around and around the iron-bound perimeter of the prison yard, listening to the beating of drums, and the sounds of the people of Paris. Screaming, weeping, pleading, cheering, taunting, jeering.

Above her the sky was blue. Tiny birds swooped in and out of the eaves, twittering joyously. She watched them longingly, wishing she could be so free.

As a little girl, Viviane had loved to explore the meadows and hedge-rows and forest, finding all sorts of secret places she could hide where no-one could find her. She'd crouch low, her hair hanging over her face, making little gardens with twigs and petals, feathers and fallen berries, bright leaves and stones. She would search for treasures, down deep in the tangle of hawthorn, wild rose and bramble, where no-one but her and the little creatures of the field ever ventured. She would crouch so still a hare might lollop past, or a red squirrel with its paws filled with nuts. She'd see dainty balls woven out of grass by field mice, or little nests built of twigs and moss and mud and feathers.

Once she'd found a nest with three tiny eggs in it, blue as the sky, speckled with brown. Very gently she had cradled one in the palm of her hand. It had been warm. The mother had darted about her head, shriek-ing the alarm, and Viviane had carefully put the egg back where she found it. Later, she had come back and found the eggs had hatched into ugly, bony, ruffled things with yellow gaping beaks, unbearably fragile, starving for love. She had barely dared breathe as she had watched their mother return again and again to feed them. As the summer had passed, those fledglings had grown feathers and, eventually, fluttered outside the warm cup of their home and learned to fly.

Every day Viviane watched the swifts dart in and out of the eaves of the Conciergerie, catching insects on the wing. Their aerial acrobatics and elfin cries were her only joy in long hollow days haunted by darkness.

One morning, two young swifts collided mid-air. The smaller bird tumbled down and crashed to earth. Its wings flapped desperately, but it could not rise into the air again. The guard stepped casually to kick it out of the way. Viviane rushed to stop him. She bent down and picked the little bird up. Its heart trembled against her fingers. It looked up at her, eyes as bright as obsidian beads. Viviane lifted up her hands and unlaced her fingers.

The swift soared away into the sky.

The *Lion* and the other ships were becalmed for ten long days.

David felt he would go mad with impatience. He paced around and around the deck, till Scotty said he was wearing the wood away. It was a shame the hot-air balloon had been left in China, David thought grimly, else he might have tried to fly back to France.

'Fret not yourself; it tends only to evil,' his grandfather had always said. David tried his best not to fret.

So David read, and played endless games of cards and backgammon, and learned to tie knots. Each morning he checked his precious cargo of rosehips. Each night he lay in his hard, narrow bunk and thought of Viviane.

The wind rose at last, but brought mist. The fleet were like ghost ships, their sails and masts looming out of the fog, then disappearing again.

'Ships to starboard!' the lookout shouted.

It was feared the ships were French. The drums began to beat out the summonses, and the men were told to make themselves ready in case it came to a fight. Quickly the decks were cleared and the cannons made ready. Pistols were loaded, swords polished.

'Tom, I want you to go below deck,' Sir George ordered.

'No, Father, I want to stay,' the boy cried. 'Don't make me go below. Please, sir. I want to stay with you.'

'It's not safe.'

'I know, sir. But I'd rather not. Surely there's something I can do to help?'

'No, Tom. Do as you are told! Your mother would never forgive me if harm was to come to you.'

Just as Tom was disconsolately making his way to the ladder, the mist swirled apart.

'She's flying the Union Jack, sir!' the lookout shouted. 'She's one of ours.'

A cheer went up, and Tom came flying back.

'Aren't we to have a fight after all?' he said in a tone of such intense disappointment it made David laugh.

'Not today,' his father said, and called for rations of grog to be passed out so the men could all toast the king's health.

In midsummer, Viviane's name was at last called.

It was her turn to climb the stairs to the courtroom of the Revolutionary Tribunal. Her turn to be accused and given no chance to defend herself. The benches were full of men and women, talking, laughing, eating, knitting. Viviane scanned the crowd, hoping to see Pierrick. She wondered if he knew her time had come. She saw a familiar face, and her heart began to pound.

Alouette's eyes met hers across the room. She grinned and waved, as if they were at a soiree. When the guilty verdict was passed down, Alouette grimaced and shrugged, as if to say bad luck, then turned back to her neighbour, laughing.

Viviane was taken back down to the Conciergerie. Her hair was hacked off. She had to surrender all her belongings, including her shoes. She was allowed to wear nothing but her loose white cambric chemise.

Barefoot, her arms and legs naked, she was pushed into the waiting tumbril. Her hands bound behind her back. Another half-a-dozen prisoners shoved in beside her, tied in pairs. Three other carts crammed full behind them.

Viviane did not know their names or crimes. One was a pale girl of no more than sixteen.

Her pulse thumped loudly in her ears. The tumbril rattled away over the cobblestones. Viviane kept her feet with difficulty.

The tumbril drove across the Pont Notre-Dame, and turned right on to the Quai de Gesvres. People swarmed around the tumbril, shouting curses. 'Death to all aristos!' someone yelled.

Viviane jerked as if stuck with a pin. She knew that voice. But she saw no-one she recognised, no matter how frantically she scanned the crowd.

It was a long drive to the Barrière du Trône, through crowds of sullen-faced people who shook their fists and shouted 'Death to traitors'. Some threw old shoes, dead cats, rotten vegetables. Others turned their faces away, as if pretending not to see.

The Place du Trône-Renversé – the Square of the Toppled Throne – was seething with people, all shouting and waving their red caps. Viviane could see the guillotine standing tall on its platform. Soldiers guarded it with sharp pikes, and the executioner stood waiting, a tricolour cockade in his hat. His face was white and rigid.

Viviane felt weak, as if her legs might give way.

A series of sharp percussive sounds, like gunshots. Whirling sparks, billowing smoke. The horse reared and neighed. Viviane was thrown down. People screamed. Sudden spouts of flame on either side. People ran for shelter, hands over their heads. Another great bang, and smoke as thick as dust. Suddenly her bonds were cut. The blade nicked her wrist. She jerked herself free of the rope and scrambled out of the cart. Smoke swirled about her. Coughing, she ran forward, her legs unencumbered by skirts for the first time in her life.

340

Another explosion. The horse bolted, the tumbril jerking wildly from side to side.

Pierrick caught her hand, pulled a red cap down over her cropped head and flung a tricolor sash about her waist. 'This way,' he whispered.

Hand-in-hand, they escaped through a haze of smoke, reeking of gunpowder and sulphur.

31

The Red Ribbon
22 June – 18 August 1794

Viviane stumbled along, clinging to her brother's hand.

He led her swiftly through a maze of narrow cobbled streets, lined with higgledy-piggledy shops and houses. People hurried about their business, their heads bowed, their faces showing the marks of hunger and fear. Many of the men were dressed in long dark robes, with broad-brimmed black hats upon their heads. Even the young men had long hair and beards. They clustered outside a grand stone building with a six-pointed star engraved above the door, a tall iron fence guarding its entrance from the street. Women with shawls wrapped about their faces stood nearby, chattering in a language she did not understand. Viviane felt disorientated, as if she had somehow blundered back in time or into a foreign country.

A street sign nearby read 'Rue des Juifs', so Viviane realised they were hurrying through the Jewish quarter of the Marais.

'It is safer here for Ivo and me,' Pierrick told her in a low voice. 'They call these streets 'the armpit of Paris'. Everyone here is poor and hiding something. It's hard enough to live from day to day without drawing the attention of the Revolutionary Tribunal. We keep our heads down, and no-one gives us any trouble which is how we like it.'

He turned into a street which followed the curve of an old medieval rampart. Roses tumbled over the crumbling stone, scenting the air. The street was called the Rue des Rosiers, Viviane read, and she thought at once of David. If only she could set out now to Wales, in search of him. But the city gates were still sealed, Pierrick had told her, and travel overseas forbidden.

If she could escape from under the very shadow of the guillotine, she could find a way to escape Paris, Viviane thought with a gurgle of laughter. But not today. She was so exhausted that the ground seemed to undulate beneath her feet.

Pierrick paused before a tall arched doorway, unlocked it swiftly and led her through into a deep shadowed passageway. Locking the door behind him, he showed her through to an inner courtyard enclosed on four sides with high walls lined with windows framed by small iron balconies. A young apple tree grew in the centre of a small vegetable patch, guarded by a low fence woven from willow saplings in the traditional Breton manner.

'Did you plant this?' she asked in surprise, for the Pierrick she had known had never liked to get his hands dirty. But it seemed the revolution had changed them all, for Pierrick nodded and showed her his garden with pride.

'Ivo wanted fresh herbs and vegetables for his cooking, and food is so scarce in Paris now, it seemed sensible to grow our own,' he told her. 'Our landlord is glad to be given a few handfuls of sorrel or some broad beans in thanks for the use of the ground.'

They trudged up several flights of steep wooden stairs. Then Pierrick unlocked a low door, and ushered her into a tiny garret. Ancient wooden beams almost grazed their heads, and the roof touched the floor on either side. The furnishings were simple – a thin straw mattress, a wooden table and a few rickety stools, and an old-fashioned stew stove in the corner with an iron flue sticking out the window. However, Pierrick and Ivo had made the room beautiful with an old velvet bedspread and soft pillows, green glazed plates and jugs and confit pots, and richly coloured rugs on the floor. There was a bunch of fresh herbs in a jar on the stove, and a view from the tiny window across the rooftops and chimneys of Paris.

'It's lovely,' Viviane said. Pierrick smiled, looking about him with pleasure.

Luna had been asleep on a rug by the stove, but she leapt up to greet Viviane, whining with joy so intense it seemed to hurt her. Ivo rushed from the stove, an apron tied about his waist, a dripping wooden spoon in one hand. He embraced her, kissing her cheeks again and again, and Pierrick opened up a bottle of apple brandy. Viviane felt utterly boneless with relief. Ivo put her in a chair, and served her a bowl of Breton fish stew, and warned her to be quiet, for a young family lived in the rooms below.

But they could not be quiet. They talked, and wept, and laughed, and danced most of the night. Viviane heard how Pierrick and Ivo had met and fallen in love. She shared something of the terrible cold endurance of this past year, and then told them that David was still – she hoped – alive.

'But where is he?' Ivo asked, sitting with Pierrick's arm draped over his knee.

'I don't know,' Viviane said. 'But I shall write just as soon as I can. He must think that I betrayed him terribly, marrying so quickly. I need to tell him I thought he was dead, and that my father threatened to send me to prison.'

For some reason, the exquisite irony of this struck her hard. Viviane laughed till she was breathless and aching, and then she cried, and then Ivo put her to bed in a nest made of cushions and rugs by the window, Luna curling up in the crook of her knees.

The next day Viviane went to walk with Luna in the sunshine, glorying in the freedom of breeches and short hair. It was a bright summer's day, but the streets of Paris were strangely empty. She saw only two carriages passing by. Most of the shops were shut, their windows boarded up. The few people she saw were dressed in dull colours, and nobody met anyone else's eyes or called a cheery 'good morning'. The park was deserted.

Viviane began to feel an eerie discomfort, as if hidden eyes were watching her. She made her way home through back streets and alleyways, turning often to make sure she was not being followed.

Pierrick was furious with her when she told him that night. 'It's not safe! You don't understand. Everyone's suspicious of everyone else. If you were caught . . . well, we would all die.'

'Am I to exchange one prison for another? I'll go mad shut up in this tiny room!'

So Pierrick sighed and said she might come with him to the Opéra National, but she must pretend to be his brother and keep her mouth shut.

So she went each day to the theatre with her brother, and helped carry props, and sew costumes, and bring wine to the artists, and breathe air that smelt of grease-paint and citron hair oil and flowers instead of sewage and death. The Opéra National had been struggling for some months, with one director imprisoned while another had fled. But the Committee of Public Safety had given it 150,000 livres to continue, as long as it only performed patriotic works.

This caused some consternation among the cast. 'Are we to address the Greek king of the gods as Citoyen Jupiter?' one man asked sarcastically. 'And have him wear a cockade instead of a laurel wreath?'

The Opéra was in the process of moving into new premises on Rue de la Loi, just opposite the National Library, and so all were busy carrying boxes and bags back and forth. It was only a block away from the Palais-Royal, and two blocks away from the Tuileries, where the National Convention now met in the apartments once occupied by the murdered Princesse de Lamballe.

One evening, Pierrick and Viviane were walking home from the theatre with Luna when the bells of Paris began to sound the alarm. A man galloped past, hatless, his face set in a fearsome grimace. Soldiers ran down the street, sabres drawn.

Pierrick drew Viviane into a doorway. 'Something is happening. Best be careful.'

The clangour of the tocsin rang from every steeple and bell-tower. Men began to form into lines in the street, pistols in their belts, pikes in their hands.

'It's something bad,' Pierrick said. 'Let's get home.'

They hurried through the streets, Luna kept on a tight leash. On the corner was a frightened-looking boy, selling the evening newspaper. 'Robespierre accused!' he shouted.

Pierrick and Viviane ran the rest of the way home, then locked themselves into the garret. They only unlocked it to let Ivo in an hour later.

'Have you heard the news?' he cried.

'Is it possible?' Pierrick responded.

They all gazed at each other in amazement and fear. Maximilien Robespierre, the architect of the Terror, the man who had sworn to release a river of blood to wash away France's enemies.

'Robespierre will never permit them to arrest him,' Viviane said. 'There will be terrible reprisals.'

'I heard he made a speech accusing the National Convention of being full of royalist spies and conspirators, but refused to name them,' Ivo said, 'and so now all the deputies fear he means to purge them all. So they ordered his arrest!'

'I can understand why,' Viviane said. 'He has turned on so many of his old friends! No-one is safe anymore. It is as if his thirst for blood can never be quenched.'

'What prison would dare lock him up?' Pierrick shook his head in disbelief. 'He will be free in a few hours, I guarantee it, and then those deputies who ordered his arrest will be sorry.'

The three friends clustered at the window, watching anxiously for any clue to what was happening in the city. Bells rang, drums throbbed, marching feet rang on the cobblestones. Then they heard distant gunfire.

At some point long after midnight, a man ran down the Rue des Rosiers, carrying a flaming torch. He hammered on doors and windows, shouting, 'They have him! The Incorruptible is in prison. Madame Guillotine shall drink his blood this day. Robespierre to die!'

By dawn, the streets were seething with people. No-one knew whether to rejoice or be afraid. Rumours flew about. Robespierre had shot off half his jaw trying to kill himself. No, no, someone argued, he would never be so cowardly. He was shot by a gendarme trying to arrest him. One of his supporters had shot himself; maybe he had tried to shoot Robespierre too. No, it was suicide, someone else insisted. To escape the guillotine.

No-one knew the truth.

The guillotine was moved back to the Place de la Révolution that day. The streets were swarming with people, every doorway and window crammed. The crowd mocked and jeered at Robespierre and his supporters, jolted along in tumbrils.

'What a lovely king!'

'Are you suffering, Your Majesty?'

'Death to the tyrant!'

Once again, Viviane knew the exact moment of his death by the roar of elation from the crowd.

The day after Robespierre's execution, gilded carriages were once again seen on the streets of Paris.

The Jacobins and their supporters were arrested or banished, and those Brissotins who had survived the purge were recalled to the National Convention. The prisons were opened, and those who had somehow escaped the guillotine released. Boards were torn off the windows of wig-makers and silk-weavers, and young men wearing skin-tight *culottes* and ragged satin coats roamed the streets with bludgeons, looking for *sans-culottes* to thrash. They laughingly called their clubs their 'executive power'.

Pierrick joyously adopted the dandified dress of these Incroyables, as they were called, though most insisted on pronouncing it 'incoyable', as the letter R – as in Revolution – was no longer to be pronounced.

He brought Viviane a severe black dress to wear, and high-heeled red shoes, and a red velvet ribbon to tie about her throat. She put her hand up to it, not entirely understanding.

'You escaped the guillotine,' Pierrick told her. 'You are most fashionable now.'

Viviane looked at herself in the mirror. Sunken cheeks, corpse-white skin, hair hacked à la victime, and that scarlet slash about her throat.

She felt giddy, disorientated. 'I don't think . . . I don't want . . .'

'It's a new world,' Pierrick said, 'and we need to survive it.'

It was a strange, feverish new world. Balls every night, with women in sheer chemises, like those worn to the guillotine, dancing with men dressed as long-dead kings. Pink satin, gold lace, embroidered stockings, tottering heels, huge plumed hats, cravats so stiff with starch the wearer had to gaze towards heaven. Suddenly, tall wigs like Marie-Antoinette's famous pouf were seen everywhere. Women wore a purple wig in the morning and an orange one in the afternoon, and gilded their nipples and their toenails. Green – a colour that had been dangerous to wear since poor Charlotte Corday bought a hat with green ribbons to assassinate Marat – was the shade of the season.

Most nights Viviane went dancing with Pierrick and Ivo, whirling from the arms of one stranger to another. At dawn she went to queue up outside the bakery with the other women, hoping for bread. Often the women curtsied to her, seeing the thin red ribbon bound about her throat, and offered to show her to the front of the line. Viviane always refused, even though it meant she missed out on bread that day.

It was strange and unsettling to be called 'mademoiselle' once more. She had grown used to 'citoyenne' and could not help but fear danger and entrapment, no matter what term of address was used.

One night, the three of them sat drinking cheap gin in a café on the Seine, watching the world pass by and arguing about the revolution.

'Was it worth it?' Viviane said. 'So much death, so much horror.'

'Could it have happened any other way?' Pierrick demanded. 'Hundreds of years of repression cannot be dismantled easily. If the king and his nobles had their way, we would have been crushed under their heels for another thousand years.'

'Evil times attract evil men,' Ivo said. 'Did you hear about the drownings of Nantes? Priests, nuns, women and children, anyone who dared speak out against the madness, all were drowned in the Loire River. They say more than four thousand died. Including babes in arms! How could murdering little babies serve the revolution, tell me that?'

He leaned forward, his eyes burning with pain and passion. Viviane thought – not for the first time – how lucky she had been that day, when Ivo had come to her rescue and given her a job and his friendship. It gave her great joy to see how Pierrick nodded and put out his hand to grasp Ivo's, and considered his answer more thoughtfully than ever before.

'You're right,' Pierrrick said. 'When we dreamed of changing the world, we never imagined such bloodshed. If we had known . . . would we have gone ahead? At what point did we lose control? Could anyone have stopped it, once the machinery was put in motion?'

Viviane remembered Alouette, the laundress at the Temple prison, and how her black eyes had smouldered with hatred as she had cried, 'Vengeance at last!'

'I feel so guilty,' she said with difficulty. 'All those years, I tried so hard to be good, I tried so hard to help. Yet I was born with blue blood, I was born with a silver spoon in my mouth. I had no idea what it was like to be poor and sick and starving, with no hope of ever escaping . . .'

Ivo took her hand. 'At least you tried.'

Pierrick grinned at her, and seized her other hand. 'And now you know! We couldn't be poorer or hungrier if we tried.'

The three of them sat, gripping each other's hands, an equilateral triangle of love and connection and remorse.

'What is done is done,' Pierrick said at last. 'We cannot help what happened. Right or wrong, the revolution has swept everything away. What are we going to do to rebuild our lives?'

A long silence.

'I'd like to go home,' Viviane said, at the same time that Ivo said tentatively, 'We could go back to Bretagne.'

They laughed and looked at each other and squeezed each other's hands, then looked rather nervously at Pierrick. He seemed to love Paris so much. He was throwing all his energies into being one of the *jeunesse dorée*, or gilded youths, who laughed and danced and drank and gambled as if they would never see another dawn.

'We will need money. Quite a lot of it.' Pierrick grinned at them impishly. 'Viviane, my dearest darling sister, what of our father's estate? Surely there is something we can sell?'

With her throat and Luna's bound with scarlet, and Pierrick and Ivo dressed in white wigs and powder-blue livery, Viviane went to see lawyers and demanded restitution of her father's property. Most of the estate was entailed, of course, and so his debt-encumbered château and townhouse were to be inherited by a cousin she had never met. It was agreed, however, that Viviane had a right to his personal effects. She was given the keys with low bows and many apologies.

The marquis's townhouse was still secured with the Commune's seals and padlocks. As she opened the door, Viviane smelled musk perfume, dead mouse. She walked through the shadowy rooms, stared at her father's collection of three-hundred-and-seventy-eight gilded snuffboxes – many with lewd paintings under the lid – and Clothilde's chests full of beribboned shoes and fans and gloves, many unworn. Pierrick exclaimed in delight, caught up a fan of white ostrich feathers and began to mince about, mimicking Clothilde and her high-pitched breathless way of speaking.

Ivo was soberer. 'It is ridiculous, the expense, the waste!' he said, looking at drawers full of quizzing glasses and jewelled watch-fobs. 'No man could ever wear all this!'

'What shall I do with it all?' Viviane asked.

'Sell it, of course,' Pierrick said, waving the ostrich feather fan lazily. 'The gaudier the better, these days.'

Looking through her father's desk, Viviane found a packet of letters written in a round, childish, awkward hand that she recognised at once. It was Briaca's. Troubled, she turned them over. One letter fluttered to the ground. Bending to pick it up, Viviane read: *she spends much time with the English gardener . . .*

An awful sick thudding of her heart. Viviane sank down into a chair and began to read.

Briaca had written down every single one of Viviane's misdeameanours, small and well-meant as they had been, and sent them to her father the marquis to read. Her tone was cringing, ingratiating, eager to please. Viviane could not bear it.

'What's wrong?' Pierrick asked her, coming in with a crate piled high with fans, gloves, parasols, vinaigrettes, quizzing-glasses and snuffboxes.

Mutely she showed him the letters. He dumped the crate on the couch, and began to slowly scan the lines, frowning a little, for reading was not his forte. His frown deepened.

'I always knew someone was writing to Monsieur le Marquis,' she said. 'I did not think it was Briaca.'

'I don't understand,' Pierrick said. 'She loved you. And she was afraid of him.'

'Sometimes fear wins out over love,' Viviane said.

Pierrick nodded, sombre as she had ever seen him.

'I knew she wrote to him,' he said. 'I carried the mail to Rennes to post. I thought it was the kitchen accounts. Maybe a plea for more money. I did not know, I promise you.'

Viviane felt faint and giddy. 'I don't want . . .' She paused, fighting the choke in her throat. 'I don't want fear to win over love anymore.' She looked up at him, tears beginning to spill down her cheeks. She dashed them away. 'Pierrick, Monsieur le Marquis was your father as well as mine. If the world was a fair place, you would inherit just as much as me. I'd like to split it all, half and half. What do you say?'

Pierrick put his arm about her and gave her a little squeeze. 'Much as I hate admitting that bastard was my father, it's worth it to have a sister like you.'

'It's yours to do with as you wish,' Viviane said. 'You don't need to come back to Belisima if you don't want to.'

He smiled at her. 'I've always wanted to have a go at making a weaving machine powered by the water-mill. And Ivo would love the kitchen at Belisima. All those ovens and spit-roasts! Positively medieval.'

'So we'll go home?'

Pierrick nodded, with a sweeping laughing gesture. 'As soon as we've sold all these bloody snuffboxes.'

32

To Invent a Rose
6–22 September 1794

'Good luck, Davy boy,' Scotty said. 'I hope you find her.'

'So do I! If I do, I'll invite you to the wedding.'

'That'd be grand.' The two men shook hands, then – as David began to walk away – Scotty cried, 'Hey, Davy, I don't suppose she has a sister?'

David turned back, grinning. 'No, she doesn't, but I do. Two, in fact.'

'Then I look forward to meeting them.'

David waved farewell, then set off to look for a boat willing to take him to Saint-Malo. Britain was still at war with France, but there was always someone willing to run the risk for profit. French silk and wine and brandy were harder to get than ever.

At last David found a boat willing to take him onboard. He oversaw the disposal of his precious cargo, then went to walk around Portsmouth, enjoying the first decent cup of tea that he'd had in a long while. It was good to stretch his legs, to see wild clematis, red haws and elderberries in the hedgerows, and to hear the English tongue spoken all around him. He had a game pie and a beer in a pub on the waterfront, and went out to smoke his pipe and watch the waves.

The news from France was worrying. The death of Robespierre had not brought peace. There were still clashes and confrontations between royalists and republicans all through the country. But David had no choice. He had to find out what had happened to Viviane.

He sailed on the evening tide, on a three-masted lugger called the *Osprey*. It began to spit a few hours later, and rained for the seven days it took to reach Saint-Malo. At last, though, he was on French soil and arranging to hire a cart filled with straw to protect his precious blue-and-white ginger jars.

The only nag he could buy was a poor old broken-down thing with a shaggy mane and forelock, and hooves the size of dinner plates. David bought him some oats, and set off to walk the fifty miles to the Paimpont forest.

Each step, he hoped, brought him closer to finding Viviane.

She stood on the lake shore, gazing across the serene waters to the château. Three towers were still standing, but one was a scorched tumble of stones.

'It's not as bad as I feared,' she said to Pierrick.

'You haven't seen inside yet.'

Viviane stood still, her hands clasped tightly. Nerves fluttered in her stomach. 'It will have been good for the fields to have lain fallow so long.'

'Shall we go in?' Ivo asked, looking about him in interest.

Viviane nodded, and led the way across the arched bridge and through the gatehouse. The iron gates stood askew. One had been wrenched off its hinges. Luna dashed around, sniffing all the new and exciting smells. Viviane had to pull her away from a rat that lay decomposing on the cobblestones.

The courtyard was a mess. Dead leaves lay in damp piles, and the windows were all broken and filthy. The parterre garden was a mass of weeds. The château, however, rose into the blue sky, seemingly untouched. A knot inside her chest loosened.

She went up the steps and tried the door handle. It was securely fastened.

'I locked the doors,' Pierrick reminded her, 'and threw the key in the well.'

'Then you're the one going down the well to retrieve it,' she said, laughing.

The château well was in the courtyard outside the kitchen. On this side, Viviane could see broken and blackened windows above her, and gaping holes in the the slate tiles on the spire. Weeds grew over the cobblestones, and the honeysuckle on the wall had run rampant.

Pierrick leaned over the well, which had a pointed slate roof that mimicked the château towers. 'It looks deep. I can't see the bottom.'

'We'll lower you down on the rope,' Viviane said. She gave the rope a sharp jerk and it snapped in her hand. 'Maybe not.'

She went to look for more rope in the kitchen garden. The nasturtium and pumpkin vines had grown wildly, but she was heartened to see a few herbs and vegetables had survived. All three were very hungry. Food had been scarce indeed on their journey.

Despite all the treasures of their father's house, she and Pierrick had not managed to raise a fortune selling them. There were too many impoverished aristocrats, too much stolen loot. They had managed to gather together only a few heavy bags of silver, Pierrick having wisely refused to accept assignats, which were now worthless. They had dressed like beggars, the silver hidden in their rags, and somehow managed to get home. A boat had given them free passage down the Seine in return for free labour, and then they had walked from Honfleur, sleeping in haystacks or under trees, and begging for food in return for work.

Some days, they got nothing. But there were always hazelnuts and blackberries and mushrooms to be foraged, and Pierrick devised a clever trap to catch birds. Filthy and footsore, they had come at last to the château, standing eerily quiet and half-ruined on its island in the lake. Viviane hoped that the hidden bags of silver they had carried would pay for repairs, and flax seed, and new looms, and labour.

'Here's some rope!' Viviane called. 'It looks stout enough.'

She retrieved the coil of rope from the garden shed, and then Ivo tied it securely to the well handle. They lowered Pierrick down and listened to him splashing about and cursing. Then came a cry of triumph. 'Got it!' he shouted and they hauled him up again, the huge rusty old key clutched in one wet hand.

Within seconds, the side door was unlocked and Viviane was inside. She found the kitchen almost exactly as she had left it. The table and dressers were thick with dust, and cobwebs were spun in grey cocoons about the herbs hanging from above the fireplace, but the copper pots still gleamed dimly on their shelves and the kettle hung on its hook above a hearth of grey ashes.

Viviane ran down the corridor to her stillroom, Luna loping at her heels, and had to rub tears from her eyes to find her book of remedies still lying open on its stand, its pages a little nibbled by mice.

'I'll get this place cleaned up and some soup on,' Ivo called from the kitchen. 'There are some potatoes and leeks in the garden, and I can hear doves cooing.'

'I'll get some water,' Pierrick replied.

Viviane went to the secret door, and climbed up the tight circular staircase to the height of the tower room. It too was just as she had left it. Here was the place where she had stood clasped in David's arms, kissing for the last time. Here was the spot where she had found his severed finger, marked by an ugly stain on the carpet. And here she had lain all night, weeping, her bloodied hands pressed against the wound in Luna's breast.

She walked about the room. *Le Roman de la Rose* still lay open on the table, a faded ribbon marking the illustration of the lover entering the walled garden. One of David's little notebooks lay nearby, a stub of a pencil tucked inside. The candelabra stood in the window embrasure, its candles burned down into fantastical shapes like icicles.

If it had not been for the dust and the cobwebs, Viviane might have believed the past six years had been nothing but a nightmare.

She went to explore the rest of the château.

At least half of it was charred and ruined, but the chapel where her mother's tomb lay was untouched. Viviane knelt beside it for a long time, her face hidden in her hands, silently giving thanks. Then she rose, whistling to Luna, and picked her way through the burnt ruins of the eastern wing to the garden David had made for her.

The yew hedges were wildly overgrown, and she had to force her way through the pathways of the maze. Her arms scratched, her face bruised, she at last made it through to the hidden garden at its heart.

The pool was green and slimy, and the statues stained with damp, but the flowers and weeds bloomed together extravagantly. Pansies, asters, sweet alyssum, hollyhocks and daisies were tangled together with grass and field bindweed and mouse-ear chickweed, below rose bushes drooping with vivid orange hips.

Swaying everywhere in the grass were the dainty seed heads of dandelion clocks.

Viviane picked one, and blew its seeds away.

David turned in at the château gates, and saw the long avenue of linden trees, blazing golden in the sunshine, their beauty doubled in the lake.

He made his way along the avenue, his horse plodding beside him. The road was overgrown with grass and weeds, and the fields were untilled and lying fallow. No sound but crickets and birds. Ahead was the château. He could see half of it lay in ruins. His heart began to pound heavily.

He passed the weavers' cottages and the barn, all empty and half-derelict. The cottages seemed to have been abandoned in a rush, for a few looms stood with cloth still half-woven upon them. David unhitched his horse under a tree, and brought it some water from the lake, then – taking up his battered leather satchel – crossed the bridge and went through the deep archway into the courtyard. Everything was deserted.

Misery heavy as a millstone on his chest.

For a moment he stood, not knowing what to do or where to go.

Then slowly David became aware of two things.

The first was the faint delicious smell of soup.

The second was the sound of a sweet familiar voice singing. He turned and saw Viviane coming through the archway from the rose garden, flowers in her hands, and Luna at her heels. She stopped abruptly when she saw him, her expression full of wonder and disbelief.

David cleared his voice. '*Bonsoir*, mamzelle.'

Her face lit up with laughter. Dropping her flowers, she raced across the courtyard and leaped into his arms.

'Good evening, sir!' she cried, and kissed him.

It seemed as if the whole world stilled upon its axis.

Viviane was alive, and she was in his arms.

At last they had to part, if only to breathe and steady themselves. Luna leapt about, barking joyously, and David had to bend and pet her and tell her what a good dog she was.

There was so much to say, and yet it seemed there was no way to say it. He kissed her again, her face between his hands.

'I'm sorry,' she said. 'I thought you were dead.'

'It's me who is sorry,' he said. 'I should never have left you.'

'If you'd stayed, you would have died. I should have gone with you in the beginning. I was afraid . . .'

She spoke between frantic kisses, her arms clinging to him with all her strength.

'I didn't understand,' he said. 'If only I'd . . .'

Viviane stopped his words with her fingers. 'No, no. No regrets. You are here now, you're alive, it's like a miracle. I was just wishing for you with all my heart.'

'I can't believe I found you.'

'Where have you been? How did you get away?'

'I skated,' he said, and saw the quick understanding in her face. 'And I've been to China.'

'To China? No!'

'Yes. I've been to China and you will never believe what I found there.' Laughing, he caught her hand and ran with her across the bridge. His cart stood under the tree, his horse grazing nearby. He rummaged through the straw.

A tall porcelain pot decorated with blue roses was revealed to her wondering eyes.

'It's beautiful.'

'Just wait till you see what's inside.' David carefully lifted off the cobalt-blue lid. The pot was full of rice. He carefully stirred the white grains and pulled out a slender briar of rosehips.

'It's the ever-blowing red rose of China,' he told her. 'It blooms again and again, even in frost. I found it for you, and brought it back all these thousands of miles.' He passed her the rose briar, and then took her in his arms and kissed her again with immense tenderness.

When at last he let her go, she was giddy. She steadied herself against his shoulder and looked down at the blood-red rosehips in her hand, then up at the château glowing in the evening sun, and then to his face, his grey eyes intent on hers. 'It seems impossible,' she whispered.

'Nothing is impossible to a valiant heart,' he replied, laughing. 'Or so my grandmother always said. You will love her when you meet her, and she will love you. Oh, Viviane, do you think . . .'

'Yes?' she asked.

'Would you marry me? Indeed, I love you so. We could stay here at Belisima, I know what it means to you. And maybe, just maybe, we could invent a new rose.'

He plunged his hands into the Chinese jar, drew out a dozen rosehips and offered them to her with a bow, as if they were jewels.

She took the briars, laughing at him. 'Yes, indeed, Davy *bach*. I would love to invent a rose with you.'

Author's Note

I first got the idea for *The Blue Rose* in March 2015 when I read a memoir called *Chasing the Rose* by the Italian journalist Andrea di Robilant, about his quest for a rare rose. In one passage he wrote: 'In 1792, Gilbert Slater, a nurseryman from Knotts Green, Leyton, introduced a dark, rich crimson rose known in China as Yue Yue Hong, or "Monthly Crimson". Europeans had never seen a rose of that colour (called pigeon's blood). The cultivar, which became known as "Slater's Crimson China", quickly spread to France ... It became the ancestor of many of the red roses we have today ...'

How fascinating, I thought. Surely Europe had red roses before 1792?

Then I thought ... 1792 ... that was during the French Revolution. I have always wanted to write a book set then, it is a period of history that has always fascinated me.

Andrea di Robilant went on to say: 'Around that time ... Sir George Staunton, a young diplomat and enthusiastic gardener, travelled to China as secretary to Lord Macartney. Taking time off from his embassy, he went looking for roses and found a lovely re-flowering silvery pink specimen in a Canton nursery, which he shipped to Sir Joseph Banks, the powerful director of the Royal Botanic Gardens in Kew.'

I had read about the Macartney Embassy before. In the eighteenth century, Britain imported vast quantities of Chinese tea, silk and porcelain, but China was buying nothing in return. So, in 1793, Lord Macartney and his entourage travelled to Peking to meet with the emperor. At that time, it was Chinese custom to kowtow before the emperor, a ritual obeisance that involved prostrating oneself on the floor and knocking one's forehead to the ground nine times. Lord Macartney, as a representative of King George III, refused to kowtow. The emperor refused to open trade.

I knew about this failed ambassadorial journey because it was one of the things which led to the Opium Wars between Britain and China in the nineteenth century. I did not, however, know the British had brought back roses.

I was so interested by this story that I went browsing amongst the many books on roses I have on my shelves. (I've always been a rose fancier.) I found out that the introduction of the China roses to the West at the end of the eighteenth century revolutionised rose cultivation. For the first time, roses could be grown that had more than one flush of blossoms. And for the first time Europeans could grow a rose that was truly red, long considered the symbol of passionate love.

I began to dig deeper. I discovered that Gilbert Slater was not responsible for introducing the Crimson China rose (*rosa chinensis semperflorens*) to the Western world. He certainly sent his gardener, James Main, to Canton. However, none of his plant specimens survived the long journey home. James Main later wrote that the Crimson China was never among Slater's botanical collections.

So it is a mystery how the ever-blowing red rose of China (as it was romantically called) was brought to Europe. Examining Sir George Staunton's record of his journey to China, I discovered that the embassy gardeners – one named John Haxton and one named David Stronach – had found not one, but two, rose specimens in Canton. Was it possible, I wondered, that the second rose found was 'Yue Yue Hong', the blood-red repeat-flowering rose that is the ancestor of all our red roses today? If so, why was it hybridised in France?

Historical novelists love the gaps and holes in historical records, because that is where the imagination can play. Nonetheless, much of what happens in *The Blue Rose* is inspired by known historical fact. Apart from Viviane and her family, most of the characters in the book once lived and loved and died. David Stronach really did travel on HMS *Lion* to China (though I doubt very much whether he fell in love with a French marquis's daughter and settled in Bretagne to invent new roses).

The research for a project like this is immense. I read everything from the diaries of the Sansons, the family of executioners who operated the guillotine, to the memoirs of Lord Macartney's valet, Aeneas Anderson, who wrote: 'We entered Pekin like *Paupers*, remained in it like Prisoners and departed from it like Vagrants.'

The most useful books for me in writing Viviane's story were biographies of Marie-Antoinette by Antonia Fraser, Will Bashor and Evelyne Lever, books about the French Revolution by Simon Schama, Eric Hazan and Peter McPhee, and books about daily life in eighteenth-century France by Jean Robiquet and James Anderson. *The Immobile Empire* by Alain Peyrefitte was my key source for the Macartney embassy's journey, as well as the memoirs of Sir George Staunton and his son Thomas.

Thank you also to my friend and horticulturist Libby Birley, who helped me understand the deep story of Chinese gardens and lent me her books on the subject; Li Jianjun, the director of the Centre for Australian Studies at Beijing Foreign Studies University, who invited me to speak to his students about my writing and suggested a number of helpful books to me, including *A Photographer in Old Peking* by Hedda Morrison, which was incredibly useful in helping me visualise the streets that the English embassy rode through; and Henrietta Harrison, the Professor of Modern Chinese Studies at the China Centre in Oxford, Great Britain, who helped me with questions about the Chinese priests who travelled with the Macartney embassy (in particular how they could have avoided the death penalty for having cut off their queues).

As always, my heartfelt love and thanks to my husband Greg and my children Ben, Tim and Ella, for suffering through another of my long obsessions. My sister Belinda for sharing my fascination with the French Revolution and lending me her books, her insights and her never-failing emotional support. My family and friends, who forgave me for long months of absence while I travelled to France and China (both in real life and my imagination). Thanks to my friend Susie Stratton, who came with me to France, and my son Ben, who came with me to China (being tall, pale-skinned and blue-eyed, he taught me what it felt like to be stared at all the time).

To my brilliant agent Tara Wynne at Curtis Brown Australia, thank you for your unwavering faith and support – and for many a glass of champagne! To all the wonderful people at Penguin Random House – but especially my publisher Meredith Curnow and editor Patrick Mangan – thank you for your wisdom, your insight and your clear-sightedness. I am so blessed to have you.

And to all of my readers, for following me on my long creative journey and for loving my stories – I thank you all from the bottom of my heart!